MAYDAY

by

GRANT PARKER

Liberty Press
Lansing, Michigan

Library of Congress
Catalog Card No.: 80-83408

Parker, Grant
  Mayday.
Lansing, Mich.: Liberty Press
260 p.
8010   800814
ISBN 0-9604958-0-0

Cover photograph of plaster cast of "Girl With
A Cat" from the personal collection of the
sculptor's son Douglas Angell.

Published by Liberty Press
2115 Mark Ave.
Lansing, Michigan 48912

To

Helen, Bill, Dan, Susan

Table of Contents

Acknowledgements

My initial awareness of the atrocity which is covered in this book came from reading a little 1927 book called THE BATH SCHOOL DISASTER, a copy of which had been loaned to me by Donna Goodwin. (That booklet, plus the school board minutes, and the transcript of the testimony given at the inquest into the death of the school superintendent were later to become three of the most important source documents in my reconstruction and analysis of the event.) When at my wife's suggestion, I determined to write the full story of Bath, I first immersed myself in the voluminous newspaper coverage of the tragedy. The result was a near paralyzing awareness of the true horror which once engulfed the small farm village. My concern was that even fifty years later, the subject might still be unspeakable for survivors and families of victims, at least insofar as a newcomer to the community might be concerned.

For helping me break the ice, I wish especially to thank Chester and Adabelle McGonigal, Mary Alice Snyder, James Hixson, and Doris Wilkins. Other critical contacts which enabled me to break through in areas which time or anguish might have erased were Mrs. C. W. Allen, Mrs. Hettie Murphy, Bonnie Swanchara, Mr. and Mrs. Larry Treadway, Edna Babcock, Sister Celeste, and Lieutenant Calvin Glassford of the Michigan State Police. In addition, I have relied heavily on Fordney Cushman for backup information throughout my writing. Others who have been helpful in making suggestions or arranging contacts are Mr. and Mrs. Milton Coe, Doris Ray, Dottie Covert, Ted deWolf, Harold Burnett, Laura Hardy, Roger Seamon, Victoria Huhn, Duane Black, Robert McKerr, Mrs. James Hixson, LaVon Simpson, Jean Rademacher, Helen Parker and Duane Beach.

Most critically important were the interviews which allowed me to reconstruct and interpret the event. My deepest gratitude goes to those survivors and parents of victims who agreed to relive the trauma for me. Those interviewed, some repeatedly, included; Mrs. Talbert Abrams, Mrs. C. W. Allen, Mrs. Edna Andrews, Mr. and Mrs. Douglas Angell, Mr. Ernest Babcock, Mrs. Benedict, Mrs. Thelma (Ewing) Cochran, Mr. and Mrs. Fordney Cushman, Ms. Marcia Detluff, Mr. Wendell Douglass, Mr. Ormond Eldredge, Mr. Raymond Eschtruth, Mr. and Mrs. Walter Kyes, Mr. Warden Kyes, Father Lee, the half sister of Andrew Kehoe, Mr. and Mrs. Walter Geisenhaver, Mrs. Lenora (Babcock) Haight, Mrs. Florence (Peacock) Homer, Mr. Floyd Huggett, Mr. Don Huffman, Mrs. Ethel (Huyck) Saur, Mr. Arthur McFarren, Mr. and Mrs. Chester McGonigal, Mr. Anson McNatt, Mrs. Hettie Murphy, Mr. Percy Patterson, Mr. Dominick

Perrone, Mrs. Patrick Porter, Mr. Earl Proctor, Mr. Lee Reasoner, Mr. Jack Rounds, Ms. Jeannine Seeger, Dr. Erwin Sober, Mrs. Roderick Schoals, Mr. William G. Searl, Rev. Salisbury, Dr. Milton Shaw, Mr. and Mrs. Larry Treadway, Mrs. Doris Wilkins, Mr. and Mrs. Roscoe Witchell, Mr. and Mrs. Howard Witt, Mrs. Thelma (Cressman) Weismiller, Mrs. B. Ghizzoni, and Mrs. Lillian Cochrane (mail).

I am also appreciative of correspondence, documents and photographs made available to me by Mrs. George Oliver, Mr. and Mrs. Douglas Angell, Mrs. Harvey Dinse, Lillian Cochran, Mr. Arthur McFarren, Mr. and Mrs. Anson McNatt, Mrs. Florence Homer, Mrs. Ethel Huych Saur, Mr. Raymond Eschtruth and Mrs. Lenora Haight.

Of the numerous public and private agencies whose services and facilities were made available to me, I wish to give special thanks to: the University of Michigan (School of Education-School Services), Michigan State Archives (Lee Barnett), Michigan State Police Records Unit, Office of the Clinton County Clerk, the Tecumseh Senior Citizens Club, the Tecumseh Herald, the Alma Morning Sun, the Michigan State Library, the Bath school system, and the Bath Township Clerk.

While assuming complete responsibility for my work, I also wish to acknowledge consultation solicited and received from Attorneys William Youatt and Raymond Scodeller, and from Paul Stimson, M.D. (Doctor of Psychiatry).

Finally, I wish to thank Mr. Harry Barnard for permission to quote from *The Independent Man*, the splendid biography of Senator Couzens, which is the key to my capsule look at one of America's truly great men.

Grant Parker
Spring, 1979

Chapter I
Introduction

Bath Village near Lansing, Michigan shares with other historic sites of battle a trait of apparent unremarkability. It looks simply like a quiet farm village—reminiscent of another time or even another place. With its main street of nineteenth century false-front buildings, it has more the appearance of a frontier Western town. Other than that, its scene is unimpressive—and yet mass murder occurred in this rolling farm village, murder of a scope and of a kind unparalleled in American history.

The fateful and fatal day was May 18, 1927, a day which had started out as a beautiful Spring morning. A light rain had fallen during the night, but the morning sun which followed was bright and warming to the ground. Bath's chief chronicler of the event recalled later that it was perfect for planting melon which he was doing in his garden at the outskirts of town. Suddenly, the planting was interrupted by a tremendous explosion which shook the earth. The explosion signaled the community disaster; and before the acts of carnage were over, 45 school children and adults were dead, including the killer.

At once, Bath, the least likely news spot in the world, at the least likely time in the world, captured the attention of a shocked world. The news of Bath spread worldwide by radio. Banner headlines saturated the nation—pushing reluctantly aside news of the Lindbergh trans-ocean solo flight which had hypnotized the world.

The 'Bath Disaster' is a story of murder, of cunning, of tragedy, of anguish and tremendous internal conflict externalized. It is also a story of great courage and rescue. It is a story of a strange convergence of political powers and automotive giants. And it is a story of unending mystery.

The Bath murders are now a long time past, but the hurt continues, and so does the healing. Evidence of the tragedy may be missed now by the casual observer of Bath, but it's there. It's there in a simple bronze plaque commemorating the dead which is located at the inner entry of the little Methodist Church. It's there in the hauntingly lovely bronze memorial statue of a delicate and timeless

1

schoolgirl which graces the entrance to the new Bath High School. It's there on the commemorative hill where the old consolidated school once stood—the salvaged cuppola visible under bright lights to the distant night football crowds. And it's there in the identity of every Bath citizen.

How could it have happened? "Mass murder in Bath?" a visitor might scoff. "Why they'd have had to kill the whole town!" In truth, that's just about the way it was.

Chapter II
The Village

The explosion of hatred, which is murder, requires a time, a setting, and a conversion of personalities, circumstances, and frustrations. With the rest of the country, the Bath of early 1919 celebrated victory and anticipated a still uncertain peace from the explosive violence which was World War I. Unknowingly, Bath was the setting for a coming violence far greater to *it* than the Great War itself. The required circumstances were all ready well in motion.

Bath, the village, was laid out to respect its two chief communication arteries. The few dirt streets of the south end of the village were properly perpendicular and parallel to the east-west running Gunnisonville Road (Clark Road as it is now called). The block long business district to the north ran roughly north and south and was properly perpendicular to the vital tracks of the old Michigan Central Railroad which were located downhill at the district's north end. Because the railroad did not parallel Gunnisonville Road, running rather southwesterly instead, a corrective adjustment was required in the Village's main connecting link, Main Street. From the Gunnisonville Road the street jogged fairly sharply to the left from its northerly direction as it dropped downhill past the shop area to cross the railroad track at the bottom of the hill. The result was and is a block and street configuration which would cause confusion in a city but which, in Bath, is simply an innocent characteristic—two street patterns in a single village of 300, evidence that independence and compromise are not incompatible.

The bow and dip of the business district to the railroad was appropriate enough. The railroad had been successfully courted by Bath fifty years earlier. With its capacity for freight and passenger traffic, the Michigan Central made Bath a natural marketing center for farms of the entire township.

Bath reflected the township. It was small, bustling, but unpretentious. Its homes were plain and simple and its people unsophisticated, lacking the opportunity for education found in nearby Lansing.

Within the village, family heads operated or worked in the many businesses which served the area. The Michigan Central depot and freight station handled the six daily passenger trains which fed into Lansing. Dan Huffman, telegrapher, a newcomer to Bath ran the station while Joe Perrone, a popular Italian immigrant, bossed the section gang which maintained the vital road beds. Overnight guests of Bath could get bed and board just up the street at the artificial brick DeLamarter hotel. Cushman and Son Grain Elevator with lumber and coal yard equalled any like establishment around. There was the blacksmith shop and garage owned by big and amiable Albert Detluff; and Detluff's competition, Mr. Wilkins, operated Bath's second garage (part time).

In addition, business bustled at a general store, a barber shop and pool room, an implement store, a brine station for cucumbers, and at the large nearby chicken hatchery.

The times were, indeed, prosperous. The People's Bank was anxious to make loans and hold money. The residents were increasing their wealth; and Alonzo Webster was there to insure them against any kind of loss they might think of.

Befitting the area's increasing communication needs, a telephone office had been installed in one room of the Vail residence. Down the street, though, a residence/post office processed the bulk of communication with the outside world; and a village cobbler upheld, perhaps, the oldest communication of all.

Although all this was complimented by the Glass pharmacy and ice cream parlor, the unchallenged center of social life in the area was the Community Hall, a kind of privately owned civic center, the property of residents calling themselves the Community Association. Lodges held their meetings there—the Oddfellows, Rebeccas, Maccabees; and church and school groups performed plays on its well worn stage. The Epworth League play provocatively titled "His Wife's Relations" was a sample. Musicians of the area also performed on that stage while the young folks danced waltz and square to their music.

Adding to the stature of the village were the churches and the school. The Methodist and Baptist Churches adequately served the predominantly Protestant population of the area. The old school, two story and brick, was located just at the jog on Main Street. Sitting purposely atop the highest ground in the village, it dominated the entire scene. Unlike the surrounding rural schools, the

3

village school educated all the way through tenth grade. The curriculum and faculty were limited, however, and the school had no facilities for community activities. It was the best country school in the area, but it was still, basically, a country school.

Last, but not least, Bath served as center of government in the township. The little brick town hall was smack in the middle of the business district.

If anything, the Bath of early 1919 was no mere close by appendage of Lansing, the capitol and industrial city ten miles southwest. It was a center in its own right, rural and comfortably isolated from the city and its manners.

Bath also had a bit of tradition. Old Zachariah Chandler, a former Detroit Mayor and wealthy merchant, had descended on Bath Township back in the 1850s. Land development, specifically Bath land development, was Chandler's hobby. With expensive experimentation involving an intricate network of drainage ditches, Chandler had converted the impossible and worthless swamplands of the district to workable agricultural land.

Chandler, of course, had other interests. He helped found the Republican Party at Jackson and got himself elected as a United States Senator from Michigan. In Washington, Chandler was conspicuous from the start. His carriage men sported uniforms with monogrammed brass buttons. Mark Twain, a coming reporter with the Chicago Tribune, covered the wedding of Chandler's daughter.

As Senator, Chandler's abolitionist tactics were instrumental in fomenting the Civil War; and after the war he pushed for the most repressive reconstructionist policies. Before the war Chandler had written, "Without a little blood letting the Union will not in my estimation be worth a rush."[1] It is one of the many ironies and strange coincidences of Bath history that this should be remembered as Chandler's most famous line. Subsequently, of course, "the great blood letter" got his blood as well as the unwanted nickname which lives forever after him. As it turned out, Chandler was to be but the first of two Detroit Mayors to play an important part in the destiny of the hamlet and township of Bath. Unfortunately, Chandler was not destined to be the only blood letter of Bath.

By 1919, Bath was enjoying more than tradition and local prosperity. Agriculture nationally was enjoying unprecedented prosperity and Bath was agriculture. During the war, enormous acreages had been removed from production in Europe because of the devastation there and the manpower shortage. The withdrawal of an estimated fiftyfive million European acres needed to be compensated somehow by an increase of thirtyfive million cultivated American acres. The burden on the American farmer was great—but so was the (short term) blessing. Ceilings which were clamped on farm

4

prices looked to be a burden to the farmer, but he was stimulated to increase acreage and production. A vast agricultural thrust was to be decisive in gaining the peace as well as the victory. To that end, the Wilson Administration created the Food Administration Board headed by Herbert Hoover, and the giant that was American agriculture was turned loose.

As additional spurs, farmers could be excused from the draft; and a National Board of Vocational Education was created. The board distributed federal funds to teachers of agriculture and domestic science in qualifying schools. Surplus explosives were distributed to farmers as an aid in clearing additional land.

Even the War's end seemed to hold no threat to the prosperity of farmers. In fact, just the reverse appeared to be true as famine in Europe threatened friend and foe alike. With a sense of security, then, Bath and its farming population greeted the end of the war with true pride of accomplishment.

Americans everywhere were thumping their chests. They really *had* "Saved the world for democracy." They really *were* something and they were looking for new fields to conquer. Least of all, were they going to take any nonsense from anybody—and when a gang of Mexican bandits wandered across the border, the American Army simply invaded Mexico and put an end to it.

Other forces were afoot, too. The super-patriotism of the war effort had spawned hatred and suspicion toward all things foreign. The KKK was reborn to take up where it had left off in its own version of the battle against "lawlessness." Lynching of blacks was commonplace. The Klan moved north—and it reached Bath.

In 1919, lawlessness was destined to be taken lightly in the country. The Prohibition Amendment which was to be ratified later in the year would see to that.

As for woman's suffrage, the Prohibition Amendment might have indicated that vote or no vote, women had the power—but just to make sure, the suffrage amendment was clearing its last obstacles. (Bath, by the way, was ahead of that. The township clerk was a woman.)

As the war ended, the strains of "Over There" and "Hinkey Dinkey Parlez-Vous" drifted into the background. Al Jolson's "Swanee" and "When My Baby Smiles At Me" came to the fore. Lansing's theatre houses featured Charlie Chaplin in a movie at the Bijou. Tom Mix was appearing in the "Dare Devil" which was billed as the romance of a hard boiled tenderfoot; and "The Little Shepherd of Kingdom Come" asked the question, "Can the young tycoon, turned off by the sophistication of high society, find happiness again with the unspoiled mountain girl he had left behind?"

Although America's first permanent radio station had not quite

5

been built, newspapers and telegraph could be counted on to give full coverage to Jack Dempsey's challenge of Jesse Willard's heavyweight championship.

In those same papers, the automobile (the "machine" as it was called) was commanding special sections—and farm tractors were surviving demonstrations that they could even function in wet ground.

But for Bath, life was still basically simple—and it was not immune from the naivete and mood which swept the rest of the country toward a myth of ever growing prosperity, good times and heroism.

Welfare as a system with paid employees was still unknown to the state. Persons who had to, scrounged to survive—or a little extra money could be made from bounty payments collected from the township clerk. The rate was 2¢ a piece for sparrows, 10¢ for rats, and 50¢ a piece for woodchucks. (Mrs. Detluff, the township clerk, didn't find this her pleasantest duty. "Yes, yes," she would say, looking the other way, "I'll take your word for it. Just put them over there.")

Even the roads were maintained by the townspeople themselves. For road gravel jobs, teams and drivers were selected from township farmers by the township road commissioner. The pay was five dollars a day, and the work was equitably distributed. The times were not so prosperous that an extra five dollars in cash could be ignored.

Each farmer was also responsible for dragging the road in front of his place. He simply picked up the drag from wherever it was last used. And in the winter, residents could try their hand at the V shaped contraption that horses pulled to clear the roads of drifts.

Nor did Bath lack for social life. In addition to the dances at the community hall, there were the church clubs, the lodges, the Grange, the Farmers' Club, the Literary Club and a popular social organization with a waiting list, The Friday Afternoon Club.

Still, the residents of the area were sensitive to the particular deprivations associated with a rural area. Their solution was not to give up the rural life, but improve it. They knew that the popular war song, "How You Gonna Keep Them Down On The Farm After They've Seen Paree?" was as much a put-down of the farmer as it was a recognition of Parisian night life.

In comparing themselves to city residents, one particular deficit stood out—the school system. The five districts surrounding and excluding Bath Village were typical of the times. Each district had its country school house, the famous or infamous (depending on how one looked at it) one room school which educated children of all ages through the eighth grade. The typical district board was made up of the Moderator, the Treasurer, and the Director. Teachers were often daughters of Board members. Sometimes when that was not the case, no board member's daughter had become qualified.

Qualifications were by no means extreme. Normal Schools were established strategically throughout the state with the single purpose of training teachers for rural schools. Entry into the Normal School required the applicant to be at least seventeen years of age and to have successfully completed ten years of high school—or to be the holder of a Second Grade Certificate, or to have taught successfully for two years. One year at the Normal School entitled its graduate to qualify for three years of teaching in that county without an exam—and this license could be extended for another six years with renewals.[2]

The existence of the Normal School was meant not only to upgrade the standards of the country school, but to also help assure a supply of needed teachers. In 1919 and 1920 this was especially a problem. School districts throughout the state were obtaining teachers only with the utmost difficulty. Some districts could find none at all.

In spite of all the advantages of being a "neighborhood school," the one room school had glaring inadequacies. Many of its graduates never went on to higher education, and the education it did provide was no longer a source of comfort in the farming area surrounding Bath. The city jokes about "dumb farmers" stuck in the craw.

The sentiment for change was one of pride. It was sparked by a growing passion of Bath area parents to give their children an education, not merely equal to, but superior to that provided in the cities. It was nurtured by the growing problems of maintaining the one room school in the midst of a teacher shortage, and by the incentives to improved teaching offered to qualified high schools. If the districts around Bath could unite, "consolidate" was the word, they could lead Michigan in bringing their children the very best. After all, this was a time for bold thinking and it was American. So what if it would be expensive? The farm prosperity brought on by the war could make it all possible.

By 1919, the idea of consolidation had truly arrived in Bath—and so had a new resident farmer by the name of Andrew Kehoe. The two were newcomers, one, an idea, the other, a man with ideas. Before they would run their course, all the ingredients of time, setting, circumstances, personalities, and frustrations would be in place— the ingredients for murder on a scale unheard of in America.

7

Chapter III
End of the Little White School House

Consolidation or not, the one room country school house was not about to give up without a battle. For one thing, the little country schools had been around since the pioneers had first started building schools. Their very sight aroused a certain sentimentality. For citizens who had either attended country schools or sent children to them, they were part of the American identity.

Perhaps just as important, several were located in each township. They were neighborhood schools. They were located within a child's walking distance, as walking distance was defined then; and they were controlled by one's neighbors. For the farm family, consolidation might loom not only as the exterminator of the eight grade country school, but as a loss of control over the education of the children. In a society where mobility had been limited by the horse, people from the other side of the township could be practically as strange as foreigners—and yet the board members of a consolidated school might be these very strangers. In short, the neighborhood, of which the school was such a vital part, was the essence of the farm family's existence. To give up any part of it was to give up part of one's way of life.

Besides that, the eight grade country school had some other diehard proponents. These were the decreasing number of farmers who simply couldn't see the sense to more than an eighth grade education. They couldn't see the sense to it; and they couldn't see paying for it. Fine if some people wanted high school education for their children, but let them pay tuition and send their children to the city.

Arrayed on the side of consolidation, however, were the impressive and persuasive forces of the state educational establishment, a federal and state incentive system, and most of the Bath farm leaders themselves.

If a local spokesman lacked for articulation, a state educational consultant could supply him with a list of consolidation arguments as long as one's arm. Something for everybody, but the arguments had substance, and they couldn't easily be sloughed off.

If these arguments didn't find a responsive ear, further inducements could be presented! The promise of state money to the district to pay for transportation; the teaching of practical agriculture and home economics (not only guaranteed, but subsidized); and a feeding program for the undernourished. Finally, there was the

8

harsh reality that it was becoming more and more difficult to find among already scarce teachers those willing to put up with the inadequacies of the one room school. It was almost like the alternative to consolidated education was no education at all.

The arguments for consolidation boiled down to the promise and the means of equal educational opportunity. Consolidation would mean better schools with better teachers and facilities at the lowest possible price. The stigma of the eight grade country school would be replaced with the same opportunity for high school enjoyed by the city child. Pride would be restored to rural education and made secure by a broader financial base.

Although the battle lines were drawn, and battles raged across the land, the area newspapers hardly mentioned the contest. However in May of 1921 the editor of the Clinton Republican noted that advocates of consolidation were "claiming great and valuable results may be secured therefrom—!"[1] His editorial reviewed some of the claims without comment, but then looked askance at the intention of feeding children in school and of teaching farming and home economics (properly the responsibility of parents). Without being specific, the editorial forecast that losses would result from the discarding of the neighborhood school. "Here's hoping," wrote the Editor, "that the final decision in regard to this important matter will prove to have been wisely taken." Only a test would determine if net benefit was to result.

When voters in nearby Meridian and Alaedon Townships elected to make that test by a vote of 203 to 93, the opponents of consolidation hotly rejected defeat by taking the election itself to court. The finding of the court was that the election had been technically illegal and consolidation was enjoined from taking place.[2]

While consolidation went down, at least temporarily in Meridian and Alaedon Townships, interest in consolidation picked up elsewhere. In Bath, the drive toward consolidation was led by the very officials who were responsible for the administration of the country schools.

Men like George Morris, Enos Peacock, G. E. Spangler, and Melville Kyes were all respected and determined farmers with a strong belief in education and its importance for the young people of the township. To a man they attempted to convince their neighbors that consolidation meant quality—the end of the country rube stigma, at a price they could afford. Unconvinced, the voters of the Bath fractional districts defeated consolidation the first time it was placed on the ballot.[3]

Undaunted, the proponents of consolidation kept returning to their trump card—the promise and subsidy of bussing! In place of the dangers which sometimes lurked along a child's way, the school buses promised child safety. They also tempted the residents with financial security. Buses required drivers; and they offered a new and valued source of employment for the township.

In Bath, the consolidation drive was possibly boosted by one other development—the membership drive for the newly organized Farm Bureau. The national Farm Bureau was an outgrowth of the wartime creation of country farm bureaus which operated under the guidance of the numerous county agricultural agents.

The Farm Bureau described itself as an organization of cooperative marketing associations—to further the economical handling of farm crops. Although its objectives were said to be commercial, legislative, and educational, it disclaimed any political objective. In 1919 it began an aggressive membership campaign, using designated solicitors.

The very emergence of the Farm Bureau would have supported the farmer in his growing sense of strength. A kind of consolidation, too, it would reinforce the need to consolidate educationally. But perhaps even more critical to the school consolidation question at Bath was the fact that Andrew Kehoe had volunteered to head the bureau's drive for membership in that part of Clinton County. Andrew Kehoe was the distinguished looking 47 year old farmer who had just moved into Bath Township.

In late April of 1921 a Bath Farm Bureau Unit was formed. It was made up of all the Farm Bureau members who made the village of Bath their trading center. Along with several other prominent farm leaders of the area, Andrew Kehoe was elected to the board of directors.[4] Kehoe was later to become the deadly critic of the consolidated school; but so long as he was engaged elsewhere, the foes of consolidation were left without any real leadership.

As mid-summer approached in 1921, the issue was still emotional and undecided. The proponents of consolidation, however, decided to make their move. The July 21st issue of the Clinton Republican carried this small notice: "A consolidation meeting will be held in Community Hall, Friday, July 22, 8 PM. The State Superintendent of Public Instruction will be present and give a talk. Everyone is invited to attend." The item looked harmless enough, just another little informational meeting; but without any further notice in the paper, the election was held just three days later! In the election of July 25th, consolidation carried by a majority of 68 votes. In reporting the victory, the Clinton Republican noted ". . . it is hoped that a central building will be ready for use within the next year or two—the building will probably resemble the modern high schools of today."[5] Overlooked was the fact that not all people shared that hope.

Two weeks later, on August 10th, the first meeting was held of the new consolidated board. As that meeting was called to order, Melville Kyes, the temporary Secretary, was proudly presented with the brand new leather embossed record book—its pages meant to record, through the official minutes, the building of the dream.

On August 12, 1921 the District Directors were instructed to turn over their district properties to the Consolidated Board.

Chapter IV
Building The Dream

The new board, Bath's first consolidated board, had its work cut out for it—but it was a consensus board, roughly representing all the fractional districts. Its leader was N. J. Sleight, the gentlemanly, distinguished farmer who knew how to organize meetings and get things done. In addition, this board was eager, and was willing to work tirelessly to meet its challenge. All it lacked was expertise and experience in running a comparatively large, quality school.

For guidance it sought consultation from the Superintendent of Public Instruction and from other newly organizing consolidations. However, because the board was pioneering itself, not much in the way of experience was available to it.

The problems were clear enough. The board needed a plant and it needed an operation. It needed a school site; it needed a building plan; it needed to raise money for the building, and it needed to build it. Temporarily, the one room schools would have to be operated until the new school was ready. A superintendent and faculty would have to be hired, and a transportation system would have to be developed. Once in operation, the goal would be to educate well while wiping out or neutralizing the opposition which remained to consolidation. The key, and the members recognized it, would be the new superintendent—but the building could not wait on that.

The first organizational meeting of the board on August 10th was hurriedly followed by a second meeting on August 12th. Instructions were prepared then to the District Directors to turn over their district properties to the consolidated board. On August 19th, the Board triumphantly named the new district "Consolidated School District Number One."

Next, the board tackled the hardest reality—the building of the school. Although consolidation had been voted in, a true cost and building plan had not yet been projected. Here, the board turned for advice to a Lansing architect, Warren Holmes. Holmes had devel-

11

oped considerable recognition as a designer of schools in Michigan, and he was not bashful about aggressively selling his product. The board would rely heavily on Holmes not only for his professional building expertise, but for reassuring the Bath area voters on the need and soundness of their investment.

True, conditions were prosperous by the standards of the times—but not by the standards of fifty years later. Public bodies might be given license by voters to spend relatively large sums of money, but those bodies were expected to scrounge right along with it—and all the way. In Morrice, for instance, voters were willing to spend say $39,000 on a new school—but only with the explicit understanding that bricks salvaged from the old burned school would be used in the construction.

In Bath, the tenth grade high school was the answer. The old building could be salvaged. It could become a part of the consolidated building to be built. Several fewer classrooms would need to be built, and the economy would be evident. Hopefully it would be evident enough to make the proposed $43,000 price tag acceptable to enough of the voters.

The old school had to be the answer for another reason. It removed site as an issue. The school would be located exactly where residents expected a high school to be located—where it had always been located—at the bend in the road on Main Street which seemed to almost point to the spot.

There really couldn't have been a better location. The street design showed it to be the juncture of divergent community interests, compromised in the interest of the community. Atop the Bath Village hill, it would stand on the highest ground in the village, towering over it as the old shcool had, symbolizing the highest aspirations of all the district's residents and clearly representing what they considered to be the number one responsibility of self-government—the preparation of the children for a better life.

Even the proposed leap in millage wouldn't be all bad. Sacrifice itself can be rewarding, and these people were raised to respect sacrifice. For the majority of the district's residents, the argument to fund the consolidation was overwhelming. The election was held in the Bath Town Hall on November 12, 1921—and it was decisive. By a vote of 56 to 20, the residents voted to bond the district for $43,000 to build the new school. The board had carried the day on this most critical issue, and it had done it the first time around.

Although the negative vote indicated there were foes still, the outcome anticipated the very great pride of these residents in providing the very best for their children. The children would be educated as they should be, and they would be safe "from the time they leave the door to the time they are brought back ..."[1] It seemed to be a reasonable expectation. The price of victory, however, may

12

have been increased bitterness among the opposition who still smarted from the earlier vote taken at a poorly advertised meeting— and from the strategy which separated that decision from the cost reality of carrying it out.

Once the bids for construction were let, and the contract awarded (to Ehringer Construction of Lansing), the board turned its attention to more operational matters. Strangely enough, this activity was preceded by a resolution of the board on November 26th that all their school meetings be private.[2] Coming hard on the heels of the voters support of the bond proposal, it could have been an unwelcome move, with the appearance of ungratefulness—but in fact it simply confirmed a practice and attitude which even today officials are loathe to give up. The practice might later deny the Bath public its opportunity for warning. Later yet, the public record of the board would be the best documentation available for retracing a murderer—but its cryptic style, (largely limited to recording actions on motions), would bar the same door it opened.

Certainly, any such early move on the part of the board, would not have gone unnoticed by the board's future antagonist, Andrew Kehoe. Although he would be unlikely to attempt to change the practice if he were on the board, as an outsider "secret" meetings could only reinforce his identification of the board as an adversary.

With the building question behind it, the board moved just as energetically to tackle its other problems, the most critical being the hiring of a superintendent. The board well knew that hiring the right man was absolutely essential. Much of the operation would be on his shoulders. Precedent and direction for the future would be under his tutelage, for the board would need to rely heavily upon him.

Quite naturally, the board turned to Michigan State Agricultural College for advice and suggestions. The man suggested by the college came something as a surprise—at first. Emory E. Huyck was the man, but he had had no administrative experience, a qualification which had seemed essential. In fact, the board was being asked to consider a man who, at the time of the suggestion, had not yet graduated from college.

There were, however, offsetting circumstances. One of eleven children, Mr. Huyck was raised on a farm near Carson City, and was president of his graduating class there. He had attended Ferris Institute before entering the service. In the Army, he served as a training officer at Camp Custer teaching new recruits how to speak and read English. Following the war he had entered Michigan State College where he majored in agriculture. Chicken breeding was his particular interest. In addition, Mr. Huyck was married to an experienced teacher.

As the board reviewed Mr. Huyck's qualifications, it had to be mindful of other influential factors. First, school teachers and ad-

13

ministrators were in desperately short supply. Next, a man with successful administrative experience would cost money—more money than the district was really prepared to pay.

Basically, though, the board became convinced that it didn't need to pay top dollar to get a man of top quality. Mr. Huyck's lack of administrative experience seemed little more than a bargain factor —for Mr. Huyck truly looked like a bargain.

At 26, he had already demonstrated leadership. He had proven he could teach, and he had proven he could control men while teaching them at the same time. Instructors and administrators at the college recommended him highly, and in his wife he brought along the bonus of another qualified teacher. The board, of course, could relate to his farming background and they could expect top quality teaching from him in the agricultural subject area.

Beyond that, young Mr. Huyck could sell himself. He was short to medium height, wore dark rimmed glasses, and brushed his hair neatly back over his high forehead. His dress was immaculate, almost slick, and his carefully trimmed mustache reminded people just a trifle of Charlie Chaplin—but not more than a trifle. There was the quality of sternness and toughness about him, no nonsense. He looked people straight in the eye, and he could obviously be in control. His youth was the last quality a person would notice in this very alert, observant, and ambitious young man. And there was one other factor. Mr. Huyck was sold on the agricultural school. Through the consolidated approach, rural education could be everything anyone might want it to be.

The board didn't need to take long to consider. Emory Huyck was their man. On April 6, 1922, the Board moved to offer young Mr. Huyck $2,200 to act as Superintendent (as well as to teach) during the upcoming school year. Even with no administrative experience, Mr. Huyck knew he could bargain. He rejected the proposed $2,200 salary and came back with a counter proposal—$2,300. Not wanting to take a chance, the Board accepted Mr. Huyck's price on April 15th—and well it did. The contract with Mr. Huyck had no sooner been signed than he requested release from the contract to accept another position. Possibly it was a more lucrative position, possibly it was at a location more to his choosing. Possibly it was even some sort of premonition. Whatever it was, a contract was a contract in the eyes of the board, and on April 29th it rejected Mr. Huyck's request. Mr. Huyck's destiny was sealed, and the Bath Consolidated School Board had itself a superintendent.

With the availability of a superintendent assured, the board members moved ahead to hire teachers and to build the transportation system. These were the two components the members had promised themselves and the residents: advanced teachers, and safety for the children from the moment they left the house. The board had

14

already made an important move toward advanced education in hiring Mr. Huyck. Good teachers would follow, this year and the years following. The bus system, however, would be strictly up to the board.

First of all, the board needed to establish routes and publicize them and then put the routes out for bids. The routes would roughly cover the former fractional school districts; and the bus drivers would be local residents doing contract business with the board. Under the system established, the board purchased the necessary bus bodies while the drivers were expected to furnish the truck chasses for the motorized routes. One route was to remain horse drawn. Its driver would simply drop the bus body over a horse drawn wagon.

Although the routes were to be put out for bids, it was to be clear that low price would not be the only factor considered by the board in deciding who would be awarded the contracts. Apparently, though, the board would be able to make average monthly commitments of about $150. The drivers would be expected to pay operating expenses out of that. This amount didn't compare too unfavorably with the amount to be paid most of the teachers. For the most part the teachers would be paid in the range of $110 to $116 a month the opening year with a premium salary naturally enough, to the home economics teacher. Given the importance placed on the bussing operation, the routes promised to be highly sought after by the respected men of the district.

By August, the faculty had been hired and the bussing contracts awarded. Construction of the school building which had started in the fall picked up in the spring and proceeded through the summer at a feverish pace. Villagers and farm families visited the site regularly, to inspect and to admire. The final stages of construction took place under the watchful eye of the newly arrived superintendent. With no doubt at all this was the grandest building ever constructed in the township. It contrasted sharply with the simple homes of the village and the contrast marked its importance.

The pupils of Bath district needed only to await the building's final completion and readiness. Actually, they, the teachers, and the community were too anxious to wait. Following a special inspection of the premises by the County School Commissioner, the construction company agreed to let classes start during the second week of October (1922)—even before construction was completed.[3]

For Bath, it was a bright day as the brand new green school busses pulled up one at a time to discharge their loads of excited students at the front entrance of the new school. The boys were dressed respectfully in knickers, clean shirts, and bow ties—the girls in fresh gingham, carefully groomed and bowed hair. It was nothing all that unusual. In 1922 and for many years after, families who could afford

15

it, and most who couldn't, dressed their children nearly as well for school as for church. Education was respected and daily celebrated that way.

On this particular morning, the special greatness of the day was in the air. Usual school dress or not, no one could overlook it. The dream had come true!

Chapter V
To Make It Work

With the beginnning of classes at the consolidated school, the board had completed all those vital tasks necessary to getting the school up and ready and in operation. The work had been done with amazing speed and efficiency. The board could be pleased with its accomplishments. Only the final goal still needed to be achieved: to educate well while wiping out or neutralizing the opposition to consolidation which remained. With Mr. Huyck at the helm of administration, the board could certainly look forward with confidence to achieving that goal.

For Bath, however, and for the rest of the country, consolidation of the rural schools would remain an issue for some time to come—an issue which would stir the lowest and the highest emotions in men. No one could have guessed then that murder would result from either the original determination of Americans to sacrifice their neighborhood schools for quality education, or from the later reverse efforts to restore or salvage the neighborhood school by killing bussing.

On the contrary, the general mood in Bath appeared to be one of well-being. Consolidation brought with it a whole new, basically pleasant, way of life. The sight of the green school busses quickly became expected and anticipated—either on the back country roads or on the still unpaved main roads. They weren't exactly a thing of beauty—but they were a welcome sight and they got the job done. In design, the motorized bus resembled a World War I troop lorry—a windowed box on wheels with the engine housing jutting out in front. The divided windshield could swing out and up from its overhead hinges; and it was even graced with windshield wipers. The round popeyed headlights stared from either side of the engine housing; and the old tin fenders, no pretenses, stood boldly over their assigned wheels.

With one exception, comfort was not really built in. The inside of the bus was, well, barren. As a forerunner of seats, benches of wood ran on either side from the front to the rear of the bus. The pupils sat facing each other and braced for the countless bumps and lurches which were built into each dirt and gravel road.

Although the benches were better than nothing, the real comfort item was the heater—the solitary three inch pipe which carried hot gasses from the engine and extended from front to rear under one bench. In the winter time no one ever complained about the fumes.

Of course, life in the village was changed as well. The new school had to have teachers and, for large share, they were young, pretty, unmarried, and fresh out of the Normal school. Aside from the superintendent, Mr. Huyck, the principal, Mr. Huggett, and the shop teacher, the entire faculty was female. For the young bucks of the community the sudden presence of these young ladies created new and pleasant tension. The young instructresses were visible enough. Everyone knew where they lived (first at the rooming house operated by the Jury's which bedded and boarded the girls, and later at the hotel at the foot of the hill). From their boarding home the young women commenced their countless walks in town and out into the countryside. Walking was the most frequent, if not the most popular, form of exercise for the girls, and the goldfish pond down at Sleights nearby farm was a favorite attraction.

Dancing was not considered to be an acceptable form of recreation for these young models, but they were expected to become members of the local Grange, perhaps the largest local social organization. However, some activities were acceptable which, at a later date would have been frowned on as unbecoming someone of academic refinement. For instance, the young teachers ice skated in the sunken front yard of the Consolidated School when it froze over in the winter time, or they caught sleigh rides on Mr. Sweet's milk sleigh when it came into the Village, or went tobogganing down Moore's hill.

In warmer weather, they could roller skate down the side walk of Main Street. One of the stronger girls would position herself at the bottom of the hill just in front of the railroad track. So positioned, she would brace herself to catch the first skater to come flying down the hill. If it wasn't for the railroad track one could probably have coasted all the way to Sleight Road.

The teachers also played softball in the road in front of the school. The real treat for them though was the Saturday rail trip into Lansing following each payday. The girls shopped at the fine Lansing shops in the morning, then lunched at the stylish Home Dairy and enjoyed a Saturday matinee movie before catching the four o'clock train back to Bath. It was a treat never to be forgotten.

Of course the men teachers were required to live in a separate

17

rooming house, but at least both sexes could and did board together. When Mrs. Frank Smith took over the hotel, she roomed and boarded the female teachers, and boarded the male teachers and transients. The room and board came to $8 a week, really not too expensive for a young miss earning the sum of $109 a month.

On the surface, at least, and in more respects than not, the school was quickly moving from the status of welcome guest to one of the family.

Young Wilkins, for instance, was very much taken with the sight and mannerisms of a cute elementary teacher by the name of Doris Lentz—but wish as he might he simply couldn't find it in himself to approach the young lady. Fortunately, his mother had no such qualms and the ideal daughter-mother-in-law relationship was born. However, not everything with the school was so perfect.

First of all, the board may have gotten off on the wrong foot in its relationship with the superintendent—not that the relationship wasn't cordial enough. The problem was partly that the board members were all pretty much officials of the former fractional districts. For such districts board members were the administration, the complete administration. The teacher was the teacher. It was natural enough, then, to carry this board responsibility into the Consolidated School—especially when the board had to wrestle with the building of a new plant even before anyone knew who the superintendent would be.

Besides responsibility for acquiring building and grounds, the board also accepted responsibility for overseeing the maintenance of the property. The board not only contracted to have the building designed—it contracted to have it built; and it hired itself a janitor.

Although the board had hired itself a superintendent, it let out the bus contracts and directly supervised the bussing operations. Clearly, the board saw its function as providing complete support to the superintendent as he interviewed teachers and ran the academic program. The board apparently believed that by relieving the superintendent of all other responsibilities, he would be free to devote all energies to achieving the academic excellence it and he sought for the children of the Bath School District. It was a division of labor which would change slowly and too late.

Of course, those who were looking for a quarrel with the board didn't have to wait long. First, there was the early motion to conduct the meetings in private. Then there was the delay in getting school actually started in the consolidated building. Why couldn't the building have been ready at the very beginning of the school year? Next, the board's direct involvement in carrying out school business was sure to bring trouble. In later years, such trouble would be called "conflict of interest."

In Bath, the latter problem was almost one of having a conflict of

18

interest or no interest at all. The board members knew personally just about everyone in the district; and had to do business with a sizeable number of these to keep the school going. With every such business contact the question could be asked, "Was the business granted out of personal favor?" Sometimes, there would be no one else to do business with, and still the question would be asked. One thing is certain—because of the times, the board's concept of conflict of interest was ill defined. Possibly the board could have done better, but who is to say? It was the way of life—but it forebode trouble.

The troubles of the board regarding conflict and elsewise were chronicled in an imperfect yet revealing way in the board minutes: At the meeting of August 6, 1922 Mrs. E. A. Rounds was awarded a bussing contract. (Mr. Rounds was the Secretary of the Board. Unlike the other board members who were farmers, Mr. Rounds was plant foreman at one of the Lansing auto plants. His wife was a force to be reckoned with in the area. Although women were not yet to be found as members of school boards, they definitely had their say.) On September 27th, Mr. Rounds was approved as substitute driver for his wife. (Substitutes were requried for each driver chosen by the Board and, typically, the substitute was the spouse of the designated driver.)

Further items of interest:
—2/9/23 Mr. Huyck was offered a two year contract with a $200 per year increase.
—3/22/23 Mrs. Huyck hired by the Board to teach vocal music at $6 a day (this was after Mr. Huyck's acceptance of the Board's offer on March 10th).
—7/16/23 Mr. Rounds was defeated for re-election, losing to Melville Kyes, a farmer already distinguished for his fight for consolidation of the shcool district.
—7/10/24 The Board awarded a bus contract for one year to Mr. Warden Kyes, a son of the Board's secretary.

For most people, these events would hardly have been cause for raising an eyebrow. After all, they could be written off as legitimate actions taken to fill very definite need. But times were changing; and critics of the board were becoming less and less willing to simply bide their time. Given the nature of the opposition leadership, no way would the board's actions be given a judgment of innocence.

Mr. Kyes had been instructed on June 16th to "look after the painting and repairing of the bus bodies." This was a typical sort of assignment for a board member. The board's award of a bus route contract to his son, Warden, though, might be seen as something else. And why, enemies might ask, should practically brand new bus bodies need painting and repair anyway?

Not only that, there was the motion made and passed on May 27th

19

to "investigate bus routes, drivers and the inner reconstruction of the school." Most of that motion was innocent enough, hardly a cause for criticism, but to have problems at this early date of any kind regarding construction was to invite censure and wrath. Obviously, the board was on top of the problem, but how could the problem have developed in the first place?

In addition, the board was having some personnel problems, with Mr. Harrington the one armed janitor and mechanic. On August 4th (1923) a motion was adopted to withhold his pay until the school was cleaned. He was also ordered to remove his garage from the school property immediately. Later in the same month Mr. Harrington's janitorial bid of $900 for the coming year was accepted by the board, but with misgivings. Obviously, parents or staff had complained about his performance of the preceding year, for his bid was accepted only on condition that he keep the school house warm or follow the instructions of someone who could.

The superintendent's performance, however was exemplary and the Board rewarded him with a two week summer vacation. Even that Board action probably upset farmers who felt their own work was never done. Grumblings might also have been anticiapted by the $200 salary increase given the superintendent and by the purchase of an athletic field and lighting plant. The image of a free spending board wasn't wanted by anyone.

If the board members had any anxiety over these happenings, they could well have thought that counter actions would more than balance them. For example, there were definite evidences of economies which could be pointed out. In October of 1923 the teachers and the board had joined a work force together on a Saturday morning to put in a catch basin. The board had initiated that move, nothing extraodinary, but it was an example of important work being done without any extra expense to the taxpayer. It also demonstrated, about as literally as it could be demonstrated, that the board and the faculty were working together as a team.

That was nice, of course, but the board could also point to an even more significant economy, one which was inseparable from the educational goals of the school. From the very beginning Mr. Huyck's chief goal had been to achieve academic accreditation. This was what the school was all about, and this is what he had been hired for. The board understood that he was well aware of the technicalities involved, of the processes required and of the basic requirements of accreditation. The board had recognized in him a man of the required knowledge and will to succeed. Very simply, if he didn't succeed at achieving accreditation, he wasn't going to be considered a success as a superintendent. Too much rode on it—the academic honor of the school, yes, but it was also the required ticket to federal state aid. For this tight fisted agricultural community, one was as imperative as the other.

Indeed, Mr. Huyck had wasted no time in making contact with the University of Michigan, the official accrediting body. In reviewing the requirements of accreditation, and the realities of the new school, he had recognized that accreditation would probably not be possible during the first year of operation, although the accreditation requirements which confronted the superintendent were simple enough: The faculty had to include at least one teacher with a degree from a four year institution! That was at the high shcool level. In addition, all other high school teachers were required to have two years of college. Besides these teaching qualifications, the school was required to offer sufficient units of instruction to meet entrance requirements of the university.

Beyond these rather concrete requirements, each school was marked for performance in more esoteric areas: the "efficiency" of the teachers, the "intellectual and moral tone of the school," "discipline," "management," "supervision of instruction," "the general estimate of the high school," and the "community school sentiment."

There were, undoubtedly, performance indicators which the consultant from the university used in his grading and in his advice to the young Bath superintendent. With his knowledge of those indicators, Mr. Huyck must have been confident by the Spring of 1924 that faculty, curriculum, and school performance were ready. The Spring inspection by the university inspectors was not dreaded, it had been sought. As was custom, the official decision of the university was not given during the inspection itself. The findings needed to be taken back to the university and carefully weighed there. Still, Mr. Huyck must have had every reason to believe that the school had indeed passed the inspection. He probably conveyed this belief to members of the board who looked forward to accreditation at least as much as he did.

In early May the suspense ended. In a letter to Mr. Huyck dated May 3, 1924, J. B. Edmondsen, the renown educator, stated with fitting pomp, "I take great pleasure in informing you that the University Committee on Diploma Schools has voted to place your school on the Accredited List for the term of one year ending June 30, 1925 . . ." There was more, of course, but most importantly, Bath had achieved its victory. In the following month, the board went through the formality of signing up for Federal and State Home Economic Aid.

Given the crowning achievement of accreditation, the board had every reason to expect a vote of confidence from the constituency. Even the details of the accreditatoin inspection report would have

21

supported that. Inspectors are not expected to find perfection even when it exists, and Bath was far from being a perfect school. Still, the recommendations were modest and in general the various areas of performance were marked "good." There were two exceptions. "Management" received an "OK" which was acceptable enough and "Community School Sentiment" received the highest mark of all, a "Very Good." This had to be interpreted as exceptionally good support of the school. Here, the inspector may just possibly have erred, relying more on past community performance as demonstrated by the new school itself than on more current realities.

The most distressing of current realities was the worsening farm picture. The high prosperity of the War years and the years immediately following had been replaced with dwindling markets. There were increasing farm failures. Individual farmers became increasingly pessimistic that they could make it. Even with this background, and three years after Bath had voted to consolidate, President Coolidge urged a resistant and reluctant farm population to revamp the rural schools. In speaking to 15,000 delegates of the National Education Association, he argued that the old one room country school must "give way to the consolidated school with a modern building and an adequate teaching force commensurate with the best advantages that are provided for our urban population."[1]

The Bath Board undoubtedly found comfort and support in the President again pioneering a battle which it had already fought. However, a speech by the new President of Michigan Agricultural College was probably more to the point. In his first address to the student body, President Butterfield said, "Any system of rural education that leaves out the stringent economic situation in which the farmers are, is a poor system; but," he went on, "any system which on the other hand makes the economic phase the main element, is wrong too."[2]

Most residents of Bath knew or felt they knew that the issue of consolidation had already been basically decided. Even so, they wanted absolute assurance that dollars were not needlessly being spent, and that the school administration and the Board were fully committed to efficient management. The times demanded it. Yet, many voters were not so sure. There were also those who never had accepted the finality of consolidation. As long as the one room school house still stood, a visible alternative to consolidation seemed to exist. For those critics, and for those others who simply wanted to survive the growing farm depression, confidence in the Bath school board members could not exist. Together, these critics looked for a leader.

The annual school meeting was scheduled for July 14, 1924. The terms of two board members had expired and there would be election to fill their vacancies. The record of the Bath School Board was on the line. The voters and the times would do the balloting.

Chapter VI
Challenge

The square-off in the first contest on the fourteenth pitted two formidable foes: Mr. Enos Peacock, charter member and treasurer of the board, life long resident of the township versus the chief adversary, Andrew Kehoe, the emerging leader of the opposition.

Enos Peacock had stood not only for education in the district, he stood for Bath. His mother had acquired title to the land of the Peacock family farm back in 1872. The patent she acquired was deeded over the hand of the Governor, himself. Basically, the Peacocks were a pioneer family, one that quickly acquired prominence in the vicinity. The road the farm rested beside was named Peacock Road, and the country school which earlier gave one room elementary instruction was named the Peacock School.

Enos grew up with a very definite respect for education. He wanted as much education as he could get as a young man, and later, he wanted to do what he could to make the best education available to others. When he had graduated from the elementary school, he was needed to work full time on the farm. Even that didn't stop him from enrolling at the tenth grade high school in Bath. In the end it had taken him four years to complete the two years at Bath, but he had done it. That was back in 1897.

Enos had married since that time and had two children in the Consolidated school: Florence, 13, and a nine year old son named simply, R. T. Now, 45, Enos no longer possessed the striking handsomeness of his youth. He had become definitely paunchy, and the corners of his mouth appeared to droop in an almost perpetual scowl, giving him a nearly Churchillian appearance.

Peacock spoke in slow, measured, precise wording and in his own way was definitely a leader. Especially because of his years of leadership on the Peacock School Board, he was highly respected by the members of the Consolidated School Board. He was esteemed as something of an expert on educational matters. He knew school law and he knew the references to it. But most of all he was a liberal and an enthusiast in education. He had identified himself with the cause of Consolidation, and had won critical support for that cause among fellow natives of Bath who respected his opinion. If the Consolidation Board had to pick its best representative, it could hardly pick a better man.

Peacock's chief antagonist in the contest proved to be a somewhat younger gentleman by the name of Andrew Kehoe, Andrew P. Kehoe. Kehoe was a relative newcomer to the area, but many newcomers had come to Bath in recent years, and several had not only been accepted by a sometimes suspicious populace, they had achieved positions of leadership. More often than not, these newcomers had been forced to overcome the suspicions first. If Kehoe had any such original handicap, it must have been lightened considerably by his wife's esteem in the township.

The great difficulty in contesting with Kehoe was that he was practically two formidable foes in one. First there was Andrew Kehoe and what he was and represented (or what the community thought he was and represented), and then there was Andrew Kehoe, husband of the former Nellie Price who had once resided in Bath. Nellie Price was not only a popular teen age girl when she had lived in Bath, she was a member of one of its most respected families.

Her Uncle was Lawrence Price, a truly outstanding American. Price had earlier farmed in Bath Township and built what was now the Kehoe residence just west of the village. Price had been a Civil War Hero, an auto pioneer, a significant philanthropist and a politician all rolled into one. The people of Bath were familiar with his history.

Price had been born in County Tiperary in Ireland in 1843, the son of an Irish mason. He had come with his family (which included Nellie's father) to this country in 1849, was raised in Lewiston, New York, and attended the Lewiston Academy for four years. Finishing the academy just in time for the start of the Civil War, Price enlisted in the New York Light Artillery and was assigned to the Army of the Potomac. The assignment commenced a series of actions which would have been a novelist's dream and a soldier's nightmare. Before the war was over, he saw action at Antietam, Fredericksburg, Chancellorsville, and Gettysburg; was wounded twice, captured, and incarcerated in the infamous Libby Prison. Finally, at war's end, he was released in time to take part in the Grand Review down Pennsylvania Avenue.

In 1866, with the war behind him, Price came to Lansing hoping to find his fortune. By 1883 Price, handsome and mustached, was ready to carry his talent for adventure into the business world. He immediately began a series of business and investment sorties that were to have tremendous impact on Lansing, on Michigan, and even on the nation itself. In this, he combined characteristics of daring and tireless energy. His aspirations for the community and for business seemed to go hand in hand; and, with other Lansing businessmen he moved boldly to establish Lansing as one of the great automobile centers of the world. Although Oldsmobile had originally commenced manufacturing in Lansing, its plant had been moved to Detroit. When fire partially destroyed that plant, Price and other Lansing business leaders led a determined and successful fight to lure Oldsmobile back to Lansing.[1] Critical to this successful fight was the decision to build an auto body supplier plant nearby which could supply Olds as well as other companies. Lansing Auto Body was formed in the Summer of 1901 for that purpose. Price became its President and guided its fortunes during the prime years of providing auto bodies to auto manufacturers. (Lansing Auto Body was to precede Fisher Body in Lansing by some twenty years.)

Lansing Auto Body was by no means Price's only effort in the auto industry. He was a director and organizer of Gier Pressed Steel, and of the Auto Wheel Company. Auto Wheel was to later merge with Prudden and with the Lansing Spoke Company to become the giant Motor Wheel Manufacturing Company. Price was also an original stockholder in REO, the auto and truck manufacturing firm formed by R. E. Olds after the latter sold his interests in Oldsmobile. With interests, successes, and needs such as these ventures represented, Directorship with the Lansing City National Bank was almost automatic.

In short, Price was an auto pioneer of the first order. His efforts helped Lansing rival Detroit and Flint as auto capitol of the world. To a large extent, Lansing spawned and was spawned by the auto industry. Oldsmobile, REO, American Motors, Fisher Body, Motor Wheel, General Motors—all had roots there. But if Lansing names like R. E. Olds, Roy Chapin, and Price competed with the likes of Durant and Ford in the industry, Price was the name inseparable from the Lansing community.

With all of his business interests Price still found time to serve variously as Chief of Police, as Superintendent of Public Works, and as first Chairman of the Board of Supervisors. Politically, he was so well thought of, that in 1916 he won the Democratic nomination for United States Senator from Michigan. As rock-ribbed-republican as Michigan was then, even a man of his outstanding qualifications was destined to defeat. Still, even in defeat, some folks took to calling him "Senator".

Lawrence Price died the year following the election. The time was February 12, 1917. Ironically, the headlines of the State Journal read, "Lawrence Price Dies In Bath City". The city referred to was actually Mt. Clemens, famous for its Sanitarium and baths.

Mr. Price had been undergoing treatment there at the sanitarium for Neuritis. Said the Journal, "Mr. Price was in every sense of the word a self-made man. He came to Lansing empty handed and by his genius of organization became one of the big business men of the city. He did more to advance the commercial and manufacturing interests of Lansing and Ingham County in the early years than any other man of his time."[2]

A Journal Editorial on the 13th stated, "No man in Lansing had more business courage than he and no man was a better judge of the possibilities of success in a younger man."[3] (Undoubtedly, Mr. Price had frequent opportunity to meet and observe the husband of his

25

brother's daughter. Probably he attended the wedding. However, if he had any apprehensions about Andrew Kehoe, he either kept these to himself or expressed them without avail.)

The general picture of Mr. Price was, that he was a quiet, modest and generous man obsessed with the idea of seeing Lansing stretch out and grow. Besides his wife, Julia—the former Julia Bradford, he left three adopted children, Justine, George, and Irene—and he also left a fortune. In his will he provided for his wife and children and for countless numbers of brothers, sisters, nieces and nephews.

Price also provided for a great number of charities.[4] His greatest gift, however, was to create a new Lansing Hospital. In his will, Mr. Price stated, "It is my desire and intention, to devote the sum of $100,000 to the establishment of a hospital in the City of Lansing, Michigan to be owned and conducted by some religious community of the Roman Catholic Church."[5] Fittingly, enough, the hospital was named St. Lawrence Hospital. For the people of the City of Lansing and the surrounding area, it was to become a major place of respite and repair—destined to serve the Price family and the people of Bath in ways that could never have been anticipated.

Now while the Patrick Price family was not precisely the same family as the Lawrence Price family, Patrick was obviously close to his older brother. They were raised together, migrated to Michigan together following the Civil War, their families stayed in proximity of one another throughout their life times; and they chose to share the same burial site in death.

Patrick however never achieved anything like the business success of Lawrence and always showed some inclination to lean on his brother. Until he moved to Lansing in 1908, he stuck pretty much to farming. He married early and Ellen (Nellie) was the first of six daughters and a son. The family apparently lived in Bath[6] on the brother's farm for most of the years of Nellie's childhood. When the mother died rather suddenly in 1893, Nellie was eighteen. Her brother and sisters ranged all the way down to three years of age. The burden of mothering the children fell heavily on Nellie since the father never remarried. Nellie was 31 by the time the youngest reached the age of 16. In the process she forfeited her opportunity for young romance and early marriage.

When Patrick moved to Lansing in 1908, he picked up a house large enough for himself and his five daughters (one had married). Lawrence Price held the mortgage. His brother also employed him as a mechanic at the Auto Body plant. Patrick's comparatively modest house on Seymour was located not more than three blocks from the more mansion like dwelling of his older brother's on Washington Avenue. It was a convenience for families which wanted to stay close together.

In moving to Bath with his wife, Andrew Kehoe could hardly have escaped identification with the famous and respected Price family. It was natural for the residents of the Bath area to make the association and to make the identification. The identification meant that Kehoe would be considered no outsider. He would be considered an insider from the very start. The identification also meant that he would be supported in the direct image he projected—a man of business acumen, with an instinct for efficiency.

In point of fact, little was known of Kehoe. People weren't sure just how he had met Nellie in the first place. One story had it that the two had met while each was taking courses at the Agricultural College. Another version had it that Kehoe had himself once lived and worked in the Bath area as a young man. If so, no one in Bath could later recall such residence. A meeting at the college may have been more likely. At the same time, no one questioned that the two had much in common. Both were from large farm families, and Kehoe's came from a first generation Irish family, and so did Nellie. Each was introverted, at least in a sense, and each had apparently opted to let the child bearing years slip by.

They had married on May 14, 1912, at the Cathedral in Lansing. Mr. Price, who had long grown accustomed to having Nellie around, honored the couple with a reception. Later, following their wedding trip the couple set up housekeeping at the Kehoe homestead near Tecumseh. Seven years later, when the Uncle died, Nellie's old farm house became available through the Price estate, and the couple seized the opportunity presented.

The move from Tecumseh was no logistics problem. Bath was some distance away from Tecumseh, but both were stops on the Michigan Central Railroad. When the Kehoe furniture and equipment was unloaded at Bath, the residents there were impressed. The shipment included house furnishings and two carloads of the finest and most up-to-date farm equipment. As the house furnishings were unloaded it was obvious they would more than become the modern and highly envied farmhouse.

Naturally, Kehoe and his wife were eagerly welcomed into the community and its social clubs. Kehoe himself was immediately recognized as a modern farmer and a frugal one. While he had a tractor which he wasted no time demonstrating, he denied himself the use of an automobile. Kehoe also became a very active member of the newly forming Farm Bureau, and volunteered to meet and discuss membership with his reluctant fellow farmers. When a special Bath Unit was formed he was elected to its board of directors. In all ways, Kehoe appeared to move aggressively and receptively into the community life. He was recognized as an advanced farmer who could get the most out of his 80 acre farm by demonstrating the latest in farm machinery, and electrical and explosive know-how.

Unfortunately for Mr. Kehoe, his small acreage left very little room for exacting the profit he needed. He had made a down payment of $6000 on the farm which had an assigned market value of $12000. With the mortgage payments being what they were, and with taxes being what they were when he moved in, he could make it. Any sharp increase in property taxes, though, would be rougher than Mr. Kehoe cared to deal with.

Possibly he had overlooked this potentially major problem when he bought the farm. Possibly no one called the risk to his attention. Probably, his newsness to the area, and his preoccupation with the Farm Bureau membership distracted him at the critical time of the campaign for consolidation. At any rate he was slow and ineffective in reacting. The consolidated school vote had succeeded; and later the property taxes sharply increased as a result of the November, 1921 vote to finance the new school.

Kehoe's apparent immediate reaction to the decision for consolidation was at one time definite and swift. For reasons he did not explain he dropped his association with the Farm Bureau.[7]

In addition, over the next two to three years, Kehoe truly made up for lost time. He became increasingly critical of the Consolidated School and the manner in which it was operated. He was not alone. Farm conditions were getting increasingly tough. As farm prices skidded, farm failures mounted and so did criticism of the board which was responsible for the sharp increase in taxes. The growing number of school critics found their leader in Andrew Kehoe.

As Kehoe approached the contest, one flaw in his Bath History could have done him some harm. The flaw was perhaps minor, depending on how one looked at it or just how it happened. Shortly after moving into Bath, Kehoe had shot the harmless dog of a neighbor. The incident pretty well broke the growing neighborly relationship, but the neighbor chose to make no big thing of the matter. As a consequence, the shooting slipped by largely unnoticed by the community, a non-issue.

The issue which was before the people at the annual school meeting was the record of the board—Enos Peacock standing for the board and its policies; Andrew Kehoe standing for the opposition.

As Mr. Peacock came into the voting assembly, he was greeted warmly by nearly everyone present. To most, he was nearly as familiar as Bath itself. Counting annual meetings for the old Bath ten year High School, the Peacock Country School, and the new Bath Consolidated School, this was the twenty eighth annual school meeting since Enos had proudly completed his tenth year at the Bath school. At annual meetings, people expected Enos to be there. His mere presence confirmed the institution. But it was no bell weather of how an election might turn out.

With Andrew Kehoe, it was different. People knew who he was and what he stood for, but they were not yet all that accustomed to his presence. No one could remember his presence at any other regular or annual school meeting. For the supporters of the board, his presence created a sense of uneasiness. Possibly some sensed a quality in him which would later be recognized by all as a very definite characteristic. Andrew Kehoe was not apt to enter contests he thought he might not win. His inclination always was to underestimate the strength of his support and to over estimate the strength of his enemies. A defect not yet recognized was the need sometimes to even create enemies where none existed.

But this night, Andrew Kehoe was expecting support. His appearance exuded that expectation. With his pretty, yet somehow frail wife at his side, he simply looked like a man of confidence. He was well-tailored and looked accustomed to the expensive suit he wore —unlike many of the other men who looked uncomfortable and simply out of place in clothing they reserved for Sunday church meetings or other special occasions.

But Kehoe didn't exactly look like a dude either. He stood five foot nine, just a cut above the average. His clothing did not conceal his muscular frame. He was obviously strong, even handsome, perhaps. His steel grey, wavy hair was parted on one side, and was marked by a clear streak of prematurely white hair. His rather striking blue eyes casually, but carefully counted the one hundred or so persons present and he made a point of politely searching out several who did not come forward to greet him. He maintained a certain reserve, still, one which some surmised reflected an exalted opinion of himself.

Mr. and Mrs. Kehoe took their seats with the other school district residents and waited briefly for the meeting to begin. The large study hall had not been designed with town hall meetings in mind, but it would do. Compared to the old town hall it expressed a relative grandeur. Nothing could be more fitting for an annual school meeting.

Mr. Sleight, who was still board president, wasted no time in opening the meeting. With the other board officers, he sat at the table placed on the elevated platform at the front of the room. The "People's Party" ballots were distributed. The tellers were appointed to count the votes of the evening; and the first contest began—the contest for Enos Peacock's seat. Under the rules of the vote, balloting would continue until one of the candidates received a majority.

On the first ballot four gentlmen beside Peacock and Kehoe competed. Following the vote, the ballots were collected by the tellers and counted. The residents waited anxiously in their seats. The tellers hurriedly handed in the results to Mr. Sleight who announced the result. On that first ballot, Mr. Kehoe received only

28 votes out of a total of 91, but it was the largest single vote. Ominously, Mr. Peacock came in only third. He could well hope, however, for a shift in his direction on the second ballot. The ballots were again distributed for the second vote.

The count on the second ballot, though, was a definite disappointment for the Peacock hopes. Although his votes remained steady, the Kehoe vote climbed sharply from 28 to 42. The Kehoe vote was still less than the required majority, but the issue no longer seemed in doubt. Those present sensed it, and their actions belied it. The only question seemed to be—which ballot?

Ballots were again distributed, and the voting began. The marking went faster this time, and the tellers hastened to collect and tally the vote. (Six more votes were cast than on the first ballot.) When the announcement was made to the hushed assemblage, the consistent shift to Kehoe from the other candidates was all too apparent: "Andrew Kehoe, 55," came the announcement, and most knew immediately that it was all over. "Enos Peacock, 16," the announcement continued, "Fred Cochran, 23; William Dryer, 1; Guy Richardson, 1; Evro Spangler, 1." There was another pause and the announcement concluded, "Andrew Kehoe, having received a majority of all votes cast, is declared elected trustee for three years."[8]

In the end, Mr. Peacock had held onto a small but loyal following, but his policies, his image as a leader of a liberal spending board were renounced. If there was any question as to, "why?" it should have been settled in the next contest. J. W. Webster, the board treasurer and charter member of the board stood for reelection to the seat he was vacating. The outcome was the same. Mr. Webster came in a poor third to Evro Spangler. The tone for the evening had been set by Mr. Kehoe, and there would be no vacillating.

For Andrew Kehoe, it was a great evening—perhaps the greatest moment of his life. He had taken on an established and popular board. With possibly only one questionable exception, he had fought fairly and squarely in the acceptable and time honored American way, and he had won. Actually, Andrew Kehoe felt he had every reason to be ecstatic. Although only two of the five member board had been unseated, the voice of the electorate was clear to him. The voters wanted a different leadership, a different philosophy —and a different board. Andrew Kehoe could make that difference.

On the way from the building, Andrew Kehoe and his missus received many congratulations, a handshake here, a pat on the back, a friendly word from acquaintances who melted into the darkness to find their way to their "machines." A few caught rides with friends, and the villagers simply walked to their nearby homes.

Among the well-wishers that night, none could have guessed the horrible consequences which were to come from that vote. In the years to come there might be endless recounts in the hearts and souls—but always with the same anguished ending. A mere switch of seven votes, it might be reasoned, would have changed everything.

Clearly, no school election in a people's history ever dramatized so sharply that the lives of children are the issue. Some parents would be tormented by the consequences for the rest of their lives.

Chapter VII
The People's Choice

Unknown to the voters of Bath was the fact that Mr. Kehoe was apparently in financial difficulty even before Consolidation had been adopted. He had made no payment on his mortgage in more than three years! Although Kehoe sent $360 on March 29, 1921 (the last money received by the estate) he had written the executor of the estate in 1922 to say that he could make his next payment only by sacrificing some of his stock and crops. When the executor, Attorney Dunnebacke, replied reassuringly that an extension would be given, Kehoe continued to default—and continued to be concerned. At roughly the same time as the 1924 election for the board, Kehoe wrote his wife's uncle, also an executor, expressing concern that he and his wife would be forced to leave the farm. Again, Kehoe received a reassuring reply.

Without the benefit of information on Kehoe's mortgage delinquency, the people of Bath came to the 1924 school election with an unmarred image of Kehoe, the astute business man, the man of honesty and integrity. Without this information, too, they could not know that a developing rage against school taxes had a companion rage developing against the Price family itself. Probably, no deception was intended by Kehoe. He was by nature a secretive man about his private life. In his eyes he could come to the first board meeting of the new year with clean hands—and with a mission and a mandate.

Kehoe's purpose on the board was to run a tight financial ship. That was the purpose at least as the community saw it. If that was the purpose as Kehoe himself conceived it, the goal was reasonable and achievable. If there was a companion goal to gain control of the board, that, too, seemed reasonable—but if the goal was to

31

accomplish big money saving through major cutbacks or return to country school education, Kehoe was misjudging the times and the power of the board membership. Time, and Kehoe's changing perception of his own situation would tell.

The first meeting of the new board took place on July 21, 1924. This time, the board met at its regular meeting place, in the room adjoining and opening into the Superintendent's office. The time was early evening, the accumstomed time for the board to meet—and the meeting was largely ceremonial.

Along with Mr. Spangler, Mr. Kehoe was sworn in by Alonzo Webster, father of the deposed board member, and local insurance agent for the Hartford Insurance Company. Ironically, the first motion after Kehoe's swearing in was Mr. Kyes' motion, ". . . that Alonzo Webster look after insurance on the school building."

Even at this first meeting, Kehoe did not delay in asserting himself. Two motions offered by him were adopted by the board. He obviously knew what he was doing and moved quickly to take the initiative.

However, if Kehoe had any illusions of gaining easy control of the board, they were shattered at the organizational meeting which took place on the twenty-third. While Kehoe might easily have reasoned that his election at the annual meeting signalled a wish for a change in leadership and attitude, the liberal members read the election literally and quite differently. They reasoned that only two liberal members out of five had been unseated, and that the majority still prevailed. Also, the little matter of seniority was definitely on their side.

N. J. Sleight, charter member of the Board, was re-elected President and Mel Kyes was re-elected Secretary. In comparison to what might have been, the election of these gentlemen represented a very real defeat for Kehoe. But Kehoe did not come away empty handed. He was elected Board Treasurer—a gesture of recognition by the Board of the unrest which had resulted in Kehoe's election to the board. Actually, it was about as nice a trophy as one could hope for in defeat. As treasurer, Kehoe would have both responsibility and status. As keeper of the purse strings he also had authority. It was an authority Kehoe would enjoy, and exercise.

With at least some basis in reality, Kehoe could have breathed easily, notwithstanding his initial setback of the evening. Besides feeling confident that the electorate was already on his side, he could realistically expect even greater support as the worsening farm picture extended its pinch.

Conceivably, Kehoe needed to do little more than stand pat. However, sitting tight while his political base slowly and independently expanded was not in Kehoe's nature. He was confident that, one way or the other, he could best his adversaries on the board by more or less direct confrontation. If his efforts to curb spending did not gain dominance there, the record would speak for itself, and public repudiation of the board majority would be doubly assured. The Kehoe strategy was to go on the attack, just as he felt mandated to do. As Kehoe had already found out, however, the board was formidable.

Serving as the consolidated board's president for the fourth year, since its inception, was wizened N. J. Sleight. Sleight conducted meetings about as informally as could be allowed for a public body—probably because most of the members wouldn't have put up with any greater formality. The members were pretty good at talking, but not so inclined to put their talk in the form of a motion. When Mr. Sleight had to, he got his motion. He might have to beg a bit for it, but he got it. Mr. Sleight could also put a member in his place. As a pioneer for the Consolidated School, Mr. Sleight couldn't much care for Mr. Kehoe. Mr. Kehoe responded. His dislike for Mr. Sleight was explicit. It was one of the few things about board business that Kehoe confided to anyone.

Mel Kyes, of course, was secretary of the board. He was the Masonic big brother of Mr. Huyck, and in the unlikely event that Huyck should need a defender, Kyes was his man. Like Kehoe, Kyes had come from Catholic origins, but his family had bolted that church for economic reasons. His family had been of French, and possibly Dutch extraction—and he was also one-eighth Indian.

Kyes was taller than the other members of the board, and just a little round shouldered. He wore a broad mustache, and with his lean frame presented something of a scholarly appearance. Nearing 60 in 1924, he was Kehoe's senior, and probably the dominant member of the board. Besides a daughter at home, one son was graduated from the Consolidated School and was now attending the Agricultural College. That was Walt. An older son, Warden, had been president of his tenth grade graduating class at Bath. Warden was nearing thirty, was farming independently, and had been awarded a school bus contract just before Kehoe had been elected to the board. Because of that award, Warden was destined to become a center in the controversy which was to develop.

Ward's father, by the way, had one other distinguishing characteric. Blind in his left eye, the elder Kyes walked a little sideways to get the best possible vision out of his good eye. He could walk all right that way, but he couldn't drive. Walking was really out of the question anyway, since his place on the Looking Glass River was several miles out of Bath in DeWitt Township. So Walt and Warden took turns driving their father into the board meetings. Often one son would sit in for the entire meeting. Sometimes Walt, at least, would even take the minutes unofficially for his father. It was a custom Kehoe would have to live with.

33

Besides Kehoe, E. Spangler, the other newcomer on the board, had also unseated a liberal and charter board member to get his seat. While Spangler's election meant some discontent with the spending of the old board, it represented more the wish for a change than the selection of a conservative spending leader like Kehoe. Much as Kehoe might have wished, Spangler was not similarly a dedicated foe of the members of the old board. Spangler was simply a ploddy sod buster who was dedicated to the education of his children. He was straight and square shouldered, and sported a youthful cherubic face. He liked a good joke, even a dirty story now and then. Those who knew Spangler best considered him a prince of a neighbor. He was ill at ease before groups, but later, when he became president of the board, he passed out diplomas to the Bath graduates like a good soldier.

George Morris, the remaining holdover of the board, had come on the board as a charter member. Morris was another farmer. He was of spare frame, thin faced, and smaller than the rest. He was a good thinker, but pretty much kept his thinking to himself until it was time to vote on an issue. Morris had the habit, disquieting to the more talkative members, of sitting through the meetings with his eyes closed. But the longer the meetings lasted, the more awake he became.

Kehoe, himself, completed the board's makeup. Compared to the others, he offered a contrast he felt comfortable in emphasizing. His dress was a cut above the others, his grooming near faultless. In argument, he was to the point and unyielding, attacking the positions of others from a real or feigned affect of intellectual superiority. It was understood that he was the only college educated member of the group, indeed, he did come across as a very smart man. Depending on how one looked at it, he had the knack of simplifying or over simplifying complex issues.

These men were to make up the board of the first "Kehoe" year. They were destined to work together, in a highly charged, but controlled emotional climate. They would work, discuss, and argue in the closest proximity. Each could examine and judge the others in the closest detail—and be examined in return. There was even the opportunity to record it all, to record tell-tale observations of their contributions, if not to record an understanding of them.

A record would exist, of course, but not a very adequate one. After all, the board had voted earlier to treat all school meetings as private. Basically, the minutes would record only official actions taken by the board. Not all official actions made it to the minutes. Those that did were given only bare bones treatment. The give and take of discussions was never recorded. In the beginning months, a reader could tell only if a motion was made, who made it, and whether it passed or failed. Later on, the vote tally was added. From the

34

minutes one could only guess the source of initiative for a motion and assume that a person who made a motion truly supported it. Since some motions were possibly made by the most insignificant party to a key move, or were made in disgust or contempt, the record was hardly reliable. In addition, many fights were fought and decided before ever getting to the motion stage. The concept of "the public's right to know" was not born yet. From looking at the minutes, even "the Board's right to know" was not all that certain. To really know, one had to have been there—and board members very very seldom missed a meeting.

The minutes still met the standards of the day. They probably met many of the practices, unfortunately, of fifty years later. In a sense, the meetings were the secret meetings the board had officially moved to make them. Only by word of mouth would Bath residents learn what was really going on at those meetings. They would miss whatever opportunity full disclosure would have given them to judge and act on their own behalf.

Whether open to the public or not, this was the arena in which Kehoe felt most comfortable. Although the stakes might not always be that clear, the board itself was Kehoe's chosen battleground.

For Kehoe, the board meetings quickly became central to his life. Meetings of the board were frequent, averaging nearly twice a month. They were also lengthy, often going until nearly midnight. Typically, meetings started with the Secretary reading the brief minutes of the preceding meeting. While old and new business got underway, the Secretary and the Treasurer carried on their fiscal transactions, keeping alert at the same time to what else was going on about them. Seated beside Kehoe, Mr. Kyes wrote out warrants and passed them on to Kehoe who wrote out the required matching checks for disbursement. The checks were later turned over to the Superintendent or disbursing officer, or were mailed or delivered personally by the Treasurer. The system, in effect, had two sets of books, the Secretary's, and the Treasurer's. They were used to balance each other. Sometimes, in the interest of fiscal responsibility, and always mindful of his very observant partner and critic, Mr. Kyes was known to stay up late at night trying to get a few cents to balance.

The Board meeting room was dimly lit by two suspended glass globes, a condition which made the tasks of both the Secretary and the Treasurer all the more difficult. It was a small room, adjoining the Superintendent's office—and Huyck was invariably there for the meetings, sitting at his desk. The five member board sat slightly apart at its three by five table. Huyck observed, and was invited to make suggestions. This was the way most of the board members saw it. Kehoe saw it differently. In Huyck, Kehoe saw a young upstart trying to tell the board how to conduct its business. It was also like

35

having four opponents to contend with instead of three, and he didn't like it. It was almost like sitting in Huyck's office, his bailwyck so to speak.

For Kehoe, Huyck's presence was a challenge, and he rose to meet it. Certainly, Kehoe's attack on Huyck was expected. Not so expected was the nature and intensity of the attack as Kehoe reacted to the threat and malice he saw in the Board's agent. As leader of the high cost Consolidated School, the Superintendent symbolized the excessive costs Kehoe was intent on wiping out. At times, though, Kehoe appeared intent on wiping out the Superintendent, himself.

In regard to certain of Huyck's responsibilities, Kehoe was much more rational, even enlightened—but toward Huyck personally, and as a participant at Board meetings, Kehoe showed only enmity. When he attempted to demand Huyck's ejection, however, he was rebuffed by fellow board members who suggested that ejection would mean loss of state aid. Kehoe relented and simply pretended the Superintendent was not present, reasoning, perhaps, that if nothing else was accomplished, the turtle (Huyck) wouldn't be inclined to be sticking his neck out and into the Board's business.

Undoubtedly, Kehoe found other irritants in the superintendent. Huyck represented authority. While Huyck was respected by the community as an honest and good superintendent, his control amounted sometimes to almost over control. At days' end, students were required to march from the building to the tune of martial music played on the piano. During the day, students tiptoed in the halls.

Staff members, needing to see him, manufactured excuses to see him in twosomes. Students felt compelled to truth by his stern eyes. He exuded self sufficiency and self confidence. He demanded respect and somehow conferred that same demand to his staff. On their way to school one day two high school girls had greeted two barely older teachers with a jaunty, "Well, hello gals." The penalty exacted by administration was individual conferences with those teachers and apologies to them. Part of it was the times, but much of it was the Superintendent.[1]

Kehoe certainly saw all this control, hated it, envied it. Huyck, a short man, was like a bantam rooster out to protect his territory. In Kehoe, Huyck perceived the threat. In Huyck, Kehoe saw an enemy he was determined to break and embarrass.

Huyck probably had allies aplenty anyway, but he chose to protect both himself and the school in the social arena. It was an arena he was particularly suited to. It was a natural, and it offered the most complete defense possible against attack on his school program. Although University examiners had earlier given high marks for community school spirit, Huyck sought to counter and neutralize the conservative attack which had been mounted by Kehoe. Kehoe

36

had won the annual election and it rightfully frightened Mr. Huyck and his staff, as well as the board. Huyck countered by organizing Bath's first PTA. In the fall of '24 (within months of Kehoe's election) it was fully operational. As such, the PTA was the only organization in the Bath District with the school experience as its focal point. It commanded wide representation—and it stood in support of the school.

If that wasn't enough, Mr. and Mrs. Huyck were both socially active as community leaders outside the school. Both were active in the dominant church of the community, the Methodist church, and both were members of the Grange. Mrs. Huyck had even brought some notoriety and fame to the community, when the Grange Chorus she directed won first place in the state competition. In addition to other club activity, Mr. Huyck was a member of the Mason's, the most prestigious fraternal organization in Bath's highly protestant community. All in all, the school/social combinations Mr. Huyck could marshal were varied and impressive.

Although the early part of Kehoe's tenure met with failure in his frontal attempt to eject the Superintendent, he pursued cost cutting relentlessly and with success. His efforts were businesslike and effective and they occasioned sharp skirmishes with other members of the board.

In July at the meeting on the thirtieth Kehoe moved successfully to reduce annual payments to the janitor by $60. At the same meeting he began a series of strikes at the Superintendent. When his argument to deprive the Superintendent of any vacation appeared to be failing, he beat other board members to the punch by success-fully moving to give the Superintendent a restricted one week vacation.

In October Kehoe tackled what he considered to be the school's sloppy purchasing policies. After the twenty-first, nothing was to be charged to the school by Bath merchants except on the order of the board member who served as the purchasing agent.

On the surface these were all good economy measures designed to give Bath residents the most for their money. The rebuff to Huyck, however, had all the earmarks of a personal slap, and from a board which previously had given him every support. By this action, Mr. Kehoe also made another point. Maybe the Superintendent was going to be present at these meetings, but he wasn't going to like it.

In December of the same year Kehoe was probably the main factor in holding a proposed Huyck salary increase to only $100. Had Kehoe had access to the minutes of the previous year, or if he had studied them, he would have noticed that the previous increase from $2300 to $2500 taken only the year before was conditional on its being a two year increase. Could he have shown that the action was not only against him, but against the position of the board itself, he might have been successful in holding the line against even the nominal raise which was given.

On March 30th Kehoe gave evidence that he was on no mission against management. He moved that the Board accept all of the Superintendent's teacher and salary recommendations. His action may have surprised and confused his fellow board members, and it probably assured him another and unexpected political victory. He could point to, and residents could see a record of tough cost cutting apparently tempered by support of the Superintendent when support was deserved.

As a matter of fact, the public's observation of Kehoe need not have been confined to an obscure written record. In some respects, Kehoe was quite visible. He was known throughout the district as a skilled mechanic and electrician, and with some exception the Board was not reluctant to take advantage of his skill. Unlike most farmers, Kehoe always seemed to have the time available, and he was willing. He was to become almost as much of a fixture around the school premises as the janitor. He had the tools as well as the skill, and for convenience, he set up a work bench right on the property. Obviously, no one was going to question such a convenient and rewarding arrangement—and, as long as Kehoe accepted no money for these efforts, the question of conflict of interest would not be raised. Very simply, Kehoe appeared to be the practicer of what he preached.

Partly, at least, it may have been due to that image that in April Kehoe received an unexpected plum. Maude Detluff, the popular clerk for the Township (also wife of the village blacksmith), became suddenly ill after the April election and died. The Village Township Board moved quickly to appoint Andrew Kehoe to fill out her unexpired term. The term had practically another year to run, and the Township could benefit from Kehoe's precise and tough business sense. No one raised any question of conflict, and Kehoe assumed the part time duties. (Not only was there some salary connected with the position, but it was a key contact position, placing Kehoe in a spot where he could make favorable personal contact with practically every adult resident of the Township of Bath. Real or not, Kehoe could well imagine himself to be the dominant political figure of the area—and growing stronger. The victory itself might not seem so much one of a string as reward for a string—a reinforcer of a job well done.)

Possibly in a mood of magnanimity, he took action with the school board to offer Mrs. Huyck a full time teaching position. Although married teachers were not generally looked upon with favor, the teacher shortage was still severe, and she could teach music as well as the second grade. Mr. Kehoe simply made sure that the price was right. At $1100 a year, it was a bargain.

38

The Kehoe string of victories was impressive. It was even accompanied by a certain recognition from within the board itself as he and Spangler were appointed to look after the school's light plant. It was like sitting on top of a wall he had barely begun to construct. However, if Kehoe thought back on it all, he most certainly would have judged the crowning achievement to have been his selection as township clerk.

Chapter VIII
A Dip in Popularity

Just before the annual school election of 1925, the Kehoe victory string came to an end. It was not a crippling defeat for Kehoe, was not treated as such by him, and it may even have temporarily strengthened his hand. Temporarily.

At issue was Bus Route number five. At least this was the surface issue. The question was the letting of contract for the route. During the year the contract had been held by Warden Kyes, son of the Board Secretary. As per board custom, the Board had advertised for bids for the coming year. This meant that Ward would have to turn in a competitive bid just like anyone else who might be interested in the contract. The Board reserved the right to reject any and all bids, of course, but in times of stress it might be hard pressed to reject low bids. When the bids were received, Ward's bid was not low. The fact that it was $80 high eliminated the chance for an easy disposition, and Kehoe must have sensed the real burden in this situation was not on him.

Kehoe, and everyone present, knew what a personal problem was being presented. Ward was the son of the Board Secretary. He frequently attended Board meetings, sitting in a chair off to one side while he waited for his dad. He was extremely popular in the Bath area and in DeWitt and he had performed faultlessly as a bus driver. Ward was a tall and muscular young man, rather loud and a rougher version than either his father or his younger brother. On the bus route he was excellent with the children. He held a strong hand of control, but loved to verbally mix it up with the kids in a good natured way. They loved it. They obviously felt real affection for him, and he obviously enjoyed them. Aside from Kehoe, the sense and the wish of the board would have been to again give the contract to Ward. No one, perhaps, not even Kehoe, would be thinking in terms of conflict of interest, but everyone was keenly aware of the relationship.

Probably it was the father-son relationship, as much as anything, that qualified young Kyes to be a popular secondary target for Kehoe—but given an opening like Ward's bid, Kehoe could zero in on the basis of economy alone. Still, friction between Kehoe and young Kyes did not seem to be fully a by-product of Kehoe's adversary relationship with Ward's father. Ward had developed a certain respect for Kehoe and his astuteness, but he was quite capable of baiting anyone on his own, including Kehoe. Ward loved an argument. He loved to argue. It was a trait he carried all his life. With friends, he loved to bait and be baited in return. Kehoe, of course was not above a good argument himself, but in Ward he saw a young man who simply didn't know his place. Kehoe also saw a young man who liked children and seemed to identify with them. Kehoe could perhaps tolerate children, but he had made it clear to Ward, at least, that he did not like them. In total, Ward's qualities of being the son of Mel Kyes, his clear enjoyment of children, and his brash brassiness, earmarked him. Kehoe didn't like him, and the feeling was mutual.

Well before bidding time, Kehoe had resorted to subtle little devices of harrassment. For instance, Kehoe often made a point of timing Ward with his watch as Ward passed the Kehoe house on his bus route. If Kehoe happened to be out in the front yard as Ward came by, he would pull out his pocket watch, as if to time Ward's punctuality. It annoyed Ward in a way, but it was almost as humorously peculiar as it was bothersome. The disposition of Ward's bid scheduled for the 6th of July could be equally bothersome, no matter how it was handled.

When the vote did come up on the 6th, after due deliberation, the Board voted to reject the low bids for bus route number five. Ward Kyes was awarded the contract for $1,000. At the same meeting the operating budget was raised from $20,000 to $21,000 for the year— and Kehoe entered the motion to adjourn. (The motion for adjournment by Kehoe was to become one of his trademarks. When he was displeased with the way things were going in a meeting, he would simply move to end the meeting. At this stage in his board career, Kehoe was just beginning to try the technique out. It was effective, and one way or another it scored.)

Although the Kehoe string of victories was now broken, it would be difficult to tell its true impact on the Bath voters. On the one hand, his opposition to Ward's bus contract might not have set well with the many families who thought fondly of "Wardy," or who respected Ward's father. On the other hand, people wanted those expenses held *down*! Kehoe had attempted to hold the line. The rest of the board had not.

The annual school meeting for 1925 was held a week later on the thirteenth of July. Mr. Sleight, who had been at the board's helm for its entire four years, chose not to run. Albert Detluff, the local blacksmith, ran for his vacancy and was successful. Like Spangler, Detluff wasn't running any martyred campaign against reckless spending, but people understood he was a man of economy and would stand for thrift. Detluff was a relatively young man, youthful in appearance, heavy-set with ruddy complexion and sandy hair—and, just as a blacksmith should be, Detluff was strong as a bull. He was the friendly bull, however, more interested in flowers than fighting. He loved having admiring children for his smithing audience and, for them, he always kept extra chewing gum handy. Detluff was a loving father, adored by his now motherless daughter, Marcia. The entire township had been saddened, with Detluff, when Mrs. Detluff had so unexpectedly died. Prior to that, Marcia's family had made its home with Mrs. Detluff's parents, the Millmans. In a way, the marriage had been one of contrasts. Maude Detluff, with a fine formal education from Alma College, and Albert Detluff, a completely unschooled blacksmith. With his wife's help and influence, however, he had become self educated and well read. While she lived, she had maintained dominance in the community, but Albert had been active with her. Like Kehoe, he had once been a strong Catholic. Now, he taught Sunday School at the Methodist Church where he had become active with his wife.

No doubt about it, Detluff was popular in the community. As a cost cutter, his popularity was probably his biggest weakness. He wanted to please every one. He wanted to be helpful and to reconcile. He tried to see each man's view point. In Kehoe, he had seen a man whose potential ought to be realized by the community. Although he recognized Kehoe's eccentricity, his tendency to perseverate, and his quickness to anger, Detluff had befriended him. The two spoke together frequently at the blacksmith shop, and they shared a love of tools, When Detluff's wife died, he undoubtedly encouraged Kehoe's interest and was probably instrumental in Kehoe's appointment as Township Clerk.

Although Detluff's nature was such that Kehoe could not count on automatic support on cost issues, or in other conflicts to be fought within the board, his election to the board had all the appearances of definitely strengthening Kehoe's hand. At the least he was not antagonistic to Kehoe. At the most, he would certainly be an ally on some issues. Events would prove, however, that Detluff was less an "ally" to Kehoe than a force for reconciliation. If Kehoe could accept some degree of reconciliation, he might accept that control of the board's spending policies was moving irrevocably in his direction.

Although Kehoe might have cherished hopes that he would be elected to the Board's presidency as a deserved reward, the choice of the meeting of the seventeenth was a more realistic one. Spangler was the choice—but he was a choice Kehoe could live with. He was nobody's enemy. He was as close to being neutral as any experienced member of the board, and he leaned just a bit to the conservative side.

The summer gave evidence once more that Kehoe, acting like a man in command, could be magnanimous. The superintendent had finally gotten his two week vacation. His vacation post card from British Columbia was like salt in Kehoe's wound. But Kehoe reacted uncharacteristically. In August he initiated action to give the Superintendent more operational responsibility. The Superintendent was given control over the timing of the bus drivers. Possibly Kehoe's mood was brightened by the $1,200 legacy payment his wife received from the Lawrence Price estate. The following month he took new action to increase the Superintendent's authority. With Kehoe's support, the Superintendent was to have authority over route changes which were indicated for pupil benefit.

Kehoe's action may well have been craftier than it first looked. In facilitating a rerouting of controversial Route No. 5, the stage was set for another showdown over Ward—if Kehoe chose to make an issue of it. Technically, Route No. 5 had become a new route, calling for new bids. Kehoe entered a motion that the Board advertise for drivers accordingly. Although the attack on the Kyes family was only thinly disguised, the membership bowed to the technicality. By a vote of 2 "Yes," one "No," and one "Abstention," the Board went with the Kehoe motion.

In a real showdown the vote might be something else. Probably, both Ward and his father knew this. When bids were called for, Ward simply didn't bid; and at the October 3rd meeting, his father moved successfully to reject all the bids which had been presented. When the dust from the meeting had settled, two conclusions were evident. Ward Kyes and his father had been discomfited, but they had prevailed. The flavor of the meetings was something else. There were no blow ups, no tempers were lost, but the hostility was in the air and its source was Kehoe.

Quite beyond the school (but definitely connected to it), something else was seriously bothering Kehoe. His difficulty with his farm mortgage was becoming a preoccupation with the belief that he had been victimized by the price he had agreed to pay. Another year of lapsed payments had gone by when the $1,200 legacy payment was released in 1925. When he and his wife dropped by the Dunnebacke law office to pick up the check, they simply picked it up without mention of the overdue principal and interest. The attorney bit his lip, but he was surprised. When no mortgage payment followed in the mail, he was perplexed. Obviously, Kehoe was not without the money to make the payments he had agreed to.

42

On September 12th, Mrs. Kehoe sent an inquiry to Judge McArthur, the Probate Judge who had jurisdiction over the Price Estate. She had written:

> Dear Sir: Kindly give me on the enclosed card the appraised valuation as fixed by the appraisers in the estate of Lawrence Price, deceased, of the following described property belonging to said Lawrence Price at the time of his death and since sold by the executors: East 1/2 of S.E. 1/4 of Sec. 18, Bath Township, Clinton County.
> Thanking you for this favor, I am
> Respectfully yours,
> Nellie Price Kehoe (signed)

The letter was both interesting and revealing. It demonstrated a persisting concern with the value of the property—a suspicion by Kehoe that the property had been sold to him at an unfair price—a price above market value. True enough, the letter had been signed by Nellie, but it was officious—it didn't sound like her. The inclusion of "the enclosed card" may simply have been accommodating, or it may have been cunning. If the Judge simply entered the information on the card, there would be no carbon copy to the executors. It *was* strange. For at least the second time, the Kehoes had gone on record as questioning the straightness of the executors. This time the attempt was by an end run on them, done in attempted secrecy. The executors and the Price family were one and the same. Would Nellie really risk a split with the benefactors within her family? The matter could be pressed only with severe risk to that very thing. Considering the closeness of the Price family, it just didn't add up.

The next month, and coincident with his second defeat over Ward Kyes' contract, Kehoe decided he needed explosives. It probably wasn't related at all. Probably something quite extraneous made him think of it. Late fall seemed a strange time for a farmer to begin preparations for blowing stumps and rocks, but maybe it wasn't. Through the years Kehoe had developed a knowledge of explosives, a familiarity and ease with them. His abilities were recognized back in the Tecumseh area and he handled dynamite free of charge for the farm bureau. If farmers wanted something blown, Kehoe was happy to show them how. In truth, he was delighted.

It was October, then, that Kehoe asked Job Sleight, his neighbor, to give him a ride to Jackson. From the farm agent there, Kehoe bought ten 50 pound boxes of Pyrotol, a World War I surplus explosive. He also purchased four boxes of caps to go with them. The idea was that back in Bath he would sell the explosives for a little more than he paid for them. It seemed like a good idea. Farmers could use explosives now and then, but most were leery of handling

43

them. In exchange for his service Kehoe would just add a little more to the price of the explosive than he had paid. It wasn't exactly a service people were standing in line for, but if they ever needed it they'd have the comfort of knowing that Kehoe was waiting to be of service. As it turned out, people knew all right that Kehoe had the explosives available, but no demand ever materialized.

On the school board, Kehoe continued his efforts to chip away at spending and in general to find fault with just about every idea that wasn't his own. He cleverly moved to have school closed *all* Thanksgiving week. (Savings on light and heat would result.)

In January of 1926 he made another head on attack on the Superintendent. It was that time of year when the Superintendent's salary for the coming year was usually discussed. The point was to come to an agreeable figure with the man. Normally, an agreeable figure for a good man required at least a token increase. No agenda had been published in advance of the meeting (none ever were), but the Secretary and the President especially needed to be prepared in advance of each meeting. This special relationship (that between a board President and his Secretary) has more than once created an attitudinal camaraderie between the two which has been decisive.

Kehoe needed no special preparation. He could expect that the secretary would make some nice little pitch about how fortunate Bath was to have a man of Huyck's qualifications. He could expect heads to nod in agreement. And he could expect that someone would naturally move to increase the Superintendent's salary. He could knowingly sit back in his chair, and maybe just grin enough. Or he could take a puff on one of his expensive cigars and float a lazy smoke ring right through the middle of the holy sounding nonsense.

Kehoe didn't wait for the motion to be made. He sought out the eyes of the Superintendent, caught them, and raised the challenge, "I move the Superintendent's salary stay exactly where it is." There was discussion, of course, but Kehoe's true estimate of the worth of the Superintendent was only too obvious without it. For Kehoe, the discussion clarified again that he could not count on a majority. His motion went down by a vote of three to two. But Kehoe had also scored. No one was going to try to make the Superintendent's raise very much.

As expected, Kyes came back with it, moved to give the Superintendent $100 more for the coming year. As expected, the motion carried three to two. Kehoe was furious. He was becoming even more convinced that the Superintendent was the one who really called the shots—that he was artfully conniving with more than one source to increase school expenses needlessly. The Superintendent would no sooner hit the board with one argument for spending money than he would hit it with another.

The big annoyance to Kehoe was the University of Michigan

44

Accreditation requirements. The inspectors always carried out their inspections in close consultation with the Superintendent—and somehow each inspection managed to exceed the previous one in the number of recommendations being made. It seemed that no sooner would one letter come down from the University than another would be on the way. A November 1925 letter noted that certain recommendations had been carried out: new maps, additional equipment for the Home Economics Room, an Encyclopedia, and lumber racks for the shop. But that wasn't good enough. Now the University wanted the school to be equipped with a second set of supplementary readers; it wanted pictures in all the rooms; it wanted World History Charts; and it even wanted playground equipment for the grade school children.

Kehoe might agree with some of these recommendations, but some weren't dealing with standards for a diploma school—they were just plain meddling. They dealt with things the standards didn't even mention. It was easy to smell the hand of the Superintendent.

It was only shortly after the Board rebuked Kehoe's effort to keep the Superintendent's salary down that the January 23rd Accreditation letter came in from the University. The Bath Consolidated School was to be accredited based upon the most recent inspection until June 30, 1927. The University was still withholding the best Accreditation plum, Accreditation for two years. The University had constantly urged Mr. Huyck to earn the two year award, but that was impossible without full board support. Actually, it wasn't all that difficult. The board need only demonstrate through various and convincing actions that it intended to exceed the standard requirements for one year accreditation. Besides more than adequate plant, equipment and teaching staff, the Superintendent needed to be relieved of teaching duties so that he was free to supervise. If Kehoe couldn't understand what Huyck was doing to earn his salary while he carried a full time teaching load, he never would be able to understand under that kind of an arrangement.

The University didn't even bother to make the recommendation this time. Instead, it came up with four more basic recommendations: (1) that a fireproof safe be provided for the records (this was the first time such a recommendation had been made—it sounded almost ominous), (2) that classes not be held where other pupils are studying (this one Kehoe could spot immediately for what it might cost), (3) that U.S. History Charts be provided (more cost), and (4) (Kehoe would like this one) that books in the library be arranged according to some system. (To Kehoe, this last recommendation showed the Superintendent wasn't actually doing his job.) That was the better of it. But it was also the kind of recommendation that could be carried out without additional cost. Kehoe questioned if Huyck could really have been a military man and still run things like that.

Kehoe loved order in things. It would please him that the Superintendent hadn't taken the interest or the initiative to establish that order in the library. Kehoe would especially keep that recommendation in mind for later reference.

At about the same time, the Superintendent and the Principal, Mr. Huggett, were commissioned by the Board to take whatever measures were necessary to get rid of the bees that were plaguing teachers and pupils inside the school. Somehow the bees had made their way inside the building during the warmer fall months, and bedded down for the winter inside the partitions. As the furnace stoked up to full capacity to give heat in the coldest months, the bees started coming out in the classrooms. They were more than pests. They were a menace; and they threatened chaos.

Now it didn't really seem that the Superintendent and the Principal required a special appointment to get rid of them, but the problem was related to the physical plant. Days later the Superintendent was back to the Board to report failure. Kehoe, who was used to fixing things anyway, volunteered to do the job. He didn't volunteer to try, he volunteered to do the job. No motion was made or entered into the record, but the job was turned over to Kehoe. For Kehoe, no power on earth would have kept him from doing the job successfully. The three swarms of bees which had plagued the students and baffled the Superintendent were doomed, victims of a strange contest for superiority between men. Were it not for the quality of uneasy contest, Kehoe's elimination of the bees would have been put down as just one more in a seemingly endless number of jobs well done. In Mr. Kehoe, the community and the school had a Mr. Fixit without peer. For most things, Kehoe never accepted pay—not from individuals anyway. But for Andrew Kehoe, as for most men, it was terribly important that someone was keeping count. Kehoe, himself, as some other men, never missed a count of what he considered to be the misdeeds of others.

In February, Kehoe went out and, completely out of character, spent a large sum of money on himself. For seven years he and his wife had gotten along without any transportation of their own. He'd relied on his tractor to get produce to the elevator; there was good train service to Lansing, and occasionally Mr. and Mrs. Kehoe relied on nearby friends or acquaintances for transportation they otherwise needed—like the trip he'd taken to Jackson with Mr. Sleight to pick up the epxlosives. The perfect answer was a little Ford pickup truck—large enough for two to ride in comfortably, but also large enough for just about any small or medium size hauling job. It was a little curious, though. All these years without transportation had been broken by the purchase—but Kehoe still wasn't finding it possible to make a single mortgage payment.

While the new pickup now made it possible for Mrs. Kehoe to visit her sisters and the rest of the Price family more frequently in Lansing, the purchase was sure to have unpleasantly surprised the family a bit. As a pioneer auto capitalist, Lawrence Price had made auto bodies and auto wheels for just about everybody in the business except Ford. Ford had been the big competition—and Ford wasn't the only auto maker to manufacture trucks. Now, money from the Price estate was being used by a close Price heir to purchase a Ford Pickup Truck.

On March 11th (1926), more money was scheduled to be released to heirs from the Price Estate—25% of the inheritance. This time, the executors as represented by Mr. Dunnebacke decided to take no chances. Instead of turning the check over to Nellie Kehoe, the attorney simply applied it to the mortgage. When Mrs. Kehoe received correspondence from him confirming this action, she replied in writing. Her reply seemed friendly enough. She indicated her gladness at receiving another payment on the legacy, and inquired about the extent of the current indebtedness on the farm. She indicated that she and her husband would be in to see the attorney about it later, and conversationally mentioned Andrew's work on the school board. The letter gave no hint of the storm the Executor's action had provoked. Probably not even Nellie knew that the letter represented a deception. In Andrew's opinion it was a deception the executor had well earned. Kehoe's anger was seething, pervasive. The executor had resorted to trickery. Once more, the executor had shown he could not be trusted. In the future, Andrew Kehoe would deal with the executors only by invoking a higher authority. Two weeks after application of the inheritance to the mortgage, Nellie Kehoe was hospitalized at St. Lawrence with frequent frontal headaches.

Coincident with the diversion of the inheritance check to the mortgage had come yet another critical school board meeting. The meeting set the stage for increased confrontation with the Superintendent and brought three strong and indomitable personalities to the crossroads. If the session had been held today, the Board would likely have gone into executive session because the issue was a sticky personnel problem. Very simply, the Superintendent and his young Home Economics teacher, Ruth Babcock, were in conflict. Superintendent Huyck asked the Board for authority to ask for her immediate resignation.

Although the board minutes were silent as to the reason for the superintendent's request, a fuller story can be pieced together. First of all, the Superintendent was, indeed, engaged in conflict. His normally real or imagined frightening countenance was being challenged. Next, he needed to ask for the board's support—as awkward and embarrassing as that might be. By the rules of the Board, the Superintendent could recommend to hire a teacher or he

47

could recommend dismissal. He could neither hire nor fire without specific approval of the board.

Going to the board was embarrassing to the Superintendent for a couple of reasons. For one, it could be interpreted that the Superintendent didn't have his house in order and, for two, couldn't regain control. The board minus Kehoe might not think that. The board with Kehoe might not even think that. But Kehoe would think it even if he didn't say so. And Kehoe would be against any motion of support just on general principles. Kehoe would also think of other angles—like, who had interviewed the girl in the first place? Who had recommended to the Board that she be hired?

Actually a thumbs down on support was not automatic from Kehoe. He had demonstrated more than once his belief that the Superintendent should be supported by the board if it expected him to earn his money. On the other hand, Mr. Kehoe's ears perked up whenever anything came up which might even remotely question the Superintendent's wisdom or competency. It was almost a knee jerk reaction. And another, Kehoe had a sense for the underdog. Or maybe it was just such intense feeling of dislike for the overdog that it came out that way.

Kehoe listened to the Superintendent's story with a mixture of enjoyment and anger. Miss Babcock's challenge to the Superintendent's unquestioned authority was humorous—no matter what the facts were. The image of the Superintendent again prevailing was not so humorous.

For the rest of the board, the matter was cut and dried. A teacher had imprudently challenged the vital discipline of the system. She simply needed to know that Mr. Huyck was boss and to learn it from the board. It was absolutely ridiculous for anyone to question the rightness of the Superintendent's position.

Mel Kyes made the motion to give the Superintendent the authority to ask for Miss Babcock's immediate resignation. The motion carried and the Superintendent gave an inward sigh of relief. He could only hope that Kehoe would let the thing go.

With one exception, Mel Kyes' minutes recorded only that the motion carried. The exception was another tell tale sign. Andrew Kehoe moved that the board adjourn. It had probably already gone through his mind that he should look Miss Babcock up.

There is no reason to believe that Andrew Kehoe felt any anxiety about the upcoming township elections. After all, no one had any fault to find with the way he conducted his office as township clerk. At least to Kehoe's mind his less relevant, but more striking record on the school board also spoke for itself. No one could approach his record for economy. If he wasn't always successful, well that simply re-enforced the need to show him even greater support.

To a degree, Kehoe's picture of himself was shared by the

48

communtiy. He worked constantly and tirelessly down at the school. Did the lighting plant need repair? Kehoe would repair it. Was there a way to muffle the generator? Kehoe would find it. Did a new well need to be sunk? Call on Kehoe. The list was endless. There was no end to the savvy of this well educated man.

And, of course, Kehoe had his own personal following. He wasn't really close to anyone, but he was neighborly. For those who knew him as "neighborly" that said a lot. Kehoe could always be depended on in a pinch. Kehoe enjoyed doing favors for his neighbors. Never took pay for work he would volunteer for. But he could take a favor as well.

That was probably pretty much the way Kehoe saw himself at the time—a good board member who had lived up to his promises; an enlightened public servant, and an excellent neighbor to his friends and those members of the community who might not be quite as intelligent as he. His war both with the school and with the estate needed to continue, of course, but right was on his side. It's unlikely that he associated the dramatic appearance of his wife's paralyzing headaches with the intensity of his reaction of her family's execution of the Price estate.

Kehoe's perception of himself and the perception of Kehoe by growing numbers in the community, however, were quite different. Kehoe stood out, of course. For a laboring man he was known to keep himself uncommonly clean, both personally and his premises. It was almost astounding that a man who loved machinery so, with all its grease and oil, could keep consistently spotless. His difference from other men was noticed particularly at threshing time. At lunch break other men would wash with only a gesture to the ritual. A quick splash of water on face and arms was about all most needed before grabbing a towel. Kehoe would not only wash himself thoroughly, he would even change his shirt. David Harte and other neighbors took note of this, just a little. Thought it humorous, nothing more.

The neatness of his tools and barn also set him apart. Never a tool out of place; barns more spotless than most people's houses. People think of these things, of course, especially in the intimacy of small township elections.

Howard Kittle, former Clinton County Agent and Farm Bureau manager, was confounded by a reply he had received from his former associate. From Kehoe and several other Bath farmers, Kittle had solicited the names of farmers willing to sell high quality seed corn. In his reply, Kehoe refused to give any information. He intimated farmers could get justice only by letting crops fail and starving the rest of the people. He had replied, "Owing to the fact that I get nothing out of it in the way of salary, I fail to see how I am benefited by aiding my competitors."[1] He expressed the belief that

49

nothing short of panic would get knowledge of the farmer's plight to the general public. The sharpness and anger in the reply had caught Kittle by surprise. But it wasn't that atypical. Kehoe believed strongly in the economics of scarcity.

Early in 1926 Kehoe had run into his friend, Monty Ellsworth, at Farmers Week (an annual event held at the state agricultural college). Asked if he was going over to the college proper, Kehoe replied, "No, they would just tell the farmers a lot of things that were impossible to do." He had gone on, "Last night I was listening over the radio to a speaker who started in by telling what colleges he had been to and what countries he had been in. I shut that off and went to the telephone and called the college and asked them what they wanted of a speaker who would just get up and brag about himself. That's the last time I am going to listen to them this week."[2]

Most critical, though, was the way Kehoe was coming off down at the board meetings. It was almost like he was a professional complainer. More and more it seemed impossible for him to find anything good to say about anything. He was building a reputation of being anti-everything. It was the kind of reputation that could damage his credibility even on positions he could assume would have broad support. Especially with the help of a more and more active PTA, his attacks on spending and particularly the superintendent were seen to be turning sour. The Superintendent was a respected man—maybe, not warm and popular, but a dedicated young professional. Kehoe's unceasing attacks upon him looked to some board members as pure maliciousness. Kehoe's withholding of support from him in the Babcock matter was just the latest incident. Coming on as it did on March 11th, it was fresh in mind, the last significant happening before the Caucus—and it recalled other things to mind. Folks questioned anew if it was really necessary for Kehoe to personally deliver the pay checks to the faculty once every twenty school days. (Kehoe made the rounds of the classrooms, knocking on each door. "Well," he would say, smiling curtly to the waiting teacher, "another month has gone by.")

Kehoe's check delivery to the Superintendent was not quite as reliable. Kehoe was known simply to "forget" the Superintendent. People heard these things and wondered. But if there was another assessment of the way he conducted himself at board meetings, people weren't going to get it from Andrew Kehoe. He remained characteristically close-mouthed. People would know only of his continuing stand against taxes. "Taxes are so very high," he said once to a friend, "I don't know what will become of us."[3] While Andrew Kehoe normally spoke slowly and deliberately as if weighing every word, he would depart from that style when his pet peeve came up. Regarding the school, Kehoe had once stated heatedly to an acquaintance, "They should have blown the damn place up."

Still, chances are that Kehoe, with his self image, never dreamt that he might be in trouble at the upcoming election scheduled for April 5th, 1926. If so, he couldn't have been more wrong—so wrong, in fact, that he never made it to the election. He was stripped of the opportunity. At the party caucuses held on March 13th and 15th, Esther Smith, Republican, was picked to run against David Watling. The Republican township board which had appointed Kehoe, fairly well stopped him at the gate. The loss was probably more personal and humiliating than if he had been beaten in the general election. His own people, so to speak, the people who had chosen him for the post to begin with, had decided he wasn't worth keeping.

As Kehoe and his wife left the caucus for their pickup truck, there was silence. Kehoe was as quiet as he had been inside the hall after the vote was announced. There had really been no trace of emotion in either Kehoe's face or movement. With his wife he sat quietly through the rest of the caucus. In leaving, he didn't really seem to avoid the others, but he didn't seek them out either. A few offered condolences. Many purposefully avoided him. He had been beaten. He had been surprised—and he had been humiliated. On the brief ride to the farm, Nellie found her husband's continued silence disturbing. Andrew Kehoe, she knew, would not tolerate humiliation.

In the two weeks that followed, Kehoe's quiet rage at his election defeat merged with his spurt in seething anger at the Price estate for diverting Nellie's inheritance. At least for the time being the fortunes of Andrew Kehoe were dangerously down. On March 24th, Mrs. Kehoe was entered at St. Lawrence Hospital suffering from severe and frequent frontal headaches.

Chapter IX
The Underdogs

If Andrew Kehoe analyzed his election defeat in a way at all characteristic for himself, he had immediately surmised that Esther Smith had not been voted in at the caucus. The people had voted Andrew Kehoe out. Yes he could reason, a very careful job had been done on him.

To Kehoe's way of thinking, he didn't have to look far for a culprit.

Mel Kyes could do for one. The thought of Kyes' possible complicity particularly angered Kehoe—and the thought would keep coming back to him. Mel Kyes wasn't even a voting member of Bath township. What went on in the township elections of Bath Township was none of Kyes business. Yet it was for sure that one way or another he had meddled and the people had listened to him. It was one more thing you could thank the consolidated school for. People started getting mixed up. They didn't know township lines anymore.

In Kehoe's mind any other list of culprits would have to include Emory Huyck, the Superintendent. And if Kehoe wanted to, he could detect a pattern in the way the little guy defended himself. First of all organize. Huyck had gotten himself his own little PTA to do battle with Kehoe and the kind of thinking he represented. Someone had definitely done a little behind the scenes organizing for the Township Election. And why not Huyck? Kehoe had seen the way Huyck operated at the recent school board meeting. A young teacher had given him a little trouble so the Superintendent set the scene to get rid of her. If Huyck acted that strongly to get rid of her, his efforts toward Kehoe must have been incomparably stronger.

Ruth Babcock's plight evoked a sympathetic reaction in Kehoe. He suddenly needed to seek her out, get her side of the story, maybe help her out. Kehoe had been enraged by the Superintendent, but Kehoe felt capable of dealing with Mr. Huyck in his own due time. Miss Babcock would probably be not nearly so fortunate.

Andrew Kehoe had to find Ruth Babcock a very pleasant surprise. Far from being a cowed and lonely petunia in an onion patch, Miss Babcock was smouldering for battle, at the same time that she was frightened. All she really lacked was an ally with power. Normally, Ruth Babcock didn't even need that.

"Babbie," as she had been known by her classmates at the Michigan Agricultural College, was slightly older than the average college graduate when she was hired by Superintendent Huyck. Her record showed she was a twenty five year old with some record of leadership at the college. She had been active with the campus Columbine Players, and was a student staff consultant for the 1924 college yearbook, the 'Wolverine.' Both the qualities of leadership and age probably appealed initially to the Superintendent. In his mind they probably added up to 'maturity.'

A couple of other factors may have led to the same conclusion. Ruth Babcock was a bit on the short and stocky side. She could be described as 'matronly' in appearance. A not really attractive blond, her hair was worn over and extending below both ears. Her hair style, the roundness of the face, and her round eye glasses gave an appearance just slightly reminiscent of Orphan Annie—perhaps an older and wiser Orphan Annie at that. Beyond that, the girl could easily impress with her intelligence, given the right opportunity and a receptive audience. The combination was attractive to the Superintendent. In the rural consolidated school the Home Economics position was second in teaching importance only to the position of teacher of agriculture, which he, himself, occupied. It would be a plum if he could manage to fill it with someone who possessed qualities of leadership, maturity, and possible immunity to quick marriage. The Superintendent guessed, probably correctly, that Ruth Babcock would not be turning her head for every eligible young gentleman in the area, and that she would not be causing many heads to turn. In short, Miss Babcock looked like a very solid and safe choice.

Shortly after she was on the job, however, the Superintendent may have begun having second thoughts. At the least, he may have early recognized that his evalution of Miss Babcock was something less than complete. She was, well, unorthodox.

For one thing, she was unorthodox in her discipline—or rather her lack of discipline. She was known to chase Ernest Babcock (no relation) around the room. Word got out that she even chased another student around the building. This sort of thing was upsetting to a Superintendent who prided himself on running a tight ship. Some pupils got the idea that she took out her frustrations on other students who wouldn't fight back. It was almost as if she was encouraging rebellion.

She was also unorthodox in her own relationship to the Superintendent. The Superintendent was accustomed to teachers who always respected him and his position, and unquestioningly followed his instructions. For Ruth Babcock, on the other hand, subservience was not in her nature. While other teachers might *think* they were the equal of any man, Ruth Babcock acted out the thought, expressed it. Expression was what Ruth Babcock had been reared to. Her parents (father and step-mother) were owners and publishers of the nearby Alma weekly, the Alma Record. (Mrs. Babcock was also a published novelist.) In a very real sense they were the community leaders other community leaders listened to. When the Alma Record spoke, which was every Thursday, leaders listened to this self appointed voice of the people. After all, the people subscribed to that voice. Ruth Babcock, as a somewhat pugnacious offspring of that newspaper family, was no more likely to be cowed by community leaders than were her parents. Mr. Huyck, community leader in Bath, was destined to find that out.

Although other teachers found Miss Babcock to be friendly, she somehow didn't take well even with them. Probably it was that certain authority quality in her personality. It wasn't simply that she had a strong personality, it was the mouthy element to it. Perhaps, her well read background gave her that sense of superiority which made her absolutely convinced that she knew more than the person she was speaking with. There was a bit of popping out with things that were not that tactful. She gained the reputation of always saying exactly what she thought. "Ruth Babcock," it was said, "never said a thing her mouth couldn't handle."

These qualities, combined with her love for argument, her need to dominate, and her need to be *the* authority, headed her straight for the inevitable collision with Superintendent Huyck. Basically, Miss Babcock's mouth was guided more by emotion than by good judgment. Unfortunately, Miss Babcock was also so opinionated that initial errors in judgment were not apt to be set aside by any retrospective insights.

The nature of the precise argument which erupted between Miss Babcock and the Superintendent was carefully omitted from the minutes of the school board. Apparently, too, the conflict was initially treated as a fairly private matter. Aside from the board, the community appears not to have been all that aware of the trouble. Gossip regarding the nature of the fight or Miss Babcock's fatal deficiencies did not materialize.

One thing appears certain, Miss Babcock chose not to accept the advice of the Superintendent regarding what she considered to be her area of competency—Home Economics. Apparently, having taken a position on a particular matter, Miss Babcock simply rejected the advice of the Superintendent. Conceivably, had Miss Babcock chosen to alter her ways, the Superintendent would have been willing to alter his evaluation of her competency. He had sought a trump card from the board, clear authority to discharge her if she did not see fit to mend her ways.

When Andrew Kehoe sought out Miss Babcock, he immediately learned three things. First, he got her side of the story. In all probability it was the story exactly as Miss Babcock perceived it: a young teacher well schooled in her teaching speciality, being brow beaten by a meddling Superintendent who didn't know the first thing about Home Economics. In Mr. Kehoe, Ruth Babcock found an attentive and sympathetic ear. In addition to her side of the story, Mr. Kehoe must have easily sensed that the young teacher yearned for his assistance. But what Miss Babcock truly sought was not so much the saving of her job, as it was the defeat of Emory Huyck. Miss Babcock was ready and eager to return to the battle. She just needed someone to get her there.

In Ruth Babcock, Andrew Kehoe undoubtedly saw a teacher being abused simply because she chose to stand up to an arrogant, unyielding Superintendent. Kehoe's sense of justice and compassion demanded that she have her day in court—better yet, if he could but arrange it, the Superintendent would be the one to be placed on trial. For Andrew Kehoe, compassion and rage were becoming blurred.

54

April, 1926 came and went. Although the Superintendent did not seek to immediately retire Miss Babcock, hers was not among the several contracts recommended for renewal during the month. At the same time, Mrs. Huyck accepted a new contract as teacher of music and the second grade.

At the meeting of the board of May 26th, Miss Babcock struck back. At that meeting, letters of complaint against Mr. Huyck were presented to the board. They were written by Miss Babcock. Albert Detluff moved that the letters be placed on file. The meeting was now going exactly the way Andrew Kehoe had planned it, wanted it. He moved quite deliberately to add to the momentum. Andrew Kehoe moved that the Home Economics dispute be laid on the table for further investigation.

Kehoe's motion to investigate the charges against the Superintendent could hardly be ignored or voted down. On the surface it wasn't a motion to condemn anyone. It simply sought some fact finding.

For the record, the situation now appeared most difficult for the Superintendent. It was hardly a turn of events he would have wanted—and if Andrew Kehoe were to have his way Superintendent Huyck would turn slowly, slowly in the wind.

As chairman, Evro Spangler was not caught off guard. In addition to the board discussions of the Babcock incident, he had the advantage of private appraisals from the Superintendent, himself. These impressions plus whatever valued assessment he might have received from the Board Secretary and the previous chairman probably led him to conclude that Miss Babcock's charges were little more than a tempest in a teapot. He reacted to Andrew Kehoe's motion by appointing Kehoe to carry out the investigation he had requested. Once again, the common sense of the board had been demonstrated. Evro Spangler showed his sensitivity to the expressed concern of a fellow board member. At the same time, he fully anticipated that nothing would come of the investigation. Nothing could.

Andrew Kehoe's apparent victory of the evening was less than hollow. Perhaps, even before the board meeting ended, he himself realized that there was nothing left to investigate. The undercover work had already been done.

In the next two weeks, Andrew Kehoe went over every detail of the conflict between Miss Babcock, the fiesty little Home Economics teacher, and her Superintendent. Kehoe's efforts simply confirmed that there were no shocking revelations to be had. That was simply the way it was. Yet, in Andrew Kehoe's mind he could still make a case—for Ruth Babcock, and against Emory Huyck. It wouldn't be what the sonofabitch deserved, Kehoe would reason, but when all you've got on a murderer is evidence of house breaking that is what you go for. In this particular case, Kehoe could conclude that the whole thing came down to a question of competency, Ruth Babcock's and Emory Huyck's. If the Superintendent had erred, as he surely had, in questioning Miss Babcock's competency, he was clearly wrong in charging her with insubordination simply because she disagreed with his blatant error.

Kehoe's preparation for the next board meeting was both masterful and beautiful in its simplicity. The board meeting itself would serve as his report of investigation. A presentation of complete clarity would be made to the board and it would draw its own conclusions. It might be too late to save Miss Babcock's job, but not too late to secure her pride and her future. This was the need, as Kehoe saw it; and it was inseparate from the need to continue the discrediting of the Superintendent.

School had been over more than a month when the board meeting was held June 7th, 1926. Miss Babcock traveled from her parent's home in Alma to appear at the board meeting. At Andrew Kehoe's invitation, she was accompanied by Miss Fregard. It was a warm Spring evening. All the board members were present and prepared for Miss Babcock's presentation. As far as the board records are concerned, this was the first time a teacher ever appeared before the Consolidated School Board to put on a program. For a precedent, it was strange. The active school year was over. The teacher presenting the program, had not been rehired. The teacher being one whose contract had not been renewed.

For the evening, Andrew Kehoe served as program chairman. As he stood up to introduce Miss Babcock, he was uncharacteristically ill at ease. He smiled self consciously, swayed slightly from side to side and appeared excitedly flushed. A stranger might have guessed that this gentleman was the proud and doting father of the teacher he was introducing.

A different uneasiness was reflected in the other board members. Evro Spangler was wondering why his term as Chairman couldn't have expired a little earlier. He was obviously eager and relieved to turn the program over to Andrew Kehoe. Mel Kyes was polite yet reserved as he greeted Miss Babcock, and then sat back to patiently last out the ordeal. Mr. Detluff was his warm, friendly and welcoming self; but Mr. Morris, like Mr. Spangler, was clearly embarrassed by the whole thing, and needed to constantly remind himself to keep his eyes open throughout the presentation.

Miss Babcock, whose sense of the dramatic was matched only by her need to demonstrate her unquestioned competence, did well by the opportunity given her. Her dialogue with Miss Fregard illustrated her command over a great range of home economics topics. Then, as if to discount any possibility that she might be judged to merely talk a good game, she concluded the program by presenting the school with a round table which was made by one of her classes. It was a product of home economics, and it was high quality. The board members were taken a little back by the gift. After all, how often does a board receive a present from a discharged teacher? Miss Babcock paused, expecting some acknowledgment. Mr. Kehoe pushed his chair back and stood up—and, speaking more gratefully for the Board than it might have intended, thanked Miss Babock for the excellence of her presentation and her gift.

With the meeting adjourned, Miss Babcock felt pleased. She had presented herself where it counted, and had done well. In her opinion, she had vindicated herself. True, she no longer had her job—but no way would she have ever consented to work again for Emory Huyck anyway. As for future job applications, Andrew Kehoe and possibly other board members would always vouch for her credibility and competence.

For the most part, the board members were relieved that the evening was over. They had looked toward the meeting as a disagreeable experience to be endured—but they had also been curious.

Andrew Kehoe could only guess at their true judgment of the meeting he hoped had become a trial. Momentarily, at least, he felt very good. He had given Miss Babcock her opportunity and she had come through. For Emory Huyck, the episode had to have been an embarrassment and a setback. Even so, Kehoe could feel a swell of emptiness returning. His hatred of Mr. Huyck had not been dissipated. Miss Babcock had lost her job. Quite automatically, Kehoe's thoughts of Mr. Huyck triggered similar thoughts of revulsion toward the executors of the Price Estate.

**

Shortly after the executors had applied the $500 inheritance payment to the unpaid mortgage, Kehoe had contemplated some sort of counter move. If payments were going to be made on the mortgage, only he would make them. It was also clear in his mind that money which was rightfully his had been improperly diverted without his permission. The fact was immaterial that one way or another the money ended up in Kehoe's hands.

Probably he would have sought legal relief immediately were it not for his wife's sudden illness which came on the heels of his emotional reaction. Although his wife had been discharged from St. Lawrence Hospital, she was still far from well. Just as important, he had become fully embroiled in the Ruth Babcock affair. He had put great energy into that. His efforts to exonerate her and to again expose the Superintendent consumed his full attention.

With the confrontation over Miss Babcock now past, Kehoe could have been expected to look with relief at the upcoming annual school election (scheduled for the evening of July 12th, 1926). He would not be standing for election, and would not be seeking any elective post (his membership on the board being good for yet another year). The very nature of the annual school election didn't allow relaxation, however. It was everyone's chance to pass judgment on the past year—to make adjustments in preparing for the new.

For those who looked to expert outside opinion on how the school was being operated, there was always the report of accreditation put out by the University of Michigan. The reports of these investigators were normally most useful to the administration in pointing out unmet needs for space and equipment which the board needed to face up to. During the past year, the University investigators had recommended everything from pictures in the rooms, to home economic and playground equipment. Especially, as Kehoe kept in mind, they had also recommended that library books be organized into some sort of a system.

Normally Kehoe looked askance at these reports. He sensed collusion with the Superintendent. A no-win arrangement meant to defeat those who would keep expenses down. The threat of a loss of accreditation was a threat of a loss of state tax support. Still some of the recommendations were down right ludicrous—like the complete separation of study and classrooms. Where did the University think children had been studying all those years in one room country schools? It wasn't that Kehoe was against education. He was for no nonsense education.

Kehoe had done his homework on the U of M accreditation report before he came to the Annual Meeting. He noted the recommendation for a fire proof safe in particular. More than once in frustration he had fancied a fate at least as bad as fire for the school. The recommendation he really liked, though, the one he stored in his mind, was the one that recommended the school's books be organized into some sort of a system. This recommendation not only pointed up a need, it pointed up another weakness in the Superintendent to Kehoe—the sonofabitch couldn't even keep a few things in order. The recommendation gave Kehoe a rare opportunity. He could go on record for quality education and against the Superintendent at one and the same time.

The annual meeting had hardly gotten underway when Kehoe made his move. Following a brief discussion over the disarray of text and reference books used by the students of Bath, he offered a motion that a school library be established. The motion was seconded, put to a voice vote, and carried. Kehoe was elated. It was like old times. He had taken charge; he had moved quicker than the others and he had won.

Kehoe's elation was to prove short lived. Other citizens had come to the annual meeting prepared, too, prepared to make this election the clearest possible vote of confidence in the administration of Superintendent Huyck, and of the leadership of the board's liberal faction. Both Mel Kyes and George Morris were up for re-election. In their corner were two highly respected school and community veterans. N. J. Sleight was the charter Chairman of the Consolidated Board. An old Kehoe nemesis, he had resigned from the school board to become the township supervisor. He was joined by Enos Peacock, the former treasurer of the Board, who had been beaten by Kehoe in the first major upset of the original board.

These gentlemen were determined to remove any doubt which may have remained after the defeat of Kehoe in the election for Township Clerk. Kehoe's actions after that election had increased their determination to give Superintedent Hyuck a full show of support. In their opinion, and the opinion of many, Kehoe had made a mountain out of a molehill. Insubordination on the part of a staff member had been completely and unfairly turned around. The constant harrassment of a fine superintendent had to end. They were convinced that if it didn't end, it would cost them an excellent superintendent. They were fearful that it might already be too late. Kehoe had come up a winner before, even out-maneuvered them on occasion. They could take no chance that most Bath voters had interpreted the Babcock business the way Kehoe intended it.

There was, of course, that chance. But the wind didn't appear to be blowing that way before the annual meeting, at least. People in Bath communicated with each other, often married each other. If the grapevine produced by an intertwine of marriage didn't work, almost everyone belonged to at least two clubs, lodges, associations, churches, granges, or government bodies of one kind or another. If a member didn't quite believe what he was hearing in one meeting, he could always check it out at another. Of course, one could never be really sure until election time, but the wind appeared to be blowing strongly in Emory Huyck's favor.

When the board meeting started, the discussion of the need for a library had come of something of a surprise. One could hardly vote against a library—but a real student of vibrations could probably pick up a repressed wince here and there.

Enos Peacock sat patiently through the brief discussion—waited for the library vote to be completed and then, without any hesitation, stood up and asked for recognition from the chair. Andrew Kehoe had returned to his seat with the other board members. From his still controlling sense of satisfaction, he was hardly aware that, Peacock, this veteran of countless township contests, had taken the floor.

"Mr. Chairman," said Enos Peacock in a firm, clear voice, "Mr. Chairman," he repeated, and paused. "I move we suspend the election rules tonight and re-elect Mr. Morris and Mr. Kyes by

59

acclamation." Kehoe straightened instinctively in his chair. With all his characteristic wariness, he had been taken completely by surprise. Before he could react, Mr. Sleight was on his feet to second the motion. Actually, Mr. Sleight had begun to rise even while Mr. Peacock was in the midst of returning to the sitting position.

"I second the motion!" exclaimed Mr. Sleight. Now, there was a flurry of excitement in the room, scattered objection to the motion. Mr. Spangler, who had appeared confused by the resolution himself, took whispered counsel with other members of the board. In the confusion, it wasn't clear whether the motion was withdrawn or had been ruled out of order. What was clear was that normal election procedures would prevail.

By now, Andrew Kehoe had overcome his initial shock. He moved that two tellers be appointed so that the election could proceed. Already he sensed that the Motion for election by acclamation was meant to trigger a landslide if one wasn't already on its way of its own momentum.

He was right. The contest for Mel Kyes' vacant seat came up first. It was no contest, Kyes receiving 79 of the 106 votes cast. Mr. Morris, who could not match Mel Kyes in popularity was returned by 57 out of 101. For Andrew Kehoe, there could be no mistaking this outcome. The route was complete.

Mrs. Kehoe had been with him, as she always was at township caucuses. She knew, not as painfully or as completely as he did, that her husband had been beaten. As they drove home she attempted some calming words, some praise for his effort to begin a school library. Kehoe's thoughts were elsewhere. With that increasingly evident fault in judgment, he reasoned that the people had betrayed him. They had chosen Mel Kyes and they had chosen Emory Huyck. They had chosen the Consolidated School. All that painstaking work undone, with Peacock, the one he'd beaten in the first place, the instigator of the undoing. The fantasy of murder and destruction which he had glimpsed before had now become a seizure of full blown hatred—blurring momentarily his vision of the road. Mrs. Kehoe sat motionless, looking straight ahead. She was very sorry, and she was afraid.

**

Mrs. Kehoe was not well. The severe frontal headaches which had brought on her first hospitalization returned intermittently and unexplicably. A persistent cold developed which she could not throw off. Her color paled and she lost weight. Tuberculosis was a thing both she and her family dreaded. Her mother had died of TB leaving her to care for the younger ones with her father. Doctors examined her and found nothing; but the worry continued over the strangely episodic symptoms.

Nellie, as Andrew called her, also worried about her husband. The worry was not steady, but it ebbed and flowed in a pattern which closely paralleled her own illness symptoms. The worry about Andrew was most markedly tied to the farm itself. Andrew had plowed in the Spring as usual and he had planted—but as the summer wore on his neglect of his fields became more and more apparent. The neglect seemed planned and purposeful—as purposeful as Andrew's refusal to pay on his mortgage.

Nellie's uneasiness over the long years of missed payments reflected the increased separation she felt from her sisters and the rest of the Price Family. To miss one's mortgage payments was unacceptable, especially to benefactors who were also close relatives. On the other hand, the executors had been tolerant to the point of being accepting—even when Andrew was questioning their integrity. While this lasted, Nellie could continue to find Andrew's steadfastness bearable.

The change had occurred when the executors diverted the inheritance money to the mortgage. It had marked the beginning of a harder line by the executors, and a determination by Andrew to break off one to one communication with them—to go to a higher authority and to bring them to heel. While events at the townhall and at the school had subsequently become a preoccupation with Andrew, his intent to take the battle to the executors only increased.

Kehoe rather relished the idea of battle with these executors. If it were to come down to who best had his wits about him, Kehoe would not be found wanting. He knew exactly who the executors were, and their strength. Executors Dunnebacke and Price were both respected Attorneys. Kehoe reasoned that the way to do battle with an attorney is with another attorney. He reasoned even better that the way to beat an Attorney is with a Judge.

To Kehoe's mind, Judge Kelly Searl of St. Johns was the perfect solution. While living in Alma, the Judge had served two terms (twelve years) as Circuit Judge for the Gratiot-Clinton Circuit. He had retired from the bench in 1917 and moved his family to St. Johns. He had continued law practice there and had been joined in that practice by his son, William. Just to confirm the soundness of the Searl legal mind, William was in the process of serving the county as the Prosecuting Attorney.

Kehoe, of course, had been around long enough to know that most Probate Judges are inclined to look upon Circuit Judges with deference—even to Circuit Judges who have stepped down from the bench—conceivably even more to Circuit Judges who have stepped down from the bench.

The Judge had accepted Kehoe easily enough as a client. After all, as Kehoe recounted the facts of the case to the Judge, it was quite clear that the executors had overstepped themselves. He easily confirmed this appraisal by a review of the Probate Court's estate records in Mason. When it was apparent that Kehoe would not be content with some simple out of court settlement of the issue, he petitioned the Probate Court for a special hearing on the matter.

Judge McArthur scheduled the hearing for late summer at the Probate Court chambers and sent notice of the hearing to the Attorneys, Richard Price (Nellie's Uncle) and Mr. Dunnebacke. Under the impression that it was to be a more or less routine review of the estate, neither Attorney made any special preparation, and neither thought that anyone other than the Judge would be present. As they entered the Judge's chambers they were amazed to find not only Judge McArthur, but both Mr. and Mrs. Kehoe. If that were not enough, they had the additional shock of learning that the highly respected Judge Searl was present for more than a simple courtesy visit with Judge McArthur. There being no need for introductions, Judge McArthur invited the two rather puzzled attorneys to join the others at the small conference table.

At Judge McArthur's invitation, Judge Searl spelled out the claim of his client. The Kehoe position was simple enough—the executors had improperly applied Nellie's $500 to the note and mortgage of Andrew and Nellie Kehoe. As executors their duty was to pay Mrs. Kehoe the $500 legacy. It could be applied to the mortgage only with the explicit consent and instruction of Mrs. Kehoe.

Judge Searl got no argument on that point. Both Attorneys agreed. They had simply assumed that the transaction would be acceptable to Mr. and Mrs. Kehoe. They reviewed the status of the mortgage, its vulnerability. Applying the payment to the mortgage would be doubly in the best interest of the Kehoe's. It would protect their substantial investment, and would be protective toward the estate as well. It really was a most reasonable position. Richard Price in particular wished to look after the best interests of his niece and the estate.

Both Judges were inclined to agree. Mr. Kehoe had made his point. The executors had been in error, but given that, why not approve the transaction now? The Judges and the attorneys present turned to Nellie. Judge Searl suggested that they let the thing stand. Nellie gave every appearance of being agreeable to the suggestion. More than anything she needed agreement. It would be Andrew's decision, of course, and she looked to her husband almost beseechingly.

Kehoe had become displeased with the discussion and with his wife. The discussion should have ended with the finding of executor error. His lawyer had no business appearing to agree with anyone without talking to him alone first. Nellie knew instinctively that things had turned against her. Kehoe fairly glared at the collection of attorneys. "No," Kehoe said, "I think you better correct the error you made. What I do is my business."

There was no use pressing the issue. The executors were advised by Judge McArthur to see that Mrs. Kehoe's check for $500 was placed in the mail. The annual account which had been dated May 24th, 1926 was corrected accordingly; and an order to the executors was entered in the record.

**

The executors left the hearing in Judge McArthur's Court perplexed, annoyed, and empty handed. What really were the intentions of Andrew Kehoe toward the estate? They could have pressed the matter before the Judge, but chose not to. They were in a difficult position. The Kehoe's were family, but the estate did need to be protected.

As Nellie Kehoe left the courtroom that day, she felt the stalemate (which held estate and husband in precarious balance) was already ending. Andrew and events were rapidly forcing an alienation with her own family. Within the month, Nellie would be hospitalized again—and would never have the opportunity to recover.

Andrew Kehoe had come away from Judge McArthur's Court a victor, but even warier about those around him. His adrenalin had been up as he had planned the skirmish with these learned gentlemen and had won.

It had carry over, enabling him one more time to carry an open battle to his opponents on the board. Just two weeks before, the board had installed officers for the new year. For Kehoe, it would have been a difficult meeting no matter what, coming off the total drubbing of the week before. The installation meeting, the week of the nineteenth, had the effect of twisting the knife around—but then of applying mercurechome.

After moving to take out $40,000 worth of fire insurance for the next three years, there needed to be swearing in ceremonies for the technically new members. As the handiest notary public around, Andrew Kehoe was picked to do the swearing in of the gentlemen he had grown to detest. (As township clerk, Kehoe had become notarized.) It probably entered Kehoe's head that these gentlemen, as much as anybody, had seen to it that he no longer needed to be notarized. Now, he was required to administer their damn oaths.

Kehoe had the oath memorized. It was a nice touch, and he instructed Morris and Kyes to repeat after him: "I do solemnly

63

swear," he read. "I DO SOLEMNLY SWEAR," they repeated. "That I will support the constitution of the United States." "THAT I WILL SUPPORT THE CONSTITUTION OF THE UNITED STATES," "And the Constitution of this State," "AND THE CONSTITUTION OF THIS STATE," "And that I will faithfully discharge the duties of the office of School Board member—to the best of my ability." "AND THAT I WILL FAITHFULLY DISCHARGE THE DUTIES OF SCHOOL BOARD MEMBER TO THE BEST OF MY ABILITY."

Kehoe was glad it was over. It was unpleasant, and it was somehow malicious. He remembered the words very well. He dwelled a moment on 'to the best of my ability.' It was both a commitment and a cop out. He reflected that he had given the voters the very best of his ability and what had it gotten him.

The evening's pain was not yet over. Albert Detluff, Kehoe's sometime friend and benefactor, helped make Kehoe's defeat all the more complete. On his motion, George Morris was elected President of the Board. Kehoe, himself, then moved in the spirit of a concensus board that Mel Kyes be returned as Board Secretary. Kehoe's Motion might also have helped guarantee that he, himself, would not be stripped of Officer rank and privilege. He might even have counted on Albert Detluff again, attempting to be fair. True enough, on Detluff's Motion, Andrew Kehoe was returned to serve one more year as Treasurer of the Bath Consolidated School Board.

For Kehoe, the evening may have had just one more slightly jarring note. On Evro Spangler's Motion, Emory Juyck was given an extra week's vacation. With that there was only one other piece of business with significance. On Mel Kyes' Motion, Kehoe and Spangler were appointed to look after the repair of school property. Coming from Kyes, it was one more recognition of the competence Andrew Kehoe.

The evening had ended for the board in a rare sense of harmony. There had been a little something for everybody. It was to be the calm before the last open board storm.[1]

Chapter X
Defeat and Withdrawal

Like so many times before, the contest over the awarding of Bus route contracts became the cause provocateur. And like so many times before, Ward Kyes was at the center of the center. Perhaps like others, Kehoe had learned that Ward was considering not going for the contract again. Probably at one point Ward had decided to give the route up. Possibly he had decided that the price of renewed conflict with Kehoe wasn't worth it—but that is far from likely. Ward Kyes loved an argument and he loved a scrap.

When word got out that Ward Kyes was ready to retire from the route, a somewhat unlikely successor emerged. Anson McNatt was a young Bath scholar who lived on Ward Kyes' route, two and three quarter miles northwest of Bath. He was a strapping young farm lad who had just finished his sophomore year. He was not a particularly studious type, but he was a student leader at the consolidated school. He was extremely quick witted and uninclined to be awed by his elders. As often as not they were targets of his sometimes ungenteel sense of humour. He also demonstrated unusual maturity for a lad of his years. A good share of the farm work had been his to perform. His father who worked at the Forge in Lansing simply didn't have time for that. Anson hit the chores well before he left for school in the morning, and helped his father finish up after he went home at night. In the Summer, the farm work took up practically full time.

Had not the word gone out that Ward no longer wanted the route, Anson would never have thought of bidding on it. The fact is that Ward was an early encourager of Anson—had even offered to sell his truck to him. As it developed, young McNatt thought the bus route was the opportunity he had been waiting for. While it was unprecedented for one of the students to bid on a route, Anson McNatt simply didn't view himself as precocious at all. This hard working young man even had credentials. In addition to all his other responsibilities, he had found time to work as a part time truck driver for a Lansing Coal Company.

Conceivably, Anson McNatt's bid might have been rejected out of hand by the board at any other time (due simply to youth, and to his student status), but his competition for the route may have caused some members of the board to take another look. In addition to four other bids, Ward Kyes had decided to reenter the competition after all.

Kehoe's interest in Bus Route Number Five became, then, at an all time high. It could have been simply his normal interest in school business. It could have been that a special interest was reawakened by the newsworthy entrance of a mere high school boy into the competition. It could have been all of these. Regardless of what Kehoe thought it was, underneath he had to see Anson McNatt in the role of underdog to a family which had been his own nemesis.

Perhaps, Andrew Kehoe didn't exactly see it as intercession, but he took a personal interest into looking into the credentials of Anson McNatt. Kehoe had made it a point to talk to the young man, to interview him. To Anson, Andrew Kehoe was 'a heck of a nice guy' who showed positive interest in him and his bid. It seemed to Anson that Mr. Kehoe was inclined to give him a chance. Kehoe wasn't for giving him a chance recklessly, but if he was responsible and had the skill, well, it should be checked out.

To check it out, Kehoe and young McNatt drove in the Kehoe pickup to the coal company in Lansing, the place where Anson had driven truck. The owner was sought out, and the three discussed Anson's performance as a truck driver for the company. Not only had the owner been pleased with the work Anson had done for him, he was sure the young man could carry out well the much greater responsibility which would come from driving school bus. Kehoe pressed the owner on the point of that responsibility, and he came away satisfied. He came away satisfied enough to support the young man's bid with the board.

The bids were scheduled for formal opening by the Board at the meeting of August 16th, 1926. The agenda called for the board to open all six bids and then come to a decision. Anson McNatt was there for the opening; Kehoe represented the boy to the rest of the school board. If bids alone were all that mattered, Anson could have relaxed through this important adult occasion. He realized he was attempting to bite off a pretty big hunk for a boy. He was proud just to have the opportunity. When the bids were opened, Anson's bid was low, and Warden's was high (for those bidding for the bus route alone).

For the actual decision, the board retired to executive session. Anson had been prepared not to win. He knew that other factors beside the bid price would be considered. He knew that among these, his youth and student status would probably do him in, but he still hoped.

In executive session, the expected and realistic argument for Warden Kyes was raised. When it came right down to it, he was the driver who had the experience. He had performed with reliability and without a blemish through the years. Any other driver would be a risk. Warden Kyes should be replaced only if there was dissatisfaction with his performance. Evro Spangler offered the motion that the board contract with Warden Kyes for the rest of the year. The motion was defeated on a tie vote. The record does not show which

66

member abstained, but certainly Kehoe voted against Ward. Probably, the abstainer was either Mel Kyes, holding off for possible conflict reasons, or it was Al Detluff, characteristically not wanting to choose between friends who were at conflict.

Most likely, the debate behind closed doors, started out as a relatively impassive presentation of the respective merits of the bidders. It quickly moved to an attack on the credentials of the bidders. Any one of the board members other than Kehoe might have zeroed in on the shortcomings of the McNatt bid. Of those members, any other than Mel Kyes might have been relatively unsusceptible to counter attack from Andrew Kehoe. Probably, Mel Kyes did join in questioning the wisdom of giving serious consideration to the bid of Anson McNatt. Such a question from Kyes would have aroused the pent up antagonism which Kehoe felt toward him. He probably countered by rebuking Mel Kyes in his most sensitive area: Was it really that the other bidders didn't have proper credentials, or that the Board Secretary was only interested in protecting his son's interests? The debate had now become intensive, and it had become personal. Spangler's Motion was then made as much to stop the argument as to decide the question. In the vote which followed, there was a single abstention (probably Kyes'), and the motion was defeated on the tie vote.

Without any further debate, Albert Detluff offered the Motion to accept the McNatt bid as the logical alternative. This time there was no tie vote. The McNatt bid was rejected. In hopeless deadlock, the Board decided to call it quits for the evening—to try again three nights later. With the clear rejection of the McNatt bid on August 16th, Kehoe may have already recognized that awarding the contract to Warden Kyes was inevitable. The question could not long be put off. "Why should Warden Kyes, by far the most qualified candidate, be denied a bus contract simply because he was the son of the Board Scretary?"

At the meeting on August 19th, Albert Detluff, the Board's chief advocate of compromise, moved to end the stalemate. His motion to 'compromise' was really a motion to end the Board's opposition to Warden Kyes. In fact, his motion was exactly that: "To compromise and hire Warden Kyes for the remainder of the year." Kehoe acquiesced, and the Motion was carried unanimously. With the Detluff switch from McNatt to Kyes, Kehoe knew that the Motion would carry anyway—so what the hell?

If the Detluff motion (and subsequent vote) did not signal the end of Andrew Kehoe's true participation as a Board member, the following motion did. The issue was conflict of interest. The subject was Andrew Kehoe, himself.

Mel Kyes had a thing about Board members taking pay for school related work. He may even have harboured some suspicions that

67

Kehoe found ways to launder money that was ostensibly directed to others for the work they did. Although he had entered the motion of a month earlier to have Kehoe and Spangler look after repairing school property, he had probably become increasingly rankled after that motion was modified ten days later to pay Kehoe $4 a day to repair the school property himself. Following the vote to award the bus contract to Ward, he surfaced the issue. There wasn't really much to discuss about the matter. He was right. Records of the Consolidated Board would support the fact that no board member had ever been hired before to carry out school business. In thinking back on their action, the members could probably agree that they had simply taken the action without thinking. Kehoe, himself, who prided his personal integrity above all else, would probably have jumped in the discussion to disavow anything questionable in his relationship with the school. The Motion to rescind any action to pay Kehoe was made by Mel Kyes. All five members, including Kehoe voted to pass it.

What Kehoe voted on the 19th and what he felt were probably two very different things. On both the bus contract issue and on the payment issue, he had voted for the motions probably because there wasn't really anything else he could do. But on the payment issue in particular, he must have experienced both the discussion and the vote as an attack on his personal integrity, an insulting attack which would be returned one hundred fold. For that future reference, he had noted that the members of the Board had voted as one. He would remember that.

For Andrew Kehoe, the manifestations of his mental illness were neither recognizable to him, his family, or his acquaintances. But there were manifestations. Although his defeat in his bid for election as Township Clerk was undoubtedly a bitter and unexpected one, his activity after the election did not change enough to be noticed by anyone outside his immediate family. However, that defeat coupled with the heightening dispute over the mortgage created strains which may well have been signaled by his wife's hospitalization and turn to chronic illness.

Although Kehoe had gotten his crops planted just as he always did, he had shortly begun to neglect those crops. If it was a beginning of withdrawal from reality, that withdrawal was first focused on the farm itself. But the withdrawal appeared to be purposeful. Besides a beginning neglect of the farm, Kehoe sold his entire stock of cattle.

No signs of withdrawal from full and purposeful participation on the school board appeared until the sharp series of defeats he suffered during July and August—but with the Board meeting of August 19th, came a change in the character of his participation on the Board. For the members of the board, it appeared to be just that—a change in the character of his participation. He appeared to have simply become more agreeable.

In retrospect, Kehoe appears to have given up. In place of an effort to make a place for himself in society, he substituted a plan of vengeance. It was the plan of a sick mind. Until the plan gained substance, however, it was still a fantasy.

Without question, Kehoe had earlier experienced some fantasies of destruction toward his opponents and toward the school. He had toyed with the fantasies but put them aside in favor of continued more or less open conflict with those he considered his adversaries.

The August experiences, however, pushed him over the brink, possibly not irrevocably, but still over the brink. Although he had won his courtroom battle with the executors, the scene most probably stamped in his mind was that brief glimpse of his wife appearing to stand with everyone else against him. The quality of paranoia would have exaggerated that scene, while blotting out the memory of her sacrifice of herself to abide by his wishes.

On August 19th, Kehoe had repeated somewhat the same experience. The board as one against him, attacking *his* integrity when he alone had fought the community's fight. The board and the community appeared merged as one against him—and the fantasy of retaliation became more insistent.

For Kehoe, he needed only to determine the method and the timing of his retaliation. That determination came naturally and quickly. His talent and love for dynamite was probably always closely associated with controlled urges toward violence and destruction. The natural object of course would be the school. Kehoe had almost immediately identified the school as the source of his financial difficulties to begin with. What better way to punish the board and the community than through the hated school?

If Kehoe arrived at that determination during the summer of 1926, he needed only the opportunity and the will to put that determination to effect. Part of that opportunity had been his practically ever since he had taken office on the Board. As a skilled electrician and the resident armorer articifer of the school, Kehoe enjoyed ready access to the school.

When Andrew Kehoe set up his work bench, it was like part of the property. There was no part of the school plant which couldn't be repaired by Kehoe or repaired under his admittedly expert supervision. When parts went bad, Kehoe knew where to get replacements. If replacements didn't exist, he would improvise—like the time he ingeniously created a muffler for the school generator. On that particular occasion, the invention didn't work—or rather it worked too well and stopped the engine from working at all. Most of the time, though, Kehoe's spare part projects worked—and work or not, faculty, students and administration were used to his familiar

69

sight both on the grounds and in the building. His avocation not only gave him the opportunity, it gave him a knowledge of the building which was more intimate than that possessed by either janitor or administrator. The episode with the bees had only increased his knowledge of the school's partitions and its underpinnings. Should anyone question his presence in the building, he had only to point to specific and continuing responsibilities. On July 19th he had been appointed to look after the repair of school property. On July 29th he had been appointed to hire someone to clean the school building. On the same date he had been hired to repair school property. Although payment for the work was shortly to be rescinded, the work appointment was not. In August Kehoe was appointed to oversee repair of the school's water system and toilets. For that, tile needed to be repaired both under the building and extending from it.

For those who made a habit of watching Andrew Kehoe at his work, there was nothing mysterious about his work. Some would recall later that bamboo poles were first observed on the Kehoe work bench during August of 1926, but it wasn't anything worth worrying about.

Kehoe's continuation on the board gave him not only the opportunity he needed. It gave him camouflage. Ultimately though he would need the undetected cover of his own house, from which he could complete his planning, carry out his preparations, and store his weapons of destruction. In short, he needed his home as base camp for his covert operation. Required would be absences by his wife. Certainly Kehoe did not plan his wife's illnesses, but as his alienation increased so did her need for hospitalization.

Chapter XI
Foreclosing

By Octorber 1 three months had passed since the hearings in Judge McArthur's court. Further delay in squaring the estate's account with Kehoe, now seemed pointless to the executors. Not only did the estate need to be protected to safeguard the interests of all the heirs, the executors needed to protect themselves. Any evidence of failure on their part to responsibly protect the value of the estate could subject them to legal action by any of the injured parties. The refusal of Andrew Kehoe to make payments was patently self centered with total disregard for the interests of the other heirs, his wife's blood relatives.

Julia Price, Lawrence's widow, was the key executor. She was key in the sense that as Lawrence's widow she, more than anyone, represented the embodiment of his will, his compassion, and his intention in the settling of the estate. Julia was herself now seventy one years old. The emphatic beauty of her younger years was more subtle now, but no less present. Her dress, her grooming and her manner were every bit as carefuly attended at seventy one as they had been forty years earlier. Her proud and distinctive rather full face was often framed by a carefully chosen bead necklace, and a grandly swept back pompadour. She was a private person, preferring to be rather less in the public eye than her husband, but bearing a quality of distinction which well complimented his need and skill for public life. Her own innate shyness and comfort in privacy might sometimes have been misinterpreted by others as pure haughtiness. In reality she and her husband shared the same empathy for those who live in pain. There was no doubt that she was a well bred lady, but she was dedicated to seeing that others also had that opportunity. Three adopted children attested to that dedication.

For Julia, for the executors, and for the rest of the Price family, the stalemate with Andrew had become more than an embarrassment. It had become a matter of trespass onto the rights of others. Julia, herself, had no need for any other complications or burden in life. Her only son, George, had died at the young age of 25 only months before. His death might have encouraged sympathy and condolence toward Julia Price. Instead, Andrew had pressed his claim against her.

Andrew Kehoe was definitely an enigma, but somehow the stalemate had to be ended. By October, the executors of the Price estate settled on a course of action which they hoped would lead to a satisfactory solution. To their minds, the plan was simple, forthright and fair. Andrew Kehoe would have to fish or cut bait. Mortgage foreclosure proceedings were to be instituted in chancery.

On a Monday or Tuesday, Attorney Dunnebacke mailed the first notice of the foreclosure process to the Clinton County Sheriff. These would be the first process papers, in a foreclosure proceeding which the Executor anticipated could take many, many months to run its course. Upon receipt of the foreclosure papers from Mr. Dunnebacke, the Sheriff would be under duty to serve them. Apparently, there had been no prior discussion of this particular plan with the Kehoe's or with the sisters of Mrs. Kehoe. The estate had already exhibited extreme patience with Mr. Kehoe and probably considered further amenities to be pointless. The fact of

Mrs. Kehoe's illness had not surfaced in the deliberations of the executors. Evidence indicates that they were simply unaware of her ill health and increasingly fragile condition.

By chance, Attorney Dunnebacke ran into Nellie's sister, Elizabeth, shortly after depositing the mail for delivery to Sheriff Fox. In the brief street discussion with Nellie's 45 year old sister, the executor explained the latest development. For Elizabeth, the news was shaking and alarming. From her near panic reaction, Attorney Dunnebacke learned for the first time that Nellie was not a well woman and that the service of subpoena might cause severe trauma to her. Attorney Dunnebacke was now alarmed in return. He had mailed the foreclosure papers in the morning. It was now afternoon of the same day. He reasoned with some calming effect both on him and Elizabeth that time was on his side and that he would be able to head off the service before it was delivered.

Relieved, Elizabeth returned to her office place of employment. Mr. Dunnebacke departed from her without any telltale outwardly of the anxiety he felt. Returning to his office, he wasted no time in phoning the Sheriff's Office in St. Johns. When his first attempt met with no luck, he tried again and again without success. Frustrated at his inability to get through, he pondered the situation with growing concern. Then, the rational solution hit him. He would telegraph. Telegrams get through quickly and reliably, and there is a written record of the communication. The attorney was convinced that the telegram would easily reach the Sheriff's office ahead of the mailed subpoena. Mr. Dunnebacke's telegram was brief and to the point. It read, "Do not serve the Kehoe subpoena pending further instructions."[1]

Somehow, the impossible happened. The mail drop had caught train connections perfectly. It was a model postal operation, carried out when excellence was routinely expected of the postal service.

At the Sheriff's end, the day had been quieter even than many of the normally peaceful days at the Sheriff's Office. The mail delivery came as a welcome relief from the boredom of the day, and the deputy was dispatched to serve the subpoena.

It was a short, but chilly drive to Bath, the Deputy driving a bit slower than he needed to, just to stretch the errand out as much as possible. When he identified the Kehoe Farm from the address, he slowed to turn into the driveway, and brought the car to rest. He leisurely got out of the car, and walked up the front steps. As he knocked at the front dor, he felt no apprehension. He needn't have. Andrew Kehoe answered the door and, in response to the Deputy's inquiry, acknowledged that he was Andrew Kehoe. The Deputy said, "I have a subpoena here for you, Mr. Kehoe," and handed him the subpoena.

Kehoe had been taken by surprise, but his manner, aside from his

72

eyes, gave no hint of it. As he reached for the subpoena from the Deputy's outstretched hand, he smiled. It was a knowing smile. He turned to go back inside. Nellie would be waiting for him there, wondering who had been at the door.

**

Winter months are characteristically cold and dreary. The winter of 1926-1927 was characteristic. It was the kind of dreariness that can drive normally happy individuals to periods of depression.

If Kehoe was himself overtly depressed, he did not show it to acquaintances or to members of the board. But things at the house were dreary.

Kehoe had wondered about his wife. He had been alert to her willingness to take the side of the executors at Judge McArthur's court. In all likelihood, he had wondered if just possibly she had known ahead of time that her Aunt was going to start foreclosure proceedings to serve him with that goddamn humiliating subpoena. For a man of Kehoe's strange sense of pride, the subpoena could only have been seen by him as demeaning, insulting. Coming without specific advance warning, it confirmed all his misgivings about the executors and the Price family. From now on he would accept nothing less than complete alienation from the Farm, the executors, and the Price's. In the meantime he would watch Nellie very carefully. The court scene wasn't the first he'd been aware of her tendency to stick with family. He was convinced that Nellie and her family were uncommonly close. From the first, she had needed to visit with her sisters constantly. He was also convinced that, contrary to his wishes, the sisters conspired to assure Nellie continued contact with the Catholic Church.

With the notice of foreclosure, Nellie knew immediately that all her hopes for maintaining ties with her own family, and for staying on the family farm were crushed. While the executors might merely have wished to prod Andrew into one course of action or the other, his reaction was almost certain to be to wash his hands of the estate. By October, Kehoe had decided to reject both the school and the estate. The only question which remained was, "How?"

For neighbors, it seemed that Mrs. Kehoe was away from the farm for hospitalization most of the time after September 1st. Actually, she was home more than that. Increasingly, however, she lived the life of an invalid. She became given to incessant coughing attacks. At one point Doctors may have felt she was tubercular. Although that condition was ruled out to her, she apparently remained convinced early in the Winter that she carried some very harmful germ.

73

As she became helpless about the house, Kehoe hired a girl to work around the house. Mrs. Kehoe confined herself to an upstairs bedroom. On one occasion, Mrs. Sidney Howell called at the house to pay her respects. She, more than any one else in the neighborhood, had been very close with Mrs. Kehoe. Mr. Kehoe wasn't home at the time and the hired girl sent Mrs. Howell upstairs to see Mrs. Kehoe in her bedroom. As Mrs. Howell appeared at the bedroom door, Mrs. Kehoe ran to her, but was immediately seized with a convulsive coughing spell. Mrs. Howell, concerned that she had upset Mrs. Kehoe said, "If I possibly hurt you, I will go out." But it was Mrs. Kehoe who was most afraid, afraid of hurting her friend.

"I will hurt you," Mrs. Kehoe warned between coughs and tears.

Mrs. Howell replied, "You know there is nothing in the world I wouldn't do for you."

"I know it," answered Mrs. Kehoe, and Mrs. Howell turned tearfully and left the room.[2] Mrs. Kehoe's condition had frightened her. There was something desperate, almost morbid about it.

No alarm was sounded or even seemed necessary about Andrew Kehoe's condition. He continued on the board, but passively, impassionately. Covertly, his actions were less dispassionate. On November 18th or 19th he purchased two boxes of 40% Hercules Dynamite at Chapman Sporting Goods Store at 1111 East Michigan in Lansing., At various other times he bought dynamite caps from the same store.

In December the Board and the Superintendent agreed to disagree. The superintendent had decided that he would not return to Bath the following year. The given reason was that he wanted more money. That possibility had been discussed with the Board, at least with the Secretary, and it had been ruled out. No one could guarantee that Kehoe would be gone the following year, even with his election coming up. While Kehoe was on the board, any substantial increase in the Superintendent's salary looked to be out of the question.

Possibly, Superintendent Huyck had simply had it with Kehoe, and his harrassment. Possibly, he was now interested in new fields to conquer. His own salary not withstanding, the recent elections indicated that Kehoe could no longer be viewed as a realistic threat to the future well being of the school. Superintendent Huyck had seen the Consolidated School through its birth, and had overseen its successful defense against the energetic attack mounted by Andrew Kehoe. Mr. Huyck could reasonably claim that he had now done his job and it was time for someone else to take over.

On December 15, 1926, the Board decided to communicate with state authorities regarding a new superintendent. Perhaps at any other time, Andrew Kehoe might have seen that action as the most sought after Christmas present he could ever have hoped for. But on

December 15, 1926 it was already too late. Far from elation, Kehoe probably more accurately felt some fear that his erstwhile target was going to elude him. Kehoe exhibited nothing untoward at the Board meeting or at any of the discussions about the Superintendent's planned departure. Before the month was over, however, he returned to the Chapman Sporting Goods Store in Lansing. This time he bought a 30.06 Model 54 Winchester rifle. With the rifle he bought one hundred rounds of ammunition.[3] If events were to change on Kehoe, he would not be caught napping. In first one way and then another, Kehoe's fantasy of destruction was coming off the drawing board. Kehoe's apparent preparations continued, along with an almost instinctive use of deception. His ability to consistently mask one move with another was characteristic yet, somehow, undetected.

Two years earlier, he had exploded a large quantity of dynamite on the Fourth of July. At that time, his wife had calmed alarmed neighbors by saying, "Oh, the little boy is just having some fun."[4]

On New Year's Eve for the new 1927, Kehoe again celebrated a Holiday. Although neighbors heard a tremendous explosion at Midnight, they were unsure where the explosion had come from. Job Sleight, Kehoe's neighbor and friend on Sleight Road, guessed that it was Kehoe. A short time later, Mr. and Mrs. Sleight were visiting with the Kehoe's during one of Mrs. Kehoe's respites from the Hospital. Sleight had commented something like, "I heard you were shooting off dynamite on New Year's Eve."

It was more of a question than an answer and Kehoe answered, "Yes, I thought I would shoot some off." He explained that he had covered some up in the garden, and had wired it to a clock in his basement. The clock was set for midnight, and it had worked perfectly. Kehoe had obviously enjoyed the trick. He laughed as he explained the explosion to Mr. and Mrs. Sleight and, referring to the other neighbors, said, "I guess I jarred them up." He laughed in a cheerful sort of way that seemed typical to some of his acquaintances.[5]

No one thought further of the episode. It was indeed a most interesting experiment. Kehoe had placed the clock in the basement. He had placed the dynamite in the garden where things usually grow. There was apparently nothing at all mysterious about it. The dynamite had blown loud enough to wake the entire countryside. For the curious, Kehoe was not the least reticent about describing his clever timing device. For those on the scene, it was simple enough, another example of the inventive Kehoe enjoying what he enjoyed most. In retrospect it seemed a devilishly masterful piece of revealing nothing by revealing all. If, on the other hand, Kehoe was looking for more insightful detection, the detectors were not out. Or maybe there was really no need for detectors.

During the same month (January, 1927) Kehoe put his place up for sale. The farm was put in the hands of a Lansing realtor.[6] Kehoe's reaction to the mortgage foreclosure notice was to get out—to sell. If he had considered any other alternative, no one knew about it.

The foreclosure process had been started in October. Possibly, for two months, Mrs. Kehoe had hoped against hope that her husband would relent, decide to make payment after all. For a brief period, Mrs. Kehoe appeared to enjoy some respite. Mr. and Mrs. Kehoe were even able to host a meeting of the Bath Social Club. Kehoe, always one to enjoy a good social evening, was a good host, and members looked forward to the evening. Eucre was the mainstay of the Bath Social Club and Kehoe considered himself a cut above the average Eucre player—or even a cut above the superior Eucre player. When other members misplayed, Kehoe did not hesitate to point out the error of their playing. It was a somewhat irritating quality in Kehoe, but one his guests had learned to live with.

On this particular evening, guests remembered most of all the fine candies which had been prepared for the occasion by Mr. and Mrs. Kehoe. They were also very much taken by the metal puzzles which Mr. Kehoe presented to each male guest. The puzzles had been fashioned from heavy copper by Mr. Kehoe, himself. Each of the puzzles was unique unto itself, and Mr. Kehoe was obviously proud of the fine workmanship which had gone into the making of them.[7] Making puzzles was apparently a hobby with Mr. Kehoe.

The big Kehoe puzzle was still in the making, and it was intriguing. Although Kehoe had gone through the formality of putting the farm up for sale, few if any of his neighbors were aware that the farm had been put on the market. If any were to find out, it was probably by accident. Kehoe simply didn't choose to talk about it with anyone. Perhaps, in Kehoe's mind, the farm was not really up for sale.

Kehoe had talked about it with his wife. He decided what he was going to do, and that was that. Family farm or not, he would no longer tolerate the insults of the executors. With that knowledge, and with that blow to her own family esteem, Nellie Kehoe still survived the early winter months. Her rehospitalization at St. Lawrence came January 26, 1927. It came quickly after the Farm was registered for sale at the Lansing realty.

Although there had been a brief period of two months during which she had been free of symptoms, her condition upon entry into the hospital was not good. Her illness now seemed almost chronic. Its severity had become increasingly acute. To doctors she described her loss of appetite, her decrease in weight. She complained of frequent colds followed by a sensation of fullness of the chest. Her state of exhaustion was such that she simply could not carry out any of her duties about the house. She appeared asthmatic. Earlier observations at the Ford Hospital and at St. Lawrence had proved inconclusive.

As long as diagnosis and treatment remained inconclusive, the increasingly grave nature of Nellie's condition surely resurfaced fears of the tubercular condition which years before had struck down her mother. The quality of the illness was mysterious, and it brought fears of morbidity. Its effect was to produce further required separation from Andrew.

After nearly two weeks, doctors determined that exploratory surgery should be performed. On February 7th, Mrs. Kehoe underwent exploratory surgery. Her diagnosis was believed to be utropic catarrhal infection.

To Mrs. Kehoe's sisters, and to the staff at the hospital, Mr. Kehoe was seen to be the attentive husband. He visited his wife regularly. He was always solicitous of her condition. At the same time, acquaintances began to notice a difference in Andrew. Kehoe had characteristically maintained an aloofness which warned others to keep their distance. Suddenly, another quality was added to the Kehoe makeup. Kehoe would carry on a conversation with friends as he always did, but now, he seemed to have something else on his mind.

Obviously, Kehoe had Nellie on his mind. While he was concerned about her, he was also angered by her. He was extremely sensitive to the fact that her increasing illness coincided with an increasing distance between the two of them. He was clever enough to sense that the illness was creating a purposeful separation of the two, one that brought Nellie closer to her sisters. To Kehoe, the illness smacked again of conspiracy—conspiracy against him.

Nellie's hospitalization increased his sense of aloneness. it increased his determination to even the score against those who were working against him. It also gave him further opportunity to transform fantasy to reality. The winter nights were still long. He could go and come during those long nights without interferences from anyone. People worked hard around Bath, and they went to bed early. Children went to bed even before their parents. There would be no one astir at the village but Kehoe. The plan would be simple enough. He could visit his wife at the hospital during the evening, come back, get into his work clothes and go to work at the school. He didn't know how long his wife might be hospitalized, but, at least, he could get started. The complete hatred Kehoe felt for the school board had taken the form of a simple fantasy. He would blow the school up—obliterate it; and in obliterating it, he would destroy his enemies. That was the fantasy. Kehoe had already given preliminary planning to converting his fantasy to reality. He had even completed some of the detailed planning which would be necessary. It took into account every feature of the substructure of the consolidated school building.

In fact, the building was two buildings. The front building, elongated to left and right, was the new structure. There was no basement under it—not under the center entrance to the school and not under either the northern or southern wings. The crawl space under it extended to its extremities, but could be entered only from special trap doors inside the building.

By clever construction, the new building had become attached both physically and functionally to the old ten grade high school building. It was this section of the school which contained the school's only basement. The basement extended under the entirety of the old building but housed the furnace which provided heat for the entire school. The basement also contained the boiler and the generator for electricity, as well as rooms for storing coal and for general utility.

The basement was the key to any plan for undetected demolition. It was the means to the crawl space under the new part of the school, and it was the only means to access the space between the basement ceiling and the subflooring of the first floor of the old building. Demolition of the building would require wiring, and explosives in large quantities. It would also require a timing device of some kind. In addition, Kehoe would need conduits of a type which could guide caches of dynamite to the near and far reaches under the subflooring of the old building.

Months ago Kehoe had discovered from only the most cursory examination of the underpinnings of the new building, that it could be had. The crawl space was hardly more than ample, but it was ample. He would have no problem bringing explosives in, affixing them to the most critical points, and wiring the charges. There would be no problem at all. Each set could be placed by hand, precisely in the spots intended. The only possible problem would be that of unexpected detection. Even that could be guarded against by clever wiring and concealment of the charges behind support posts and beams. He reasoned that he would take that precaution, if it every came to that, even though there was practically no likelihood that anyone would ever find reason to explore the area. Kehoe, himself was the only likely intruder.

The area under the old building presented much more of a challenge. At a quick glance, there was no evident means for concealing the kind of destructive charges which would be needed. When Kehoe had first pondered the situation, he had made mental, almost accidental note of the grade locations which matched this or that location in the basement or within the underpinnings. Much more purposefully he estimated the exact spot which was

78

perpendicularly below the office of the Superintendent. Kehoe considered the fact that the superintendent's office was on the second floor. He dismissed that as presenting no problem.

The problem which was presented by the basement was no easy one to solve. When Kehoe first gave study to the problem, he cut his analysis short. After all, it was only a fantasy. But as he found himself returning to the fantasy, he gave more and more attention to the puzzle.

When the mental solution did come to Kehoe, it was simple enough. The beams supporting the sub flooring ran in parallels perpendicular to Kehoe's access to them from the new section crawl spece. Moving along in the crawl space with his flashlight, Kehoe could command an unobstructed view to the far end of the old building. If light could penetrate that distance, so could properly spaced charges of explosives, pushed gently and carefully into position so as not to disturb the detonating wiring. The trick would be to push the explosive over the very rough divisions and gaps and ridges of the top side of the basement ceiling. Kehoe's mental solution was to connect several pieces of eavestrough together, forming a smooth conduit through which explosive packets could be pushed without danger to the fragile soldered connections.

By February, Kehoe could test his hypothesis. Using bamboo poles which he had salvaged from work on the school well some four or five years ago, he confirmed that he could successfully place the dynamite where he wanted it.

Kehoe was also able to reason that he could unload required materials at the school with a minimum number of trips in his pickup truck. It wasn't going to be like he needed to make a trip every day in broad day light.

However, before Kehoe could begin to complete his preparations, Mrs. Kehoe was discharged from the hospital on March 1st. She was recovered, at least temporarily from the exploratory surgery she had undergone. With her return home the possibility existed that Kehoe's terrible isolation from humanity might be arrested. The possibility existed that his beginning excursion to destruction might be detoured, and returned to being the frightening, but harmless fantasy it once was.

**

Other events were now becoming decisive. In February, the LaNoble Realty in Lansing located a buyer for the Kehoe farm.[8] LaNoble was himself from a prominent Bath family, and could hardly have been a better agent. With farm prices continuing their downward plunge, he miraculously came up with an offer of $12,000. That was the price Kehoe had paid for the property. With the depressed farm market he was unlikely to ever do better. The buyer, or rather the prospective buyer, was an instructor from Michigan State College. He wasn't really buying the property for himself, but for his father.

Although Kehoe had made it clear to his wife that he would never consider staying on the property, the offer raised another question. Kehoe was adamant against staying on the property, but was he truly interested in selling? Was his dominant plan to start life anew somewhere else with his wife, or had any constructive planning been thwarted by the fantasy? If talking told the tale, he had no plans outside of Bath.

Possibly it was procrastination born in ambivalence, or possibly it was the delay of clearly intended rejection, but Kehoe moved with slow deliberation in reacting to the offer. When he made his move toward acceptance of the offer, the instructor withdrew the offer. The reason for the withdrawal was relayed to the executors of the estate. The prospective buyer had reportedly balked at the amount of taxes on the place! The incident did nothing to change the course Kehoe had set upon—may even have confirmed the course. Then, again, the incident may have been determined by Kehoe.

The episode had brought together an interesting cast of characters. The prospective buyer was an educator, a profession both envied and despised by Kehoe. He was going to acquire the Farm for his father! Father was somehow a code term for conflict. Kehoe was again in the position of negotiating or rather contesting with an educator. Kehoe loved contests such as that. He could outwit and he could manipulate. He could even manipulate a loss, a defeat—and he could, with deception, prove his victim a deceiving clone. Whatever, the result was the same. Kehoe was confirmed in his own mind in the position that he had always held; the school taxes were intolerable. He had paid much too much for the property. And the record, scanty as it was, would indicate that the sale fell through because the taxes were too high.

In spite of some letdown over the collapse of the sale, Attorney Dunnebacke's attitude toward the Kehoe portion of the Estate had turned to relative optimism. The stalemate with Kehoe had been broken. When forced to the wall, this aloof and uncompromising farmer had decided to sell. He had not only made a decision to sell— he was obviously trying.

Even Nellie's sisters must have been somewhat pleased. A stigma on the family name was being erased. They may have been concerned with Kehoe's silence regarding future plans for Nellie and himself, but by nature he wasn't talkative. They had learned not to pry. They also knew that his gift for mechanics and for electricity more than qualified him for any number of possibilities in Michigan's booming industry. For that matter, a respectable job could have been his for the asking anytime he wanted it with the now defunct Lansing Auto Body.

Had Attorney Dunnebacke been aware of any Kehoe alternatives to disposing of the property, or had he been aware of certain salient facts, he would have been deeply disturbed. Unbeknown to the Estate and the executors, Kehoe had allowed the fire insurance to lapse. This may have been just one more example of letting the farm fall to disrepair or it might have been more. Neither Kehoe nor the insurance agent let the executor know. The executors, on the other hand, had felt it unnecessary to take the precautions which would have assured them this information.

Early in March, however, another prospective buyer popped up and was even sent to the Price girls to talk about it.[9] The record holds no indication as to why the contact did not materialize into a sale. Possibly the asking price was more than the buyer wanted to handle.

As late as March 31st, Kehoe actually dropped into Dunnebacke's office to discuss another offer he was considering.[10] There was something about the offer that bothered Kehoe. He had dropped in to chew the situation over and to get some needed advice. As Kehoe laid the proposition out, it appeared to the attorney to consist of a one-sided agreement in disfavor to Kehoe. Kehoe would not be getting cash out or even in delay. Instead, Kehoe would be giving up the farm in exchange for a return which included an option to buy. Unfortunately, the option to buy appeared to be upon property which Kehoe knew nothing about. Attorney Dunnebacke discouraged Kehoe, but not so strongly as to prevent Kehoe from considering the matter further.

As Kehoe left the office, he gave Dunnebacke some impression of friendship. Dunnebacke's optimism was increased at the same time that he underlined his continuing faith that Kehoe would in fact come through. Were it not for such faith, he might have leaped for closure on any offer made to Kehoe. Actually, Dunnebacke was confident that Kehoe would ultimately reject the latest offer based on his advice. He felt comfortably sure of that. Never did it enter his head that Kehoe might have been any less than completely sincere in wishing to consider the offer.

A continued reliance on Kehoe was even exhibited at the school board meetings. If anything, the disappearance of his quiet, but steady combativeness might have increased the board's respect for his competencies. When the board had an occasion to consider the safety of the children, it looked to Kehoe to eliminate a potential danger. On March 23rd the occasion of the members' concern was the reliability of the brakes of the fleet of school buses. After some discussion of the possible threat to the children, George Spangler made the motion, THAT A.P. KEHOE INTERVIEW THE BUS DRIVERS IN REGARD TO THE BRAKES BEING SAFE ON THEIR TRUCK CHASSES.[11]

81

It was a good precaution, something that should have been done before. The motion carried without any hestiation on anyone's part. It was the kind of motion that make school board members feel good.

Undoubtedly the action was pleasing to Kehoe—in either confirming that his deception was, indeed, undetected—or, in encouraging him to believe that an option was still open to him.

Only a week earlier the Citizens Caucus had chosen him as their candidate for the office of Justice of the Peace. With his preoccupation with justice, Kehoe had obviously thought about that particular office quite a bit. He could sense intuitively that his grasp of justice was somehow better developed than it was in most men. He might even expect that this talent had not gone unnoticed among the countryfolk in the township. Certainly, events since the election for township clerk had demonstrated to all his persistence for justice. Given a judicial position, he need not find that justice so elusive. Kehoe as Justice! After all, it was what Kehoe was all about. A pleasant fantasy of vindication. A fantasy coexisting with his fantasy of destruction. The fantasy of justice might displace the fantasy of destruction—or they both might be acted out, the first protecting the latter and making it all the more poetic.

In reality, Kehoe's candidacy on the Citizen's slate probably meant the odds were against him to begin with. The opposing Republican slate was generally conceded to be more powerful. Around Bath, Democrats calling themselves Citizens were only slightly more popular than Democrats calling themselves Democrats. Still, personal popularity could make a shambles of party labels. Kehoe probably harboured that hope.

The township election was held on April 6th. Just as he always did, Kehoe showed up for the election with his wife. Somehow, at election time, Nellie always seemed to be well enough to be up and about.

Kehoe's opponent, the Republican candidate, was Roy Reasoner. Without the party labels, and for any other office, the voters might have had second thoughts about who to vote for. For true justice, however, they might hestitate to vote for someone with an axe to grind. When the votes were counted, one Citizen's party candidate had overcome the party labels and won but the candidate wasn't Kehoe. Roy Reasoner, man without an axe, had beaten Kehoe decisively, 142 to 76.[12] Kehoe didn't bring up last place on the ticket, but he was beaten. Once again, the fantasy of Justice was to become one fantasy.

With the election over, Nellie suffered a severe relapse. She had left the hospital about the first of March looking quite good. Doctors were optimistic about her prognosis. It wasn't the first time she had been released from a hospital in apparently good condition. The pattern was the same. Good prognosis, followed by a relatively short time back home, followed by almost uncontrollable attacks of coughing spells. Her chronic condition was asthmatic, or at least it appeared to be, but the acute attacks came on always at home. On April 10, Nellie returned to a hospital bed in Lansing.

Quite possibly, it was while on his way to or from visiting his wife that Kehoe ran into Attorney Dunnebacke five days later. On their meeting, Kehoe mentioned that he had taken the attorney's advice after all. He had decided against the last offer.

Chapter XII
Preparations—The Last Month Begins

Between the time that Mrs. Kehoe had last been discharged from the hospital and her reentry on April 10, 1927, nearly six weeks had gone by. During that time, Kehoe had no opportunity to further implement his plan of revenge. He may have considered discarding the plan. Possibly, he did discard it, temporarily, as he lived through a period of brief, but ego boosting experiences.

With Nellie by his side, he sought once more to extend his role in public life. He was rewarded with a show of trust from both the Citizen's Caucus and the school board. He had pursued sale of his farm and even sought out Mr. Dunnebacke in an apparent posture of trust. At the worst, his pursuit of the Justice post, and his effort to sell the farm looked like ambivalence between two fairly healthy goals. But then came his defeat, followed in just four days by his wife's return to the hospital.

On the surface, Nellie's hospitalization didn't seem to be a cause for desperation. Doctor's had confided to her husband that there was really nothing to worry about. She needed a little rest and building up. After that, she should undergo some minor surgery, but then her outlook should be good.

That was their word, but Kehoe was not one to take professionals at their word. Certainly their earlier diagnostics and treatments hadn't produced any cure. Kehoe probably sensed that his wife's condition was far more serious than the doctors let on. More painful, her increasingly serious illness, her incapacity, and now her hospitalization created in Kehoe the belief that she was continuing her betrayal. She was deserting him. He could control the rage he felt toward her only while she remained in his presence.

With Nellie's return to the hospital, Kehoe quickly made up for the six weeks of lost time. Either he had been standing pat, biding his time while she was home, or her return to the hospital coupled with his final defeat at the polls signaled the end of any remaining controls against complete and irreversible madness. When she left, he returned almost immediately to his intent to destroy the school.

Because Kehoe could not know just how soon his wife might return, he needed to move with speed and cunning. He needed to give the greatest possible priority to his preparations to dynamite the school. To guarantee the success of those preparations, he needed to maintain his complete cover. His daytime activities would remain basically unchanged—complicated only by his mission of faithfully visiting his wife at St. Lawrence Hospital.

Kehoe had already decided that his supply of explosives was adequate to do the job—and without skimping. Of one variety or another he had accumulated nearly a ton of explosives. His largest variety was bulk Pyrotol, the World War I perfection which was made up of 20% dynamite. Of that, he had between 10 and 20 thirty pound sacks. In addition, he owned large quantities of stick Pyrotol and 40% Hercules which was also in stick form.

In his calculations, Kehoe took into account that the three feet crawl space under the entirety of the new building made it the easiest section to work in. It also required the largest amount of explosive charges. The work would be dirty under there, but the weather was warmer, at least. It could be almost comfortable.

Kehoe considered the possibility of detection, but assured himself that with precautions detection would not take place. He would determine ahead of time the exact amount of dynamite he would be placing in one evening. He would drive to the school with that, unload it from a spot that would not ordinarily be in view of the citizenry, and then deposit it behind the trap doors leading from the basement. Driving immediately back to the farm in his pickup, he could then return to the school on foot. Once back at the school he could leisurely go about his work without any fear that his truck might be spotted by someone whose curiosity might be piqued. Under the new portion of the building, Kehoe could work slowly and methodically, compensating for the visual handicap of working by flashlight. If he should happen to hear strange and unexpected footsteps entering the building, he could purposely work more quietly— or he could cease work altogether.

A main supporting timber ran the length of the new building which extended north and south from its center. Kehoe decided to attach the main wire to the timber itself. To the side of the timber facing away from the trap doors, he would attach the wire by stapling it to the timber precisely every three feet. It was precision work. Kehoe needed to be very careful that no staple actually punctured the electrical wire itself. From the main wire, tributaries could branch off to the twelve or more explosive plants which were either covered or placed behind supporting pillars. From his drawing board Kehoe knew precisely how long both the main and tributary wires needed to be. He could prepare this wire network in the daylight at home, carefully soldering the necessary wire connections.

For Kehoe it would be interesting, challenging, and tension filled work, a last contest with his compatriots. He would play his deadly game, and they would either discover it or they would not—but he would leave the planting of explosives in the old building for last—just before he set the timer itself.

On April 26th Mrs. Kehoe underwent surgery once more. Andrew was there, just as he was every day, and even more solicitous. Doctors reported that the operation was a success. If she healed properly, she could be out in little more than a week. For Kehoe, the news almost had to be upsetting. He wouldn't show it, of course, but he wasn't ready. One, his preparations for the destruction he was planning at the school were not complete. Two, he had not decided how he would wrap the whole thing up. It was Kehoe's nature to finish things neatly, completely. He had not yet decided how to dispose of his wife.

For some time it had occurred to him that she would have to die. One thing simply led to another. She was either with him or against him; and Kehoe had been haunted by the recurring belief that she was against him. He had thought of killing her earlier at such times. It would have gotten her out of the way. He could work unimpeded to right the wrongs he had suffered at the hands of the community and at the hands of the likes of the Superintendent, and Mel Kyes. Even when he had such murderous thoughts, he had seen immediately that killing her would not work. It would only rob him of the time he needed. He knew that Nellie was so close to her sisters that a day of silence from her would not go by unnoticed. Those damned sisters! Anyway it wasn't simply a question of getting rid of a barrier so that he could get on with his enemies. She and her family were also the enemy.

With the operation over, the sisters themselves provided Kehoe with the respite he needed. The suggestion was made that Nellie spend a few days recuperating with her sisters before returning to the farm with Andrew. Considering her condition, what could be more reasonable? She would be handier to the hospital just in case anything went wrong. She could be practically on outpatient status. Also, she could be attended to with great care by her devoted sisters. They could wait on her with the woman's touch. She needed that. In her own mind she preferred it to an early return to the home, a home which she now associated with disease and loneliness and even repugnance for the dream's end it had come to signify.

Andrew may have protested the sisters' suggestion, but not too much. Although he certainly wanted Nellie home at the earliest possible opportunity, he could recognize with them that their offer made sense. It would be good for Nellie. He would visit her regularly, of course, until she was ready to come home. So he agreed. It was a good plan. Nellie would recuperate in the hospital for a week or so— and then Andrew would take her to her sisters for her final recovery. In the meantime, Kehoe would have all the time he needed.

To all outward appearances, Kehoe conducted himself almost as though he was expecting no change in his life. Uncharacteristically, he began giving some things away. To the recipients, the gifts were sometimes puzzling, sometimes not.

To the Witt girl who had kept house while his wife was ill at home, he gave a valuable tripod camera which had been in the family for sometime.[1] It was an expensive gift, but its offer wasn't questioned. Edith Witt had been a real help to the Kehoe's. Although some people referred to Edith as the Kehoe's hired girl, that description was incorrect. The Witts, like many others, had been on friendly terms with the Kehoes. They considered that any help their daughter could give the Kehoes was just plain neighborly. She would never accept wages for work of that kind, but a token of appreciation was something different. If there was a quality of finality in the gift, that quality was apparently missed. They expected that if the Kehoes needed help again, they would give it. That was as certain as the knowledge that Andrew Kehoe would more than return any favor he was given. An example was the new electrical installation Kehoe offered to set up in the Witt Farm. Kehoe knew about installing lighting systems. Witt didn't. Kehoe also knew how to order the necessary equipment. Kehoe's offer to take care of the ordering and the installing was typically Kehoe. The Witts were just thankful they had friends like Andrew Kehoe around.

It was about the first of May that the electrical equipment arrived, including a generator and a switchboard. By Kehoe's reckoning the installation would take several days time of leisurely, but purposeful work. Some of the work would be on the inside of the house and some would be on the outside. Inside or outside, Kehoe could be expected to have an audience. He loved to work for an audience. An electrician, he was a magician with a black box. Each movement was embellished and with flair, and yet so subtly done that onlookers were only aware of watching fascinating work.

Naturally, the Witts and their children, were among the audience. Actually, the children were more young adults than children, but they could admire Kehoe's work nevertheless.

In return, Kehoe apparently took kindly to the Witt young men, just as he had with Edith. To one brother, Kehoe made a gift of his buffalo gun, possibly a remembrance from his younger days west of the Mississippi. He offered the boys yet another gun—but Mr. Witt wouldn't let them accept that.

The Witts were both beneficiaries and audience to Kehoe. They were by no means the only beneficiaries or the only audience. Neighbors dropped in from time to time during the day to see how Kehoe was coming in the work. Among these, and perhaps the most appreciative of Kehoe's skilled workmanship was a closeby neighbor of the Witts, Allen McMullen, a long time acquaintance of Andrew Kehoe. That is, they had known each other for a long time, known who each other was, but had never been close.

By 1927, McMullen was an old man. He was crippled and moved about only with great difficulty. A widower, he lived alone now with his old maid sisters on the farm, but still managed to keep body and soul together. McMullen was a proud old gentleman. He was not one to be easily separated from his dignity. He was sometimes overly inclined to worry, and had never been comfortable with the occasional slight kindnesses Kehoe was wont to show him. McMullen's wife had been friendly with Mrs. Kehoe in the past—and once or twice Kehoe had bought McMullen a cigar in town. McMullen could always sense that Kehoe had a liking for him, but he could also sense that Kehoe wanted intimacy with no man. If it wasn't for that sense of guarded distance, the old man might have responded more. He could have used that friendship—but even an old man has to be careful. Mr. McMullen was especially careful.

For the old man, the days weren't that full of activity anymore anyway. Kehoe's activity at the Witt farm offered a nice diversion, something to help pass the time away. On occasion, when Kehoe was through working for the day, he would drop the old man off at the latter's farm. It was on Kehoe's way home anyway so there was no special obligation.

One day while McMullen was being dropped off, Kehoe unexpectedly asked him, "Have you any need for a horse?"[2]

The old man hesitated a moment and then answered, "Oh, I don't know, I expect I could use one once in a while."

"Well," Kehoe said, "there are two horses over in my barn tearing the barn down." The pickup had stopped at the McMullen place now, and the old man pushed down on the door handle to get out. "That's right," said Kehoe, "you might just as well come over and get one."

The old man didn't say whether he would or whether he wouldn't, but the prospect of having his own horse did cause him some excitement. He would have liked to have a horse all right, but he didn't think that he would ever be able to go over to Kehoe's and just pick one up—not just like that. It didn't seem right. The whole thing puzzled him a bit. He had heard about Kehoe giving away the camera. He had heard about Kehoe giving away the buffalo gun and trying to give away another. Somehow, the old man sensed a relationship between these offerings. It didn't sit easy with him. A horse was just too valuable a gift.

Two days later, though, Kehoe appeared unexpectedly at the McMullen farmhouse. He had the horse with him, harnessed and ready for work. Kehoe had perceived that the old man really wanted that horse. He had also perceived that he would have to lead the horse to the old man.

The old man was truly touched. He just stood there in the doorway looking at that horse. There was a slight quivver to his chin. Not quite speechless, he managed to say, "This is pretty nice to have someone wait on you like that."

"Oh, I don't mind that," Kehoe answered, and he walked back to the Kehoe farm across lots rather than wait for a ride from McMullen's sister. The day was May 4th.

For Kehoe it was a day to remember. Not in a long, long time had he felt as good as he did when he gave old man McMullen the horse or—better yet—when the old man accepted the horse.

The day was critical for another reason. By the fourth, Nellie had so well responded to her surgery of April 26th that she was ready for discharge. When Kehoe picked her up at the hospital, he was obviously in a good mood. Nellie must have been pleased to see him that happy to see her. They drove the short distance to the sisters' residence on North Seymour, and were greeted by Nellie's equally happy and receptive sisters. They, too, were undoubtedly impressed with Andrew's good humour. Andrew was in one of his more conversational moods. He was happy to stay for dinner and even a little after. The time passed quickly as Andrew stimulated a more than ample exchange of witticisms and pleasantries before begging leave to get back to chores awaiting him at the farm. He left, however, only after reassuringly kissing Nellie goodbye. It was clear to everyone that Andrew would be anxious for his wife's return in ten days or so. He would be counting the days even while he was visiting her in the meantime.

Chapter XIII
Signals, Blunders, and Rebuff

When Kehoe returned to the farm, he carried out some chores in the horse barn, and waited for darkness. It was a wait he had now become accustomed to. On this particular night he was keenly aware that his wife's discharge placed a definite time limit on his preparations. Everything would need to be in place when his wife was ready to come home. There could be no loose ends. This night he again drove to the hidden spot adjacent to the school, unloaded additional wiring and explosive, and again returned home. And just as before, he returned to the school on foot to further set and conceal explosives. The work under the new building was nearing completion now. He yearned for that partly because of the dirt and dust he was required to work in. He could never wait to get back to the house to wash up. Normally Kehoe was very careful to remove any possible trace of his presence in the building—but on the night of the fourth he committed one of a series of potentially key blunders. When he left, he forgot to replace the trap door from the fan room.

The next day, Frank Smith the Janitor noticed it. He was with the Superintendent at the time, and both had something else on their minds. The Janitor made a mental note of it, but dismissed it at the same time. Possibly, he would have given it a little further consideration if he had been aware of an earlier report of a door left open. Only three days earlier, one of the students, O. B. Rounds, had discovered the north door to the building open and unlocked. It was the same door which had been found badly split only two weeks earlier. That split had been so bad that the door had to be repaired before it could be locked.

The split door may have been completely unrelated to Kehoe. It probably was. The other findings, however, were something else. Plainly, Kehoe had a great deal on his mind. He could not remember everything he needed to remember all of the time.

On the night of the fourth he might well have been thinking of his wife and the homecoming he would need to plan for her. On the other hand, he could have been giving further thought to Allen McMullen. He wasn't quite satisfied with his gift to McMullen yet. He needed to do something further to sooth the old man's worries. He needed, possibly, to make the gift secure for the old man, even after—.

On the fifth, Kehoe maintained his perfect attendance record at the regular board meeting of the school. Basically, it was an uneventful meeting. On the way into the school, though, Mel Kyes noticed that the front door was jammed. From a cursory examination it seemed as though someone had tampered with the lock. Again, no great significance was attached to it. Things like this happened to school property. It just happened that the superintendent missed this particular meeting. On an earlier occasion the superintendent had expressed some concern over security of the building to his Principal, Mr. Huggett. Had the superintendent been along with Mr. Kyes that night, he might have reaffirmed his concern.

Just days before, Kehoe had also made the monthly round of delivering pay checks. Actually checks were issued every twentieth school day. As was his custom, Kehoe not only handed the checks out personally to each teacher, he did so with each and every employee of the system. As each bus pulled up to park in front of the building, Kehoe approached the bus, check in hand. As Kehoe approached the bus driven by Ward Kyes, he stirred the usual mixed feelings in Ward. Kehoe had been repeatedly Ward's adversary as well as his paymaster. Neither man was there because of the other's choice. As far as Ward was concerned, if Kehoe had to insist on making these payments personally, he would be regularly reminded of his regular defeats over Ward. As far as Kehoe was concerned, he would have preferred never having to pay Ward a single pay check. As long as Kehoe did, however, he could remind Ward by the ritual that he, Kehoe, was still in control.

On this particuar day, Kehoe approached in unusually good humor. As Ward was taking the check from Kehoe's outstretched hand, it slipped from his hand and fell to the bus floor. While Ward stooped to pick it up, Kehoe said good naturedly, "You'd better keep that. That may be the last you will ever get." Ward looked at Kehoe and laughed, and said, "Why? Are you going broke?"

"I guess not," Kehoe replied.[1]

Ward was a little puzzled by Kehoe's remark, but laughed it off. Kehoe's quip, though, was really better suited to a final pay check of the year. This was not scheduled to be the final pay check. Although graduation was scheduled for the 19th of May, the 23rd was to be the official last day of school—and final pay checks were due to be issued then. As Kehoe walked away from the bus, Ward watched him for a few steps. He laughed to himself and shook his head. Kehoe was a strange one, all right.

Although Kehoe was keeping amazingly good control over his scheme of reprisal, his conscious and unconscious were beginning the process of merger—a merger which might truly culminate in an orgy of death and destruction. Were sufficient merger to take place ahead of the culmination, it might bring about a fatal detection. Were Kehoe's remarks to Ward really a slip, or were they intentional? Were

90

the trap doors intentionally left open, or was it a slip caused by Kehoe's preoccupation with his gift to the old man?

On May 6th, Kehoe had the opportunity to make his present to McMullen secure. Kehoe, with McMullen looking on, had concluded his electrical work for the day. The Witts, knowing he was alone had insisted that he stay for supper, and Kehoe had agreed. Kehoe and McMullen lounged under a shade tree waiting to be called in to the table. Suddenly, as they were discussing this and that, Kehoe handed the old man a sheet of paper with some writing typed on it. Mr. McMullen unfolded the paper all the way, looked at it briefly and quizzically. "Would you mind reading it to me?" he asked. "I don't have my glasses with me."

"Glad to," said Kehoe and read, "May 4, 1927. Received from Allen McMullen. One hundred and twenty dollars in full payment for one bay mare, ten years old, blind in left eye, weight 1,800 pounds, Named Kit. $120. A. P. Kehoe." Kehoe folded the paper, and tucked it into the breast pocket of the old man's overalls. "That's your story," Kehoe said to him, "you stick to that."[2] It was said forcefully, knowingly, and reassuringly. McMullen said nothing. He was dumbfounded.

The Kehoe note was characteristic of the man's wile. It was designed ostensibly to allay the old man's worries. If anyone were to ask the old man how he came about having such a horse, he could simply pull out the paper. Besides that apparent purpose, the note confirmed to McMullen that he had received a very expensive gift— just in case he hadn't thought about that. There was a hint, too, that Kehoe might have had a special affection for Kit and a handicap the horse shared with Mel Kyes.

Between the lines, the note carried a more ominous message, one which might have been missed by someone less astute, and less inclined to worry than McMullen. The bottom line was that accepting the horse as a gift from Kehoe was wrong, or that it would be judged badly. McMullen guessed and probably, properly, that Kehoe might be attempting to protect him against any criticism of accepting charity. But, McMullen reasoned to himself, why would he need to *stick* to the story Kehoe had given him? Wasn't Kehoe planning to be around? McMullen did not quite comprehend that Kehoe had given him a clue—even though he had picked up on the message he mis-read it. His fears put him in a unique class—but he could not guess that wittingly or not, the note might serve to protect him later. It could cut him apart from a suspect group of those bearing gifts from Kehoe.

The date Kehoe had given McMullen the bill of sale was May 6th, 1927. Through the bill of sale, Kehoe had presented a fiction as a fact. By May 9th, McMullen had worried himself into a real stew. His worries were for himself. He had made up his mind that he was going to get into trouble in some way or form if he kept the horse. There was only one thing to do, go to Kehoe and get the thing off his mind. McMullen walked back lots to Kehoe's place and was there by 8 o'clock in the morning. When he got no answer at the back door, he tried the front. When he had no luck there, he walked across the road to David Harte's farm and tried to stir Kehoe by telephoning. Still no luck. The old man then walked back across the road and sat himself down on Kehoe's back step. He was determined that he was not going to go back home until he had shed himself of this problem.

After sitting for more than an hour, McMullen tried pounding at the door one more time. As he was pounding, the thought even entered McMullen's head that Kehoe might be inside, dead. Possibly he had hung himself. He was almost surprised, then, when Kehoe suddenly appeared at the door clad only in pants and slippers. As Kehoe opened the door for him, McMullen said, jokingly, "What is the matter? Are you going to kill yourself sleeping?"

Kehoe grinned and replied, "It wouldn't be a bad way to die, would it?"[3]

Inside, the two talked at the dining room table. Kehoe brought out a jug of cider, and filled their glasses as they talked. McMullen couldn't bring himself to come out with the real reason, but presented Kehoe with various other reasons for deciding that he couldn't keep the horse. Kehoe was surprised. He didn't say much, but the old man kept coming up with a new reason, just as though he was responding to an objection from Kehoe. It was a difficult meeting for McMullen, but he held his ground even in the face of Kehoe's silence of disappointment. He would liked to have gone back home the way he came, but finally he gave into Kehoe's insistence that he be driven home in the pickup.

On the twelfth, McMullen returned Kit to Kehoe. Kehoe's only comment as he took the horse back was, "Al, you made a mistake by not keeping that horse over there." For Kehoe, it was almost the final rebuff.

What special reaction if any it might have triggered in Kehoe is not known. At this point in Kehoe's preparations, any change in him one way or the other was unlikely.

Aside from a facade of activity as usual, the electrical work for the Witts, school board attendance, visits to his wife and so on, Kehoe's overall activities had picked up feverishly beginning with or shortly after his wife's lastest hospitalization. As a precautionary measure, a necessary piece of insurance, Kehoe went out on the first of May and bought himself a complete and new set of tires. His pickup was an absolute necessity to his plans. He could ill afford to have it break-down at that point. Most of all he could not afford a breakdown at some untoward time or place when the car might be loaded with explosives. With the new tires the countless trips necessary to town, to Lansing, to the school, and even to his house, would be possible and secure.

Some of that activity was noticed, but it didn't really register. Other activity was observed with interest, even increasing interest, but never with alarm. But even the most curious were held off by the sense, consistently observed, that it was better not to ask Kehoe anything about his business.

On May 1st, Ida Hall had moved back into Bath, into the house on Main Street which was adjacent to the Consolidated School. Coincident with her move back to the Village, she frequently heard the sound of a car driving in and out of the school late at night. On one occasion, about two o'clock in the morning she was awakened by the sound of a motor. Out her window and aided by moonlight she observed a Ford pickup truck parked close by the front steps to the school. Twice the driver carried objects inside the school. Further back of the pickup was a Ford touring car. Mrs. Hall was puzzled by the activity. On three other occasions she had observed a car driving around the school building. It was puzzling, but beside discussing the observances with her niece, La Donna Reutter, the matter was dropped.[4] At about the same time, Kehoe's neighbors across the road noticed that almost nightly, Kehoe was making trips to the East toward Bath.[5]

Coincident with his wife's discharge, Kehoe had also needed to face more squarely the question of the disposition of the farm. On May 2nd he had made his initial attempts through McMullen to have Kit taken care of. On May 4th, Kehoe sold his remaining hogs to Monty Ellsworth. On May 9th he may even have paid some token attention to the University's final inspection report of the year.

On May 10th, however, a piece of activity was observed which would have led neighbors to believe that things were basically normal. Leonard Hyatt, the Bath Standard Oil dealer, made his usual Spring fuel delivery to the Kehoe Farm. He added 80 gallons to the ten gallons of gasoline which Kehoe maintained for running his machine. He also added 118 gallons of kerosene to the thirty gallons of that fuel which Kehoe already had on hand. Kehoe seemed in a restful mood. With Hyatt he stretched out lazily on the grass waiting for the fuel to be emptied. Kehoe chewed on a piece of grass, apparently reflecting on just about anything. He took note of a pheasant strolling naively in the nearby field. Almost absent mindedly Kehoe commented, "If I had my gun, I'd shoot it."[6]

Kehoe paid Hyatt in cash and took his receipt. Hyatt drove off knowing Kehoe was set for another month with gasoline—and for a whole year with kerosene. Kehoe, on the other hand, knew that he had barely enough for a week—but enough to begin and complete the final stage of preparations.

Kehoe had now made arrangements to pick up his wife on

Sunday, the fifteenth of May. In arriving at that agreement, neither he nor his wife made any mention of the fourteenth of May. It would be the couple's fifteenth wedding anniversary. Possibly neither noticed. More likely, Kehoe did notice, if only to note the slight—the lack of favorable importance his wife attached to the occasion, and to him. Possibly the oversight was decisive. Probably it wasn't—but with Kehoe, such an act of omission was always worth remembering, even repaying.

With the receipt of the gasoline and kerosene, Kehoe needed to move even more swiftly to complete the work at the school. He would need to devote all his energies to preparing the farm house, the farm buildings, the equipment, and the grounds.

On the night of May tenth, Kehoe was able to complete the bulk of his explosive setting at the school. Some days earlier he had completed his work in the new portion of the school—except for setting the timing device. He had then turned to the more difficult task of setting the explosives in the old building. Painstakingly, he had pushed the wired charges of stick dynamite through the two inch eavestrough piping. The charges were pushed into place by using long poles of bamboo, and male and female sections of well poles which Kehoe had obtained from the school. To eliminate the chance of error, and of needless probing within the darkened eavestrough, Kehoe had fastened the charges to the end of the poles. As each charge was guided into its strategic destination, the pole was left in place with the charge.

Amazingly, Kehoe again neglected to close the trap door when he finished his work for the evening. Once more, on the following day, the janitor noticed the open trap door. The time was May 11th.[7] Once more the janitor made a mental note of the open trap door. Again, however, no cause for alarm was seen. After all, the board members took a direct and personal responsibility for the well being of the physical plant. Frank Smith was used to their working on this or that part of the plant whenever they felt like it. If they occasionally left trap doors open, it wasn't his place to comment to them about it.

On the same date, Kehoe drove to the Gould-Spencer Auto and Radio Supply store in Lansing. His purchase was one hot shot battery. Another hot shot battery was already in place in the sub basement of the school. The second battery, fresh, would complement the first. Set in parallel, the batteries would provide sufficient charge to demolish the entire school.

On the same date, the neighbors across the road from Kehoe, noticed something new. Kehoe began the first of daily trips from the West. He pulled into the driveway with his pickup truck, then backed it up to the hog house. The back end looked like it was loaded with boxes of some kind, but the boxes were covered with blankets. Unfortunately, the unloading zone was just out of Mrs. Harte's range of vision. Naturally, the curiosity of Mr. and Mrs. Harte was aroused; especially as they saw this precise activity repeated each day over the next several days. Their curiosity was further sharpened when Mrs. Harte noticed wiring running along the ground from the farm house to each of the outbuildings. The only guess they could make was that Andrew Kehoe's activity was linked to a plan of his to tie into the Consumer Power line which was being installed into Bath. It would be like Kehoe to have electricity installed in every barn and shed on the place.

On May 12th a hitch, but only a minor one. McMullen returned Kit to Kehoe. Possibly there was something in the return of the gift horse which reminded Kehoe of his need for target practice. He and Monty Ellsworth had planned a little friendly target competition for some time. On May 12th, Kehoe reminded Ellsworth of that. They agreed to shoot the following morning.

The next morning Kehoe drove the short distance to Ellsworth's, bringing his rifle and pasteboard targets with him. It wasn't a lengthy match, just long enough for Ellsworth to recognize that Kehoe was a superior marksman. Even at 300 feet offhand, Kehoe shot cooly and accurately. He gave no indication of anxiety or tension. As Ellsworth walked Kehoe back to his pickup, he noticed a box of rifle shells in the back. Just at a glance, it looked like a considerable number, perhaps as many as a thousand shells.[8] For no reason at all, Ellsworth made a mental note of his perception, and then dismissed it from his mind.

The time was Friday the thirteenth. As the day passed, Ellsworth and most Americans may once more have judged the superstition to be a silly one. Even Michigan's more deadly felons might have guessed that these were lucky times. Both houses of the Michigan legislature had voted to restore the death penalty—only to have the bill killed after a trip to the conference committee. Kehoe, himself, might have taken passing interest in new reports of the legislative battle. The battle was immaterial to him, but he still might have taken that passing interest.

For most, there were more exciting or more pleasant things to read about. 1927 was the time of the hero. Americans needed heroes, searched for heroes, created heroes and worshipped heroes. Heroes were everywhere. Johnny Weissmuller was shattering everyone's swimming records, including his own. Names like Jack Sharkey, Jack Dempsey, and Gene Tunney were making this the great golden age of boxing. In less than a month, Sharkey and Dempsey would be fighting an elimination bout to get at Tunney and his World Title. In baseball, Babe Ruth led a similar parade of stars destined for immortality.

Even tragedies were dominated by the inevitable heroes which accompanied and overcame them. Tornadoes and flooding had hit

95

the Mississippi flood plains with unprecedented force, but there were heroes aplenty to apparently cope with even that.

Even the comic strips featured a variety of a new kind of hero, each with the stature to be worshipped by Americans for a generation and more. Names like Andy Gump, Out Our Way, Our Boarding House, Freckles and His Friends, Gasoline Alley, Smitty, Moon Mullins, and Winnie Winkle made life just a little pleasanter for nearly everyone.

But the greatest American hero of all, then, and perhaps for all time was just walking on stage. Lindbergh! Captain Charles Lindbergh was scheduled to try his great solo flight across the Atlantic the following week. Something in his manner, something in his smile, something in his courage combined to make him the great household word long before takeoff. Newspapers across the land were becoming little more than Lindbergh chroniclers. Even the invention of Television could not compete with him.

Kehoe, with his love of the magic of machines, might ordinarily have been more excited by the unfolding Lindbergh drama than anyone. Instead, all of Kehoe's interests and energies were now devoted to accomplishing his own all consuming objective.

Saturday, the fourteenth of May, was the Kehoe's fifteenth wedding anniversary (was less than a week away from Lindbergh's scheduled takeoff); and it was also the day that Kehoe's acquaintance and shooting partner, Monty Ellsworth, needed help. Ellsworth lived just down the road from Kehoe, and across the tracks nearer to town. On the fourteenth, Ellsworth was going about the business of installing a new Shell Gasoline station on the front of his residence. On Saturday morning he was attempting to set up his air compressor in temporary working order. Finding he was in need of a piping union, he walked over to Kehoe's. Aside from a union, Ellsworth wasn't looking for anything unusual, and apparently he found nothing unusual. As expected, Kehoe had the union he needed. As Ellsworth was leaving, he mentioned that he would be converting to a permanent installation in about a week. Kehoe replied, "When you get ready to do that, come down if you need any tools. Yes, and I will come up and help you."[9] With that statement, Kehoe was either lying as a continuation of his cover, or was becoming critically confused as to time.

Chapter XIV
A Matter of Timing

With Ellsworth safely out of the house, Kehoe was free to attend to certain preparations which had been delayed until the most appropriate time. It was a matter of squaring accounts. Kehoe was always very particular about that.

After pecking out what was perhaps a final letter; Kehoe commenced loading an empty wooden box. Ominously, the box was marked DYNAMITE, and Kehoe packed the contents with deliberation and care. After closing the container, Kehoe addressed it with stencil and set is aside for delivery at the proper moment. It was a matter which had been gnawing on him for some time. It pleased him that he could handle it so well, and with such finality.

With that task done, Kehoe had very nearly completed his preparations—for the school, for himself, and for his wife's return on the following day. By Saturday he had also completed the rounds of his creditors, dropping by each personally to square accounts. In doing so, he didn't forget Judge Searl. In addition, Kehoe's preparation of the house, the buildings and the grounds were complete except for those things which would need to be postponed to the last possible moment. Significantly, the preparation of the farm overlooked not the slightest detail. The preparation at the school could hardly compare to it. On the next day, Kehoe would drive to Lansing and return his wife to the farm.

Sunday the 15th was rainy and damp. Early in the day Kehoe's telephone rang. It was a message from his wife. She didn't feel up to the ten miles or so in the damp weather. Monday would be warmer, sunnier. At least, that was the hope. Kehoe expressed disappointment to the caller, but of course he would honor his wife's wishes in such things. Dampness probably was not good for Nellie's condition. It was left that if Monday was a nice day, Kehoe would pick up Nellie early in the evening. For Kehoe, the call in behalf of his wife meant that his plans would need to be delayed for at least one day.

On Monday, Kehoe continued to put some finishing touches on the buildings. He was busying himself carrying straw into the hen house when he was interrupted by David Harte, his neighbor from across the road. Harte understood that Kehoe was attempting to sell his horses, and he wanted to help. With Harte was Semour Champion of Lansing, a potential purchaser. Kehoe was agreeable to bargaining all right. He excused himself momentarily so that he could wash his hands in the house, and then joined Harte and Champion for a little price bickering. The bickering didn't last long.

Kehoe insisted on getting $100 for his eighteen year old. Champion just couldn't give that—not for a horse that old. The risk was too great. Probably, Harte felt like an unappreciated good samaritan. Kehoe was being offered more for the horse than he could hope to get, but there was no moving the man.[1] As the disappointed gentlemen left, Kehoe returned to his work.

For Kehoe, a sign of relief was in order. The sooner the men were off the premises, the better. At the same time he had gone through the bartering process from a position of strength. Unknown to either Harte or Champion, Kehoe had nothing of material value to win or to lose. He could trade or pretend to trade without fear of being bettered in the trade. The time was past for Kehoe to give anyone the chance to undo him in trade.

**

Monday afternoon was now coming to a close. In Lansing, Nellie packed her things, and noted the little time remaining before Andrew was due to pick her up. She had picked out one of her favorite dresses. She was by no means robust yet, but she was prettier and healthier than she had been in some time.

There was a certain attempt at gaity in her conversation with her sisters. She had been with them, and away from Andrew for more than a month. She was not only grateful for their care, but saddened at leaving them. The sisters had been extremely close all their lives, and they got along well. Added to the tension of leaving them was the tension Nellie felt in rejoining Andrew. A somehow strange and aloof man, she faced an uncertain future with him. It was to be a future of drastic change for them, of drastic uncertain change, yet Andrew appeared unconcerned. Had she the slightest inkling of just how well Andrew had planned their future, her apprehension might have been uncontrollable.

Once it had occurred to Andrew that she must die, he had given studied thought to the time and the method. To await circumstances would have been totally unlike Kehoe. In addition, he had the capacity certainly to contemplate any variety of murders. He could handle guns with ease. He knew both primitive and technical means of muffling sound. He was experienced in both farm butchering and the use of various farm poisons. He had witnessed death by fire. Kehoe would simply have needed to pick the safest, most appropriate method for the occasion. That the choice was made well ahead of picking Nellie up seems a certainty.

When Kehoe did arrive at the residence of the Price sisters, evening was just approaching. As would have been typical for such an occasion, Kehoe was well dressed, and in good spirits. There was certainly nothing in his speech or manner which would have given either Nellie or her sisters any sudden concern. Undoubtedly, Kehoe presented himself as the dutiful husband, happy at the opportunity to be reunited with his wife.

Within minutes of their reunion, Andrew and his wife were approaching the pleasant and rolling Bath countryside, enriched as it was with the smell and sights of spring. The day had been sunny and the evening was now warm and comfortable—just the kind of weather that could be agreeable with Nellie, the kind that could give flesh and strength to her still frail body. Nellie was so taken with the beauty of the dusk, that she hardly noticed that Andrew had become almost completely silent.

The pleasant ride ended too quicky. Andrew pulled the pickup into the driveway and parked by the back door. Solicitously, he went round to the other side of the machine, as was his custom. As was her custom, Nellie waited for him to open her door. Andrew opened the door with one hand, and reached for her suitcase from the back end with the other. He helped her off the running board and then went ahead of Nellie to open the back door. As she went inside, Andrew followed, shutting the heavy farm door behind them. Murder, on an unparalleled scale was about to begin.

**

That evening, Blanche Harte, the fifth grade teacher telephoned Kehoe from her in-laws across the road. She had called to ask his permission to bring her pupils to Kehoe's woods on Thursday for a picnic. In the course of the conversation, Mrs. Harte inquired about Mrs. Kehoe. Kehoe replied, "She is getting along fine. I have got her here at home with me and she is fussing around." It was an interesting choice of words.

Shorty after Kehoe hung up from giving Mrs. Harte permission for the picnic, he thought better of it. He telephoned her back and suggested that the picnic be changed to Tuesday as it might rain on Thursday. Kehoe obviously knew as a certainty that Thursday was out. . . .

On Tuesday, Kehoe found time to seek Ellsworth out once more. During the meeting, Kehoe unexpectedly offered to trade rifles with Ellsworth. He offered his rifle in exchange for Ellsworth's plus $25. There was a certain logic to Kehoe's terms. He had bested Ellsworth in their recent shooting match. Very possibly, his superiority was due to a superior gun. Very possibly, Ellsworth would like to have that gun. On the other hand, Kehoe had absolutely no need for twenty five dollars. Perhaps, there was another reason the gun was in Kehoe's mind. Perhaps it was the same reason which prompted

99

him into a gesture of getting rid of it. However, when he was offered just $10 in addition to Ellsworth's gun, Kehoe refused. He explained that he had paid $50 for the rifle alone—plus an extra $11 for a special sight. When Ellsworth wouldn't pay more than he offered and Kehoe wouldn't take less, the trade aborted. A weapon which perhaps had committed one murder was left in Kehoe's hands for deeds which had yet to be enacted. From Kehoe's diseased perspective, the onus might be on Ellsworth.

Definitely, Nellie Kehoe was already dead at the time Kehoe and Ellsworth approached gun trade on Tuesday. Kehoe had been away from his home at least that part of the day when he talked trade with Ellsworth. That evening he telephoned his wife's sisters to give them a little innocent information about Nellie, comforting information. He was calling, he explained, just in case they might have been trying to telephone during the day. "Nellie is over to Jackson," he informed them. "She was lonesome here, and we have some friends by the name of Vost who we used to know at Tecumseh, and it occured to me to take Nellie over there because I thought it would be a good thing for her. I am to go back for her on Thursday."[2] Kehoe waited for questions, or for any telltale silence which might suggest something less than complete gullibility—but there was no such suggestion. Kehoe hung up the receiver, and breathed easier.

Kehoe's story was both a lie and a ploy—but the sisters swallowed the story completely. Had they been prepared to be suspicious, they might have seen through the story, might at least have seen its poor construction and its unintended revelation.

Nellie's death had undoubtedly occurred sometime before Kehoe met with Ellsworth on Tuesday. Had she been alive during the trade session, she might have called her sisters or received a call from them. Kehoe could speak assuredly with the sisters that evening only if he knew positively that Nellie could not have communicated with them during the day.

Kehoe's ploy, however, was necessary to give him the short additional time he now needed to carry out the heart of his plan. He had decided to put the sisters off until Thursday, knowing that Thursday would be too late for them to interrupt anything. It was the second indication he had given that Thursday would be too late. First, he had said that Thursday wouldn't do for a picnic—it might rain. Tuesday would be better. Nellie would be away until Thursday, he had said. Wednesday, or possibly Tuesday night, appeared to be his target date.

Of course, nothing was detected in Kehoe's comments—not even the relationship with his wife which he indirectly alluded to.

He had described his wife as 'lonesome' less than one day after she had returned to him following a month's absence. Did he feel that he truly meant nothing to her? By the term 'lonesome' he also suggested her and possibly his social isolation in Bath. It was an isolation which he had fostered in recent months. Kehoe was attributing to his wife, a rejection of her home of the past eight years, and of her family's earlier Bath heritage. Either this did reflect an isolation Nellie felt and communicated or it simply slipped by the sisters or was shrugged off. Probably, Kehoe's reference to Nellie's lonesomeness was overshadowed by Kehoe's overriding theme—the concerned, solicitous husband, making a little sacrifice for his wife's pleasure and well being. "I," Kehoe had said. "I thought it would be a good thing for her." Kehoe did the thinking, made the decisions, Kehoe the paternalistic husband of a wife still seen as an invalid in a marriage which had become nothingness.

Kehoe made at least one additional contact that same evening. The Bath PTA was meeting at the school. As a group, its membership was looked on with antipathy by Kehoe. No where else could Kehoe ever hope to find a better congregation of those who had worked to unseat him. As often as not, Emory Huyck their willing sponsor could be found with them. If Kehoe's rage was still selective, this group would sorely tempt him.

Kehoe apparently did look in on the group, but then left. Fordney Cushman, a high school boy, met him or rather passed him on the sidewalk in front of the school at about 8:30 PM Eastern Standard Time.[4] For whatever reason, Kehoe decided not to explode the school at that particular time, possibly the Superintendent or other targeted somebodies were not present at the meeting. Possibly Kehoe had selected another, more devastating occasion.

If the precise time for detonating the school had not been previously determined, Kehoe was now ready to make that determination. When the PTA meeting had adjourned, and everyone had left the building. Kehoe returned for his last preparation. Entering the building at the obscure entrance, Kehoe made his way through the trap door into the crawl space under the new part of the building. Aided by flashlight he quickly found himself at the detonation switch under the main entrance to the building. His timing device was a manual alarm clock, rigged to complete the deadly circuit at the selected alarm time. Kehoe examined his watch and the alarm clock most carefully. The alarm clock had been previously set by Kehoe to go off at 9:45. From pretesting, he knew precisely the exact time it would go off. The clock was accurate, and it was reliable. He could count on it. As he wound the alarm the time was now well into the night, leaving no danger that the 9:45 a.m. alarm would ring in the evening instead of the morning. Nine forty-five a.m. was to be it. Nine forty-five a.m., well after the start of school. Kehoe took one last look at the wire connections, and then crawled back out of the sub basement. Nothing short of a miracle could now save the Bath Consolidated School. Nothing short of a miracle would now save the children of Bath. Through clear and revengeful purpose or by circumstance, Kehoe had decided on a fate worse than death for most of his fancied adult enemies. Their children would die; not they.

His preparations completed, Kehoe made his way home. He would rest as best he could through the night, waiting for the climactic day.

Chapter XV
Daybreak—The Nightmare Begins

Before the first shades of light began to challenge the night skies, Kehoe was up and attending to business. In darkness he wheeled the empty hog chute up to his back door, loaded a heavy object into it, and placed a small box beside the object. Kehoe then pushed the loaded chute to the north east corner of his large group of farm buildings. He left it just west and slightly north of the large corn crib located there. Returning to the house he washed up, properly grooming and dressing himself for the morning ahead.

Kehoe may have been oblivious to the light rain which had fallen just before dawn. The clouds were already clearing at daybreak and the warm sweet smell of Spring was in the air. Although Kehoe's fields had lain fallow, most of the neighboring farm fields had been plowed. Some were just freshly plowed, others, from a distance, showed the green fuzz which was later to become crops of grain or corn. Spring leaves were on the trees, but delicate of the lightest green, and only indecently covering the branches and twigs with their flimsy covering. Here and there lilacs blossomed and scented the air with their fragrance. The day promised to be a good one, full of the excitement and the expectation of Spring.

School buses would be on their way soon, picking up students for the last real day of attendance. For all classes but the senior class, it was exam day. Although the seniors wrote exams the week before, those with special graduation program assignments were to rehearse in the Methodist Church later in the morning. They were to meet with the rest of the senior class at one o'clock in the afternoon.

Observing Kehoe from her farm across the road, Lulu Harte first noticed Kehoe out and around about seven o'clock in the morning. She would notice him off and on until nearly ten o'clock in the morning. At approximately 7:10 a.m., however, Kehoe slipped out of his driveway unnoticed. He drove the very short distance into the village and parked the pickup in front of the post office with him was the box he had withheld sending until the critical hour.

Possibly because the Post Office wasn't yet open, or possibly because he simply thought of a better idea, Kehoe walked with his package the few yards to the bottom of the hill and to the office of the railroad ticket agent, D. B. Huffman, who also served as the agent for American Express. Kehoe spoke with Huffman very briefly, only long enough to leave the package to be expressed to the Lansing address. Although speed of delivery was not really what Kehoe was after, Huffman routed the package away from Lansing to Laingsburg where it could catch the first train to be arriving in Lansing. In the brief conversation between the two men, Huffman detected nothing in Kehoe that he considered unusual.

As soon as Kehoe had paid for the express delivery, he walked up the street to his machine. Just as he crawled in behind the steering wheel, however, he was hailed by Albert Detluff, his fellow board member. This was a distraction Kehoe had not really counted on. Up to that point everything had gone perfectly in the young morning.

Detluff asked Kehoe to go to the school basement with him. He explained to Kehoe that the well was apparently out of commission. The school wasn't getting enough water. He wanted Kehoe to go to the basement pump house with him to take a look. Suddenly, Kehoe was afflicted with a rare feeling of uneasiness, but he thought it best to comply with Detluff's request.

As they walked to the school house, Detluff asked Kehoe the date of the next school board meeting. Kehoe replied that it was the nineteenth. The uneasiness heightened in him. Was it the nineteenth or was it the twentieth? Kehoe's accountant mind was suddenly showing a confusion which others might have accepted as normal, but which caused Kehoe a surge of concern. He corrected himself to Detluff—the meeting was the twentieth after all.

Just as the two were about to enter the building through the front entrance, Kehoe pulled out his pocket watch. Indicating the time to Detluff, he said, "It is about time for school to begin." Kehoe's watch showed twenty five minutes after eight o'clock. Detluff, who kept Central Time instead of Eastern, was showing only twenty past seven.

"No, it isn't." Detluff contradicted Kehoe, "We have got more than an hour."

Kehoe hestitated a moment, thinking, then conceded, "Yes, we have." It was an awkward, possibly even calamitous moment to be confused as to time, but it was inevitable. Fantasy and reality were only minutes away from a complete merger.

In the basement, the two found their way to the pump room where they made a cursory, non-productive inspection of the pump. Kehoe then invited Detluff into the section of the basement which housed the generator. There, the two met Frank Smith, the janitor. As Detluff and Smith began to engage each other in conversation, Kehoe interrupted to say, "You know, I am in an awful hurry." With that, he whirled on his feet and left. Shortly after that, Detluff and Smith left the building to see if they could locate Mr. Harrington, the pump repairman. As they looked downhill through the business district, Detluff observed that Kehoe's car had disappeared from its parking place.

For Kehoe, it was now a matter of time. His cold, calculating, and deliberate plan of murder and revenge was threatened by a mounting confusion and disorientation which he could not have foreseen. The outcome would depend on the success and timing of the challenge to Kehoe which was coming from within himself.

Kehoe's rush from the school may have resulted from his knowledge that much still needed to be done at the farm in a very short time. On the other hand, it might have resulted from his disbelief through confusion that the start of the school day was still more than an hour away.

As Kehoe returned to the farm he fought to regain his composure, to overcome his temporary disorientation as to time. He was determined to see the plan through.

Once again in control, and with all other preparations complete, Kehoe walked briskly from his farmhouse to the corn crib. The time was approximately 9:45 a.m. school time. Neither the corn crib nor the loaded hog chute were electrically wired as were the remaining farm buildings. They could only be ignited directly and manually. Once lit, they were prepared to burn to ashes. Once lit, no power could dowse the fire. Lighting a makeshift torch inside the double corn crib, Kehoe ignited first the corn crib and then, outside, the hog chute with its contents. The instantaneous flames were all engulfing. Black smoke billowed into the air.

Kehoe did not wait to watch. He ran for the house, the excitement rising within him. His face flushed slightly and he was aware of a pounding in his ears. The pounding became so intense that he was unsure which pounding signaled the ultimate act of destruction, the demolition of the school—the murder of the children of Bath. As he raced for the house, he simply knew it had happened and that the whole destructive system was in motion and working toward its climax.

Inside the farmhouse, Kehoe paused only momentarily to catch his breath before pushing the switch which would ignite each and every building on the premises. Once pushed, the switch would ignite and fire the buildings, and begin a series of dynamite explosions calculated to guarantee destruction and to thwart any attempt at rescue. As Kehoe pushed the switch, he was aware of fire flashing immediately within the house, and of an almost instantaneous explosion.

When a fragment struck the Harte brooder house across the road, Mrs. Harte, who was in the brooder house, ran out to look. She saw nothing at first, then thought she heard something like a gun firing from the direction of the Kehoe farmhouse. Suddenly, she spotted it, smoke about the roof of the Kehoe corncrib, followed momentarily by an engulfment of flame. When Mrs. Harte tried unsuccessfully to call her husband, she gave the alarm on the telephone.

Almost simultaneously, Kehoe looked impatiently out his back window for the expected reaction from the remainder of his farm buildings. It seemed longer, but the reaction came—and almost instantaneously. A stream of smoke shot out the east gable end of his sheep barn. It was followed by a similar burst out from the big barn. Suddenly, all the buildings were afire with the exception of the hen house. Kehoe probably noted that exception, but dismissed it as a temporary cloaking by the building itself.

It was now time for Kehoe to leave, and to leave quickly. Neighbors who had been alerted by the billowing smoke and by the call for emergency fire assistance were already enroute to help. Driving fast up from the east, Kehoe's loyal friend, Sidney Howell, came with his boys, Robb and Alden, and with Mel Armstrong. As they approached the Kehoe driveway, Kehoe was spotted rushing from the back of the farmhouse. He was halfway to the tool shed and running in the direction of the big barn. Out of respect for the growing flames, and to avoid blocking the driveway, Armstrong let the Howells out in front of the house and drove to a safer parking place. The Howells sprinted up the driveway. Just as they reached the Kehoe back door, Kehoe, driving his pickup emerged from the dense smoke surrounding the barns. Driving up to them, Kehoe stopped the pickup, jumped out and removed a funnel protruding from the gasoline tank. He peered down into the tank, and then screwed the gas cap back in place. (It was one more indication that Kehoe, at the most critical time had lost his ability for careful planning, and was now driven almost totally by compulsion in the place of reasoning.)

As Kehoe moved to remount his pickup, he hesitated, apparently recognizing the Howell's presence for the first time. He was breathing hard, excited. "Boys," he said, "you are my friends. You better get out of here. . . You better go down to the school." Howell had no way of knowing that Kehoe was in the very midst of his act of mass murder, but he recognized a demeanor, a wild-eyed quality that he had never seen in him. It was a warning given in desperation, a fleeting last bit of possible compassion. Howell and his sons didn't need a second warning. They ran for the road and were well on their

105

way east as Kehoe's pickup passed them. Kehoe was travelling at a moderate rate of speed, and he was heading into the village.

Kehoe could hardly have planned it better. The great explosion at the school alerted the countryside for miles around. Country people on either side of the village were startled by it and looked around them. What most of them saw were the huge columns of billowing black smoke coming from the general direction of the Kehoe farm. Some, of course, thought it was the Ellsworth place, just across the tracks and toward town from Kehoe's. They knew Ellsworth was installing gasoline tanks for his new station. As they approached the scene, however, they saw that it was not the Ellsworth place, but Kehoe's.

As farmers dropped whatever they were doing to race for Kehoe's, they had no knowledge of the greater catastrophe in the village. They had heard an explosion. They could obviously see where it was coming from. Some knew of the fire alarm which had sounded, followed moments later by the telephone general alarm—the request to clear the lines because of an emergency.

The Howells were only the first on the scene. As they heeded Kehoe's warning and ran for safety, they were replaced by others. As the Howells pulled out, a construction crew of Consumers Power arrived. En route to their job at Bath, the crewmen came accidentally on the Kehoe fire. (At that time it was standard Consumers policy to stop and render assistance whenever a crew was in the vicinity of a fire.)

Parking their truck a safe distance away, some crewmen ran inside the house to save furniture. Racing the flames, they worked frantically to move furniture to the window where other crewmen standing outside waited to take it from them. Several pieces had been removed before crewman Wesley Campbell discovered dynamite in one of the bureau drawers. His first instinct was not to run, but to rid the house of the explosive to save the house. It had not yet hit either him or the other crewmen that the dynamite was purposely set.

As the crewmen worked with increasing desperation, a strong northerly wind gusted, broadcasting the 100 foot columns of black smoke, and sending burning shingles dangerously in the direction of the Harte farm. Now, numbers of other people were reaching the vicinity to help. As they arrived by foot and car, a secondary fire started on the roof of the Harte farm. Simultaneously, word was received of a disaster at the school house—but that news was quickly rejected as a piece of mis-information. Wendell McFarren and his teen age daughter, Cassie, had just arrived from the school, and they could assure the others that the school was all right.

As Fordney Cushman and his father drove up over the hill from the west, they quickly evaluated the hopelessness of the Kehoe farm buildings and joined others in the effort to save the Harte farm barn.

106

At the same time the Consumer crew across the road discovered yet more dynamite in the house. Suddenly they were to give in to the unbelievable. The dynamite was purposefully set, and distributed throughout the house! Still other potential rescuers were arriving. Walt Geisenhaver and his father had hitched up their horses at Rikers to drive to Kehoe's. As they came into the yard, so did Mrs. Zeeb, mother of two small children, and George Hall, another Kehoe neighbor with children in the Bath school. They were joined by Will Horning. As they approached the window where the furniture unloading had been in progress, Wesley Campbell threw a handful of dynamite from the window into the Kehoe garden. As he completed the throw, he climbed quickly out the window himself. Spying the others, he yelled, "You better get out of here. The place is loaded with dynamite!"

The warning was enough. Mrs. Zeeb, who had her children waiting in the car, sprinted for the road. Some ran in the direction of the tool shed. Once in safety they followed the Consumer crew which now carried its ladders across the road to the Harte farm.

As they left, they were replaced by others at the Kehoe farm. Mrs. Sydney Howell had run on foot up the road from the Howell farm. She arrived just as Herb Fizzell and Fred Krull had driven up. From four miles away, the smoke had drawn Fizzell's attention while mending fence. Immediately following Fizzell and Krull, came Dave Watling and his son-in-law, Roscoe Witchell. A passing motorist had shouted to them that the school was afire—but on seeing smoke to the west they had bypassed the school for the Kehoe place. As they arrived, a second section of the Consumers crew arrived with their truck—Jess Curtis, Dart Lang, John Snively. But if the farmhouse wasn't already burning much too hotly for entry, the first of a series of violent explosions rended the building. The newcomers retreated in the direction of the Harte farm—all but Mrs. Howell. She wasn't worried so much about the farm—or the buildings, or the livestock, if there was any. Perhaps it was a sudden insight. She looked very hard and longingly into the increasing inferno—and she hoped that Nellie Kehoe was not there.

Across the road, ladders had been thrown up against the barn. The rescue group there now numbered about 50—all intent on snuffing the barn fire out in its infancy. As they worked, messages persisted against all logic that help was needed at the school and Forney Cushman was sent in with the family car to see if there was any truth to the story. He had hardly left, however, when the Harte's received what sounded like solid verification by phone—a ten ring general alarm. Suddenly, David Harte's barn no longer seemed important. He, and most of the rescue crowd ran for their cars and trucks. George Hall, Wendell McFarren, and Walt Geisenhaver, all with small children in the school, led the way. A section of the Consumer Power crew was a little behind—but driving rapidly.[1]

Chapter XVI
Mayday

Drivers speeding in from the Kehoe and Harte farms probably hoped desperately that the general alarm message was a false alarm, the work of a prankster with a morbid sense of humor. Cassie McFarren, 17 year old senior, and her father couldn't believe otherwise. When Cassie had missed the bus which took her younger brothers into school, Mr. McFarren had offered her a lift. They were parked in front of a serene school when they identified smoke coming from the direction of the Kehoe Farm.

Serene. Serene had been an apt word for the school that morning of the last exam day. Serene, at least, for most—for those who did not have to agonize through exams which might mean pass or fail.

There had been little annoyance for students, teachers and the principal when Mr. Detluff had the generator shut down. After all, it would be back on just as soon as the pump could be repaired. Fortunately, it was a bright, sunny day and artificial light was hardly necessary to see the exam papers. The bigger inconvenience was the starting of the school itself—and even that inconvenience was minor. The down generator simply meant that the school bell wouldn't work automatically. As had happened on other occasions when the generator wasn't working, Mr. Hugget simply walked into the hallway and yanked on a chain which was connected to the school gong.

With that task done, school was officially underway for the day. Mr. Hugget rather enjoyed the break in routine. With that done, and with Mr. Huyck holding forth in the study hall, Mr. Hugget walked leisurely out of the school, and took the few steps necessary to go next door to the Methodist Church. There, he was to be joined by Mrs. Huyck in rehearsing senior girls for the graduation ceremony. Mr. Hugget knew the girls would be bright and attractive. He looked forward to it.

Down the street, the business district had already come to life for the lazy spring day. One of the customers was Frank Flory, Hugget's best friend, and Bath's shop teacher. He needed to buy a few things for the class. It was a nice day.

At the local switchboard, Lenora Babcock was on duty. Barely seventeen, Lenora was the oldest of eight children. She had quit school to take some of the burden from her mother. As telephone operator she not only earned some money, but was given room and board by her bosses, the Vails. The exchange was a typical country exchange located in the Vail's residence, but the job was a responsible one. It not only paid Lenora, but gave her the experience she might need to one day work at the demanding switchboards of the city.

Down the hill, the barber shop was open for business, too. Jay Pope, one of Bath's seniors, decided to drop by early for his shave. He could avoid waiting and be clean shaven for the whole day.

Other locals would be stopping by the village drug store to do business with the proprietor pair from Canada. Doctor Crum and his wife (a nurse) were a bit of a strange pair in Bath—he with his pinz-nez and she with an occasional air of caustic condescension. Crum had been a skilled surgeon during the Great War, but when he came back from overseas his nerves were casualties. He needed steadying and a quiet, but respectable existence, the kind of existence Bath could offer a man. The well-appointed drug store which he and his wife operated was the pride of the community; and when the Doctor practiced medicine as he still did on occasion, his patients felt honored. As Crum and his wife readied the pharmacy for business on this Wednesday morning, they looked forward to another rela-tively quiet day in Bath, precisely the kind of day that attracted them to the village.

Across the street young Harry Barnard had fishing on his mind. With pole and fishing tackle he was approaching the Crum Phar-macy and Ice Cream Parlor.

Up and down the business district, there was a more unusual sight. Bath was getting electricity it could count on. Linemen from Consumers Power already had the utility poles in place. Today, the strong young crewmen with tanned faces were to begin stringing the high voltage wires. Merchants, who could find the time, watched in fascination as one young man or another went agilely up the pole. The crewmen exuded strength as they easily spiked their poles and hitched themselves nonchalantly upward. For the crewmen it looked to be a good day for an audience. And all the props were there—chaps, climbing spikes strapped to the legs, hitches, climbing belts and tool belts.

In the village houses, residents were up and attending to Spring chores. It was such a nice day that Mrs. Huyck delayed just a little longer going to the Methodist Church so she could complete hang-ing out wash to dry.

The clock at the school now showed precisely 8:44 a.m. Classes and examinations were well underway—windows opened to take advantage of a pleasant breeze.

In the large assembly room, the superintendent presided over an agricultural exam; Miss Matson busied herself in the library room, preparing for the English and Latin exams she would give. Most of the other pupils who were in the school at the time were now actually into their exams. The exceptions were the very youngest pupils.

109

Miss Sterling, the kindergarten and first grade teacher, had just finished cranking up the phonograph for her charges. She and Miss Weatherby, the third and fourth grade teacher, and Miss Gutekunst, the second grade teacher, had also chosen to entertain the pupils in their classes. Both teachers were reading stories. Miss Gutekunst sat with her second graders at a large circular table away from the blackboard. She had planned to read just one story; but the children begged so that she had gone on to a second.

In the road in front of the school, and at a slight angle from it, four teen age boys were practicing catch with a softball. Don Ewing, 17 year old son of the Township Commissioner, was there. He and his companions were all seniors—Arthur Woodman, William Robb, and Charley Havelin. Charley had just lofted a high arching fly ball. Art Woodman adjusted his position and waited for the ball to begin its downward plunge.

And then it happened—before the ball ever came down—the school house literally exploded in front of them!

The tremendous force of the dynamite tore giant chunks of foundation from under the north wing. The accompanying compression forced floors up and walls out, leaving nothing for the rising and then crashing roof to rest upon.

Within the school, students, teachers and administrators experienced the blast without comprehending it; many without surviving it. Most never heard the gigantic detonation which rocked the countryside for miles around. Most were not conscious of the deadly silence which followed momentarily after it.

Some students were aware of a severe tremor, followed by an explosive "whoof." Anson McNatt, the erstwhile young competitor for Ward Kyes' bus route, was seated in the assembly room in the upstairs of the old portion of the building. Instinctively, he gripped the top of his desk with both hands. Plaster fell from the ceiling filling the room with white dust. Globe canopy lights which were suspended from the ceiling swung dizzily. One or two fell to the floor and smashed. Students seated in front of Mr. Huyck looked back over their right shoulders—almost as a reflex action. Looking through the French doors toward the new part of the building they saw, instead, nothingness. As a few pupils ran toward the French doors to see, Pansy Wilson yelled, "Get back! Get back!"

Children and teachers of the elementary grades bore the brunt of the explosion. Like a fickle tornado, the blast hurled, tossed, singed, and crushed some children and teachers while leaving others relatively unscathed. There was the sensation of suddenly flying through air, of glimpsing timbers and open sky, and then blackness. There was the impression of floors spinning, of earth quake, of being propelled upward—and falling, seemingly, hundreds of feet downward. There was the experience of deafening roar, of whirring

110

shrapnel, of stabbing pain and crushing weight. The numbness of shock mingled with the terror of being buried alive. For some there was the emerging sense of escape, or of night mare—and for many there was nothing, absolutely nothing—forever.

Away from the center of the explosion, in other parts of the school, and in the neighboring and nearby buildings, the shock was severe, but not mortal. At the next door Methodist Church, the principal had just started rehearsing two of the Senior girls in their graduation responsibilities. Any musical rehearsal would need to wait on Mrs. Huyck, but Mr. Hugget concluded that he might just as well proceed with Bertha Komm and Thelma Cressman. Thelma had only a short poem to recite. As she concluded the three stanza poem, Mr. Hugget began his critique on her method of delivery. From her platform position looking down on the pews, the young lady listened attentively and appreciatively. More than anything she wanted to be just right for this most important occasion.

With the shock of the explosion, the church itself heaved. The tremor uprooted pews from the back of the church, and they slid forcefully but unevenly toward the front. The girls and their principal struggled to maintain their balance. Thelma Cressman steadied herself on a pew to avoid falling.

Then—as the shock lessened, the principal and his senior girls ran out the front door of the church and looked toward the school. A haze of dust obscured the view, confirming that it was, indeed, the school. From their angle, the main entrance appeared destroyed, and the principal ran toward the secondary South entrance.

Up and down the street, windows were shattered. Door hardware was wrenched from its wooden moorings. The windows from the telephone office flew apart, completely perplexing the operator whose earphones blocked the sound of explosion. In the kitchen of his nearby house, Willette Whitney was helping his wife houseclean. The chair he was standing on was knocked out from under him.

A few houses away, Mrs. Warner was reaching to put up a new curtain at the front window overlooking the main street. The window glass disintegrated in front of her. In utter disbelief she looked anxiously toward the school.

Down the street, toward the base of the hill in the business district, the shock sounded like a deafening sledge hammer. From his work room upstairs over his blacksmith shop, big Albert Detluff thought a car had fallen off the hoist below him.

Across the street, Consumer Power linemen who were up their utility poles, clutched tightly at poles which shook briskly and simultaneously with the roar. The sound came unmistakenly from the direction of the school at the top of the hill.

From her upstairs window facing easterly, Mrs. Monty Ellsworth looked automatically in the direction of the explosion. She could see nothing more of the school building than the chimney—that was all she could normally see. But she could see one thing more—a mushrooming cloud of white dust or smoke ascending rapidly from the school's location. She was sure the school had blown up.

More than three miles east of the village, Ora Andrews was plowing his back fields—but thinking of his wife. She'd lost a baby at childbirth the day before. The explosion shook Ora from his preoccupation. He hitched up the horses and drove off toward Bath in the direction of the explosion.

Ward Kyes had just returned to his farm from the morning bus run to the school. He was just slowing the school bus to a stop when it happened. He was sure the explosion came from the direction of Bath. Ward turned the school bus around and headed back.

In the basement of the old building, George Harrington had commenced working on the pump with Frank Smith the janitor. Miraculously, the explosion which centered in the foundation of the new wing of the school, spared them. Though they were below explosion level, the blast was thunderous and engulfing. Its force doubled Smith over and thrust Harrington sharply against the wall. As Smith attempted to straighten himself up, he gasped, "For God's sake, what happened?" The first thought had to be of the boilers—but the boilers were not in use. From their suspended positions they had crashed to the basement floor closing passage between the north and south ends of the building.

As widow Warner ran to the school, she could momentarily see classrooms and children made visible by the disintegrating walls. The North roof held briefly, anchored at the rear by a surviving wall. Then, as the walls and supports collapsed in front, the giant cover shuddered and came sprawling down with enormous force on the children of the second floor. The force was irresistible. The crashing roof smashed all before it, bringing both the second and first floors to undistinguishable union in a mass of rubble. The rear of the crumpled roof still leaned precariously against the back wall. Then just as suddenly, the deadly explosion and the after tremors were over. Ominously, momentarily, a nearly complete silence filled the air—followed by the screams and moans of small children. Except for the few children's bodies, or parts of bodies, which were visible, the roof formed a formidable albeit partial shield from the view of the shambles and obscene slaughter beneath it. It also created a nearly impenetrable barrier against rescue. A child's head, unrecognizable in the cast of plaster dust, extended into view from under the roof's edge. Here and there protruded still and whitened arms and legs; and in plain view was a young boy pinned between the collapsed top floor ceiling and the rafters.

Although Mrs. Warner could see the face of the school well enough, her view of the high school section to the rear was still obstructed. As she started around the northern end of the school to see for herself, she was unmindful of her shortness of breath. She feared the worst, thinking that the entire school might be down—she also feared that she alone of the villagers was present to effect rescue. Not another person was in sight.

Coming upon the rear of the school, Mrs. Warner passed a young boy lying dead in the grass, but she was distracted by shouts coming from the rear of the high school section. "Thank God," she thought, for standing near the back edge of the roof was Mr. Huyck, the superintendent. He was alive, and he was giving instructions.

From the shattered hallway outside the French doors to his assembly room, the superintendent had assessed roughly the same scene of destruction which had nearly overwhelmed Mrs. Warner. He had also clearly seen that exit down the stair way was hopelessly blocked. Emerging from the billowing black dust of the hallway, he hurried back inside the assembly room bent on maintaining order. Already students were pushing toward the back windows. Some were sitting on the sills preparing to jump. Others had already jumped onto the lean-to roof. One or two students were already jumping from the high lean-to roof onto the ground.

Fearing serious injury to panicking students, the superintendent sought to gain control. Knowing that complete control was out of his hands, he half ordered and half beseeched students not to attempt the jump to the ground. He reasoned that ladders would shortly be on the way. Then, everyone could exit calmly and safely. To be sure that his reason prevailed, the superintendent made his way to roof's edge to commandeer those ladders himself.

As Mrs. Warner came into view, so did young Harrison Ewing, another teen age son of the Township supervisor. Unknown to both Harrison and Mrs. Warner, both had been preceeded by elderly Mr. Whitney, who had survived his fall from the kitchen chair. At Huyck's urging, Whitney had hurried back to his home to get a ladder.

From his roof-top perch, the superintendent shouted to Mrs. Warner to bring ladders and axes. Young Harrison Ewing ran back with her. He didn't think Mrs. Warner would be able to handle the ladders. With mixed emotions the superintendent watched Anson McNatt jump from an assembly room window, onto the roof, and then onto the ground. Anson shouted that he would be back with ladders and headed for old man DeBar's home which separated the school from the Methodist Church on the south. Seventeen year old Arthur Woodman, running for ladders too, mistakenly concluded that Mr. Whitney was doing house painting when he encountered the latter struggling with a ladder a block away. It was a moment in a time of confusion. In the confusion, no one had yet thought to phone in the general alarm. Had minutes gone by? Hours? or only seconds? Perhaps only four minutes had gone by. In another minute ladders would be in place, freeing the upper classmen and Superintendent Huyck.

Other villagers near the school were almost as quick to react as Mrs. Warner. They went quickly through the same reflex reactions—shock, followed by mental beaming in on the explosion source, followed by selfless rushing to the scene. On Main Street merchants charged from their untended stores without a second thought. Consumer Power linemen scurried down their poles and almost in the same motion dropped climbing rigs, spikes and tool belts at their feet and took off up the hill on foot. Housewives simply dropped what they were doing and ran, and farmers who were not deceived by the distraction at the Kehoe place stopped short whatever they were doing to hitchhike, drive or ride into town. Some took off on foot and some on horseback.

Leonard Hiatt, the young Standard Oil Dealer, locked up his warehouse and started up the hill. Harry Barnard took his cue from the Consumer Power linemen. He dropped his fishing gear at the front of Crum's Drug Store and dashed up hill and diagonally across the street.

Simeon Ewing, the township's chief officer, was open for business at his grocery store (just down the street from Warners'). With children in school, he reacted quickly, as did his clerk, Mrs. Ione Smith. Both ran for the school, leaving the grocery unattended.

Monty Ellsworth and his wife barely gave a backward glance toward the Kehoe conflagration as they jumped into their machine and sped toward town.

Glenn Smith, the personable young postmaster, was one of the first to reach the school from the business area. He had foot raced the older Jay Pope who came running out of the barber shop to charge up the hill. As they first arrived at the front of the decimated building, only a total of four men seemed to be present. Muffled screams and moans were now coming from the debris still largely hidden by the roof. Almost spontaneously, Pope had sensed the immensity of the disaster, and the absolute necessity for outside help. Momentarily he reasoned that the whole world already knew of the explosion. This was followed by the sudden and frightening conviction that it didn't. Pope hurried back to the front sidewalk and jogged the one block back to the telephone office. As he burst in the front door, he yelled to the startled young operator, "The school house has blown up!" Mr. Pope spit out instructions which were short and clear. He left, however, as abruptly as he came, running back toward the school.

Lenora, with three sisters and a brother in the school, reacted without hesitation. She relayed the call for help through the DeWitt exchange, and gave the general alarm—ten rings to all parties on the line. Suddenly, the keys on Lenora's switchboard dropped, all of

114

them, as if by prearranged signal. Lenora had never seen nor experienced anything like it. Shaking off her momentary shock, she realized that only she could get those keys back up. As she reacted, news of the disaster crisscrossed the nation by telephone within minutes—creating an abrupt and near endless demand for information. With amazing coolness, the young operator fought to control and unscramble what was probably the greatest communication jam in the state's history.

Dan Huffman, the local station agent and telegrapher tried to share the burden, at least temporarily, but he had children in the school. While he waited anxiously for permission to be relieved of his post, he remained at his post, sending and receiving messages.

The situation in the school's south wing was a different story. The explosion had completely terrified children and staff on both floors, but the destruction was minimal and not mortal—and help was on hand almost immediately. High school students from the south wing second floor joined Mr. Huyck and the assembly room students in their route of escape.

The first floor escape was not quite as easy for the second graders, first graders and kindergartners. Twenty one year old Bernice Sterling needed little help in maintaining order and leading her kindergartners and first graders to safety at the southeast entry to the building.

The second grade teacher, Leona Gutekunst, was not so fortunate. She and her charges were in the room immediately adjacent to the devastated area which had been the upper elementary grades and the main entrance. The wall which divided the second grade from the entrance had almost withstood the explosion, but not quite. For a split second it stood defiantly—then toppled into the vacant end of the room. Students and their first year teacher were in a state of shock. The entrance from the hallway was blocked. Giant shrapnel had ripped a gaping 5' by 8' hole through the wall at the south end of the room. Principal Huggett coming from the church, and Frank Smith and one-armed Mr. Harrington coming up from the basement reached the first grade room at about the same time. Seeing that entry into the second grade room was blocked from the hall, Huggett broke through the partition separating the second and first grades. The three men looked into the room with relieved disbelief. The pupils and their teacher were OK. They were huddled in the corner of the room for protection. Miss Gutekunst, who was near a state of collapse herself, was trying to comfort the stunned and crying children. No one was dead or critically injured. They were OK.

Harrington, Smith and Huggett evacuated the children first, leading or carrying them through the partition. Then they returned for Miss Gutekunst. The principal made one last check to see that all the children had been taken from the room. Outside he positioned the children and their teacher at a point of safety near the first graders. After leaving instructions with Miss Gutekunst to record attendance and stand pat, he headed for the devastation at the front of the school. Frank Smith and Harrington were already in front of him. Had any of the three the time to look back, they might have sensed that Miss Gutekunst was herself to become a casualty. The growing awareness of utter destruction of life was overcoming her.

The East Wing of the school which housed the high school classes was relatively unscathed—but it was far from undamaged. The upstairs which housed the assembly room was least damaged. Below was the shop on one side and girls' home economics classrooms on the other. In that room, the blast had shattered the windows, and had punished the floor with such force that a section of flooring was threatened with collapse. Miss Evelyn Paul was in the sewing room with a few of her teen agers as the explosion hit. A Michigan State College graduate, Miss Paul was another first year teacher. She had replaced Miss Babcock.

As the shock of the explosion subsided, Miss Paul jumped through a broken window and waited impatiently, yelling for the girls to follow her. As the girls crawled hurriedly out, at least one was seriously cut on the jagged glass. An artery in Marcia Detluff's ankle was severed. Big Albert Detluff who had raced up hill from his blacksmith shop, was already beside her—so was Marcia's grandmother, Mrs. Millman. The two hurried the bleeding and plaster dusted girl home. Without comprehending the plaster, the old lady gasped involuntarily. Choking with emotion, she kept repeating, "She's turned white—she's turned white..." Ahead of them, on the horizon, clouds of black smoke arose from the Kehoe farm. Periodically, the sound of explosion came from the same direction. Behind them, villagers rushed in and about the devastated school.

As Marcia disappeared quickly from sight with her father, Miss Paul led the other girls to the comparative safety of the opposite direction—not stopping until they were in the farm field to the rear of the school. There, Miss Paul sought to hold the girls until their parents arrived. As they began their brief wait, they could see ladders being thrown up against the back of the school—could see the students and Mr. Huyck climbing down swiftly, but carefully. As Huyck reached the ground, he ran for Mina Shaw's home—to phone for outside help. The time was approximately 9:50.

At the devastated front of the building alarmed mothers and housewives were arriving. Desperately some began digging with bare hands to uncover the debris at the edge of the roof, to crawl under the roof—to get at the children. As parents began arriving, they headed straight for that part of the building in which their children were known to have been seated. As one mother, Mrs.

116

Johns, raced to the school from her home a block away, she was halted by the scene of devastation which had been her children's classrooms. Glancing protectively away, her eyes were transfixed on a suspended object in the destroyed entrance to the school. The object had the appearance of a large inverted discarded doll. Horrorstricken, the young mother recognized that the figure was no doll—it was her third grader, Doris, hanging upside down—and dead. The force of the explosion had blown her completely out of the third grade room, and she had come to rest on a piece of protruding metallic hardware. An unidentified man quickly entered the entrance area, and mercifully and gently removed the child from the death scene. Mrs. Johns was left with the slim hope that another child in the uncovered ruins was still alive.

Joining rescuers Jay Pope and Glenn Smith at the front devastation were still only a handful of other men. Tallman was there as was Pope's son-in-law, Lawrence Harte. Monty Ellsworth had arrived, as had Ed Drumheller, the township highway commissioner. Beside Glenn Smith was his father-in-law, Nelson McFarren. They were unorganized and the roof blocked or enfeebled their individual efforts to pull away timbers and two by fours.

Shortly, the group out front was joined by Glenn's brother, Frank, who had come around from the south side entrance. He had Harrington with him, and Principal Huggett wasn't far behind. As Mrs. Warner came to the front of the school after getting ladders and axes over from her home, Glenn Smith hailed her. Further help was needed from her, partly precautionary, partly not. He asked it she would go back and open her house, and get the beds ready for children. And one other thing. He asked her to prepare sandwiches and coffee. He saw only too well the long, strenuous and difficult rescue work which lay ahead. Mrs. Warner left quickly.

The men worked feverishly at tearing away debris, but their progress was painfully slow. The individual efforts were unorganized, and hampered and all but stymied by the oppressive and sprawling roof. Rescue could little more than begin until organization began first by accident and then by design. As the rescuers worked, children, unrecognizable with plaster dust, screamed and called out to them by name for help.

From under the avalanche, the sixth grade teacher could hear men digging, and it gave her hope. Miss Gubbins had awakened from unconsciousness in near darkness and in pain. Blood trickled from cuts about her head, and she had the sensation of other cuts on her body. In the semidarkness she saw clearly though—too clearly. A small boy, crushed to death, was pinned over her legs. His open but lifeless eyes looked directly into hers. Instinctively, she moved to turn her head away, but it was locked in position. Miss Gubbins shut her eyes tightly and screamed. It simply couldn't be true!

117

Opening her eyes again, she found that she could neither move her head or her legs. The legs were pinned under a massive concrete beam, the same beam which had crushed the boy before coming to rest against her legs. Above her was a mass of suspended beams and masonry. Beneath her was one of the school radiators. All the young woman could do was pray.

Frank Flory, the manual arts instructor, was the first to reach her. Crawling through a small opening in the wreckage to get to her, he comforted her. Flory knew that he alone was helpless to get her out, but he could assure her that she wouldn't be trapped long. He gave her assurance and then scurried away after help.

Out front, timbers and two-by-fours were torn aside to free a first dead child from the burial. The youngster was carried carefully and gently to the grassy knoll just to the north of the devastation. There, a blanket from a nearby home was placed over the lifeless form.

As the first injured child was removed, Frank Smith carried the limp body across the street to his small frame yellow home. Although his wife was gone, there was no question about it. It was the nearest house and just slightly removed from the furious attempt at rescue. The house was a natural as a temporary hospital. By the time Mrs. Smith returned to the house from successfully locating her own son, at least one more injured and bleeding child had been bedded down in her home.

Frank had hurried back across the street to the school, but by now the roof was posing an almost impossible barrier to further successful rescue. Someone yelled that they should get rope—pull it away with rope. They could put their strength together better with rope.

Ellsworth suddenly remembered the rope he owned which was sitting in his slaughter house. Running to his Ford pickup, Ellsworth turned the machine around and headed back up the gravel street. As he turned the corner to head west to his place, he recognized Kehoe approaching in his pickup and driving in the opposite direction. Kehoe was on his way from his burning farm, and from the Howells who he had passed on the road. It was not a time for pleasantries, but as the Kehoe and Ellsworth machines approached each other, Kehoe waved his hand in greeting, and grinned. The picture of Kehoe registered in Ellsworth's mind, particularly the clear rows of Kehoe's teeth. It registered. It wasn't right. But Ellsworth was on a mission; his mind was on something else. It was not a time for drawing conclusions. The time was approximately 9:59 a.m.

As Ellsworth had left the school, other area people were reaching it, and the scene was one of growing confusion. Besides parents seeking their children, there were other rescuers—but children of all ages were now on the grounds. Efforts to control and contain children from the rescued classes had collapsed. Actually, Huyck hadn't attempted to contain the upper classmen, and efforts to control children from the other grades began breaking down almost immediately. Some children out of pure fright had broken instinctively for home on foot and on bicycle. Small children could be seen fanning out, running across lots like rabbits—in all directions.[1]

Other children either chose to remain on the grounds or just didn't know what else to do. The oldest boys and girls were themselves helping in the work of rescue. Some simply stood and watched the furious work of rescue. Some of the smaller children rested against the embankment which separated the school grounds from the DeBar lot at its southern boundary. Some sat below street level, back to the street, watching the rescue efforts from the depressed front yard of the school. No one, it seemed, had considered that these children could be in a continuing danger. It was beyond comprehension that such an already horrendous disaster could expand.

It was not, however, beyond Kehoe's comprehension. He had driven into the village prepared to complete the circle. He may have been armed with any of the firearms he was known to possess. Definitely the pickup was armed. Driver and machine constituted an unbelievably lethal weapon, a weapon in search of a target.

As Kehoe slowed his machine on approaching the school, he was stunned—not by the destruction he saw, but by the destruction he didn't see. He had fully anticipated seeing the entire school down. Instead, only the entrance and north wing appeared to have been devastated. Possibly, no probably, many children and teachers had been spared. Probably, even Superintendent Huyck had survived. He took careful note of the Superintendent's car parked out front of the school, but saw no sign of the superintendent, himself. Kehoe was now in a sudden state of intense confusion and frustration. He needed time to think, to rethink the entire situation. He headed slowly on through the business district, and turned left on Sleight Road. He might even meet Mel Kyes, being driven into town. If nothing else, Kehoe could always do a complete circle, taking Sleight to Chandler, turning left on Clark and then passing his place again to come back into town. Kehoe had hardly left town when he met Job Sleight, riding a running board into town. He waved at Sleight, but ignored the young Witt boy who was bicycling home on his escape from the school. He also bowed sociably to Homer Jenison who was on his way into Cushman's Elevator with a load of wheat, and waved recognition to Mrs. Rounds. Kehoe was going in a circle, but he was once again deliberate and purposeful. Ellsworth, meanwhile, had already reached his slaughter house. He had picked up rope, block and tackle there, had thrown them in the back of his pickup and had driven hard back to the school.

It was the equipment the rescuers wanted, but once it was in their hands, they realized it wasn't enough. They needed to get the roof

119

up, and then over. Without an overhead, the rope, block and tackle wouldn't work without risk to children underneath.

Jay Pope had the idea. (He had long since rushed back from the telephone office where he had placed possibly the first call to get help to the school.) Pope suggested that the roof be pried up and over, using a utility pole as a lever.

The idea was practical enough. There were extra poles here and there in the area—waiting to be put in place by the linemen of Consumers Power. Monty Ellsworth knew where there was one on the ground down by Charley Wilkin's barn, only six blocks away. He and a companion drove off in Ellsworth's car to get it. The time was approximately 10:05 a.m.

Lawrence Harte had the same idea. He said he knew of a pole eighty rods away at Tom Lowe's corners. He cursed himself for not having a car, and felt cursed. Mrs. Huyck, who had come up, offered her husband's machine, but her husband had the key. With no time to look for the superintendent, Harte simply tripped the ignition with his jack knife. The engine started, and Harte and Frank Smith drove off for Lowe's corners and the second utility pole.

Chapter XVII
End To An Orgy

At the county seat in St. Johns, word of the disaster reached the county shortly before ten a.m. Bart Fox, the Sheriff, had gotten the word then. He was a simple, straightforward, and physically strong sheriff whose weather tanned face reflected the rural life of the county. Perhaps from some instinct of experience, the Sheriff headed directly for the office of the county's young prosecutor, William Searl.

The two had developed an attachment and respect for each other. In young Searl, the Sheriff saw a prosecutor who could handle himself in court. In Fox, the prosecutor saw a man who, though a Klansman, would mete out justice with plain and simple fairness regardless. (Aside from a little Prohibition trouble, Clinton County's farmers and villagers were generally a pretty peaceful lot. Normally the Sheriff and his deputy or two could handle just about any trouble that came along.)

It was ten o'clock when the Sheriff summoned the prosecutor. As he opened the door to the latter's office he leaned in and called, "There's been a disaster of some kind at Bath. I think the two of us better get over there." The prosecutor didn't question his man. He didn't have to. The two walked swiftly down the court house steps, jumped into the Sheriff's car and headed down Route 27 toward Bath.

Lansing had received the alarm earlier. Almost immediately after the explosion, State Police (then called the Department of Public Safety) at the East Lansing Headquarters received their first reports of tragedy. A call reporting fire at the Kehoe farm may have become garbled with a call attempting to report the tragedy at the school. The trooper taking the call noted the time: 9:45 a.m. On the log he entered the alarming information he had received: The Bath school house was afire. The children were still in the school. The Lansing Fire Department was immediately notified, and four troopers were dispatched toward the scene (Troopers Dora, Carpenter, McNaughton, and Glassford of the Lincoln Flyer Unit). They were slightly ahead of Assistant Chief Lefke and the unit of the Lansing Fire Department. Somewhere in between those small speeding forces was Dr. Shaw of the Lansing American Red Cross. None of these units yet knew the true nature of the tragedy. They understood it to be a tragedy, but at best, the trip to Bath from Lansing would take at least thirty minutes. They would reach Bath painfully or, perhaps, mercifully late—but considerably ahead of the authorities of Bath's home county, Clinton.

**

As Ellsworth and his companion had driven toward the Wilkin's farm in search of a utility pole, neither took any note of the other's identity. In the rush, there was no time for that. It didn't matter. By 10:07 a.m. they reached the farm. In only two more minutes they had the pole secured to the pickup and were heading back to the school. As they pulled in front of the school house, other men quickly untied the rope and helped Ellsworth run the pole to the edge of the roof. Ellsworth's weight now was a decided disadvantage. He fought for breath and shook off a slight wheezing attack. At the same time he took some note of the quickly changing conditions.

The moans and screams of children could still be heard from under the debris. Lyle Zufelt, a road worker, dug frantically in the ruins for his six year old youngster, Bobby.[1] At another spot two youngsters were pulled out of a hole barely large enough for one. One boy's leg was broken as rescuers fought to free him from the wreckage.

C. Chapman,[2] who had rushed in from the field, tore at similar

121

wreckage with his bare hands. As he struggled to remove debris he heard the voice of his nine year old son, Russell, "I'm all right, father, but get me out of here quick." Chapman dug frantically then, with renewed hopes. His boy knew he was coming! But it was too late. Russell's body was already lifeless when his father reached him—his neck all but severed by a falling beam.

On the perimeter could be seen the blanket covered bodies of additional children who had been pulled dead from the destruction. Mr. and Mrs. Ewing were standing at one side of the front entrance sidewalk. Their arms were around each other, their faces convulsed in tears. On the bank near the school sat Mrs. Eugene Hart. Ellsworth recognized her, but immediately blacked out the emotion he read on her face. Vivian and Iola lay dead on either side of her. Percy, mortally injured, was held securely in her lap.

Across the street, the superintendent was looking in on the injured children being sheltered at Frank Smith's place. He had just come from the telephone office where he had made more detailed calls for help from the State Department and the State Police. Detluff had been there, too, after dressing his daughter's wound; and had then rushed off to find a doctor.

In the Smith home, the superintendent's eyes were taken by the limp body of a little girl lying in one of Mrs. Smith's makeshift beds. The superintendent sat down on the bed momentarily, holding the child in his arms. She breathed—but only weakly. "I'm afraid she's dying," Mr. Huyck said sadly.[3] Mrs. Smith shook her head in agreement.

The superintendent gently laid the child back down. Standing up, he asked Mrs. Smith to open up her remaining beds. As Mrs. Smith walked upstairs to get the additional beds ready, the superintendent walked out the front door and past the cots lining the front porch with injured youngsters. Suddenly, he paused to look back. Ever so briefly he contemplated the children, painfully, and then hurried on across the street.

Mrs. Smith, working to make the beds up, didn't hear him leave. As she worked, she was aware of the tremendous reassurance the superintendent had given her. He had appeared calm and collected, while being genuinely solicitous of the children. More than anything, though, he was in control. The nightmare would end, she concluded. He would steady and organize the rescue—and the nightmare would end.

As the superintendent crossed the street diagonally toward the school, he entered the maelstrom. Behind him, a first makeshift ambulance parked close by the front porch of Frank Smith's house, the house the superintendent had just left. Huyck's young principal approached the ambulance from the direction of the telephone office to help. Dr. Haines was there now, needing help in transferring children to the ambulance.

In the street and on the grounds of the school, children were mixed with adults, distraught and shocked parents with rescuers, the living with the dead and dying. Glenn Smith, the postmaster, had been working at rescue tirelessly within the ruins. Feeling nauseous, he walked away and toward the road for air—for a breather. To his rear, men sought to prop up the arch over the front entrance to keep it from falling. At one side, Job Sleight knelt with a pail of water, cleansing the plaster dust from the face of a stricken child laying motionless beside him.

As men dug to free the dead and injured from the ruins, women in housedresses carried them away. Jay Pope had just relieved one woman of the child she was carrying, and started for the road. Ahead of him Harry Barnard carried a young woman teacher in his arms. Miss Gubbins was conscious but in great pain. Her face was bloodied and her foot looked badly crushed.

Atop the ruins, Eddy Drumheller and Kehoe's neighbor, David Harte, were working with Ellsworth's utility pole. Consumer Power men had an organized party working with them. No longer needed at the pole, Ellsworth walked toward the road. He could see Lawrence Harte and Frank Smith driving up in Huyck's car—arriving with the badly needed second utility pole. Glenn Smith and his father-in-law saw them too and rushed to help with the pole.

Other incoming machines were parking further up the road—the first of a stream of machines now heading in from the Harte and Kehoe farms. When confirmation of the school explosion had finally reached the crowd there, they had scurried for their machines and trucks and pickups and they were coming in.

Wendell McFarren and Cassie had parked just short of the school. Jumping from their machine, the elder McFarren ran for the school. Virgaline Zeeb, parking a bit further from the school, left her children temporarily in the car and walked toward the school. Just behind her came the crewmen from Consumers Power who had been helping at Kehoe's and Harte's. They had parked their truck and car a block away. Curtis, jumping from his car, ran ahead of the younger lineman. Dart Lang and John Snively had followed him in the Consumer's truck and were seconds behind him. Dismounting from the truck, they ran down the middle of the road to catch up— Snively in front, Lang behind him. As Lang ran, he heard a machine, a Ford pickup, was almost on top of him. He shouted a warning to Snively, "Hot rail!" and dove for the ditch at the side of the road.[4]

Snively heard the warning and stepped aside. Curtis, further ahead, hurried to cross the street ahead of the machine. As it went by, the driver suddenly struck out his left hand and raised it, the

123

pickup veering sharply to the right. Kehoe, driving nearly mindlessly, but with consuming attention had located his mark. Huyck was there on the sidewalk—standing there, right there. Kehoe saw no one else. Lurching his pickup to a stop, he leaned far to his right to call out to the superintendent. In apparent response, Huyck appeared to step toward the pickup, and then turned as if to view the school. It was a school he had dedicated his life to.

In one final and gigantic engorgement of energy, Kehoe's orgy of hatred, guilt, and self-hatred climaxed and discharged as he triggered the deafening explosion. Without warning it came—sharp, crashing, and of tremendous power. Fire flashed under the Kehoe machine and under the machines parked in a row along the street. Above the machines, a belt of blazing fire swept along the whole length, firing the car tops as it went; and a huge ball of smoke shot straight into the blue sky from the remains of the Kehoe pickup. Shrapnel, machine parts, and hunks of flesh were propelled in all directions and through the trees, spreading death, destruction, and fear as they went.

It was a battlefield, and to men's minds came the possibility that Bath had actually come under shellfire from some unknown enemy. In the distance, the periodic crack or dull thud of explosion from the Kehoe farm continued and seemed almost peaceful in comparison. Nearer by a section of wall of the ravaged school shuddered under the new shock, and bricks came tumbling down. Next to the school, the little home of old man DeBar was riddled with the equivalent of canister shot. Beside it, the front of the Methodist Church took additional punishment. Up and down the street were wrecked and burning automobiles.

From all directions, from men and boys came shouts of, "Get away from there." Children, who had been watching the rescue effort, flew for home. Injured children in cots across the way, sat up almost in unison and screamed. A rescued but bloodied youngster,[5] placed momentarily by the school sidewalk, jumped up on his broken foot and hobbled frantically across the street toward shelter. Men burst for cover, others were too shocked or stunned to run. Still others simply stood, reacting to the new horror about them.

Bodies, dying and maimed, strewned the thoroughfare. Both adults and children were down. Mr. McFarren, the father of the post master, was dead, propped up against a tree in the school yard. Superintendent Huyck lay dead where his body had dropped slightly in the direction of the Methodist Church. Glenn Smith was horribly wounded, but still alive and conscious. One leg was sheared off and clothing had been blasted from the side of his body which was blackened as if shocked from the inside. As he tried to right himself at street level, he fell back and rolled down the embankment. Further from the Kehoe vehicle, nine year old Steve Stivaviske lay with both legs broken and a bolt protruding through his upper arm. Seventeen year old Perry Hart had been dropped to his knees by a piece of shrapnel which ripped into his ankle. Fifteen year old Thelma Medcoff, who had been standing across the street from the school was also hit with shrapnel and was bleeding with cuts in both legs. Francis Fritz, young father of a child caught in the first explosion, was felled by a bolt over the heart as he attempted to remove children from the wreckage. Lying mortally wounded in the street was Cleo Claton, an eight year old who had successfully escaped the first explosion. Finally, in the opposite direction, perhaps 60 feet from the Kehoe machine, lay Anna Perrone, wife of Joe Perrone, the popular Italian immigrant section foreman. Walking back from the Detluff's, she had been hit as she crossed the street, carrying her baby Rose in one arm and holding four year old Dominic by the hand. A large piece of shrapnel had struck her directly in the eye. Somehow, she had protected both Rose and Dominic as she fell.

As Anna Perrone was carried from the street to the front yard of a nearby home, other men rushed to aid Glenn Smith. While Ellsworth ran for rope to bind the severed leg, Eddy Drumheller stripped off his own belt and made a tourniquet. Still conscious, the postmaster let him know when it was tight enough. To his brother, Frank, and to his distraught wife, he comforted, "It's all over with me, but I don't want anybody to feel bad if I go."[6] There was little more anyone could do for him until the ambulance arrived. He remained conscious, but paled and grew visibly weaker.

Parents, meanwhile, were recovering quickly from the shock of the second explosion. As they recovered some became even more alarmed at the increasingly desperate plight of their still buried children. Fathers became uncommonly strong. Children were injured while being pulled free over protruding nails or jagged pieces of wood, glass, or metal, but they were free.

Although few of those present, if any, knew exactly what had happened with the second explosion, men were beginning to put two and two together. The odor of dynamite was clear. It had been clear from the start—but the villagers were looking for children, not explosives. When Job Sleight was told it was dynamite, he went home. He was sick.

Huggett, on the other hand, had gone right on helping with the children out in front of Frank Smith's. As he worked, someone grabbed him by the arm and said, "It was a set job. They got Mr. Huyck, and they will get you."[7] The young principal listened, nodded his head, but went right on working—hardly comprehending that he was the sole surviving administrative officer for the shattered school and faculty.

Chapter XVIII
The Relief Columns

By 10:20, bells, growing distinctly louder could be heard in the distance coming from the direction of Lansing. It was the strong advance guard of the relief force from Lansing. Slightly ahead of everyone else were the state troopers of the Lincoln Flyer unit. They were dressed militarily in their uniforms. With cross over leather shoulder straps, flared out riding britches, and stiff leather leggings, they closely resembled air force pilots they modeled themselves after.

Troopers, Dora, Carpenter, McNaughton, and Glassford of the motorcycle unit were the advance guard. As they turned off Clark to enter the village, they could have been army scouts first entering a besieged city after an artillery barrage. The reports they had received from their headquarters had left them competely unprepared for the scene they entered. At the front of the school were the wrecked automobiles including "the front end of a Ford with parts of a human body hanging on it."[1] Truck parts were found 125 feet in one direction from the machine and thirty feet in another. Flesh dangled from overhanging telephone wires. A solitary automobile spotlight hung loosely from yet another overhead wire. Just to the east of the school's front sidewalk lay the bodies of the Superintendent and Mr. McFarren. (It was conceivable that Kehoe's body had simply disintegrated.) Glenn Smith, mortally wounded, had already been transported by local ambulance into a Lansing hospital. As the troopers observed, "There were several school children dead and dying from the explosion. People were frantic, trying to dig the children out from beneath the ruins with bare hands, poles, and every available object they could get."

Very shortly, others of the initial Lansing contingent arrived. Dr. Shaw, a Lansing physician summoned to duty by the Red Cross, was the first Lansing official to come in after the State Police.[2] Just behind was Assistant Chief Lefke of the Lansing Fire Department, accompanied by four other firemen and the Department's chemical truck. Racing them was Lieutenant Lyons, coming fast on the heels of his motorcycle unit. As they entered Bath, they saw there was no fire. But fire or no fire, the scene was clearly one of devastation and mortal emergency greater than they had comprehended.

As Shaw did a quick check with local physicians on the scene, Lyons and Lefke ran to the telephone office and cleared the lines.[3] In calls to Lansing officials the two made it clear that Bath was in a complete state of emergency. If there had been any doubt before, Lyons and Lefke dispelled it. All available doctors, nurses, fire and policemen were to move on Bath.

Rushing back to the school, Lieutenant Lyon began organizing rescue crews under Assistant Chief Lefke. Then, recognizing the supremacy of the medical emergency, Lyon placed himself temporarily under the direction of Dr. Shaw.

Dr. Shaw of the purely voluntary Red Cross physician's force, had received a distress call relayed from the Lansing Social Service Bureau to the Red Cross Office across the hall. Officials normally in charge of the Red Cross Office were out of town on business, but the Red Cross never performed better. A stream of pre-selected telephone calls by an inexperienced secretary,[4] jerked the emergency organization into action. In Doctor Shaw, there could hardly have been a better emergency operations chief. Not only did he beat about everyone but the state police to the scene, but he was prepared—by disposition and experience. Shaw was a youthful and energetic thirty eight, a little guy who had spent some of his earliest practice on the battlefields of Europe. Serving with the 119th field artillery, he had won the Purple Heart and the Silver Star with Oak Leaf Cluster.

Although he had left the military at war's end as a Lieutenant Colonel, the military never really left him. In the civilian life of the community he saw a need for a semblance of order which didn't exist there. For the slightly built and cocky physician, it was an observation quite compatible with his own love to give orders. As he arrived amidst the bloodshed and confusion of Bath, he was just what the doctor ordered. Assuming command of local physicians already on the scene, he took charge. The temporary hospital already set up by Doctor and Nurse Crum, he converted to a Red Cross First Aid Station. Recognizing that there was no real system for separating the merely injured from the dead, he put Monty Ellsworth and two others to gathering the dead by stretcher. The dead youngsters were laid in a row on the grassy knoll at the north end of the school—a temporary outdoor morgue, until a more permanent morgue could be set up. With speed and sureness, the doctor began examination of each child for sign of life. Those that were dead were dead. There simply was no time to think of each precise cause of death. The cause of death was simply and universally recorded as "death by explosion." It was nothing fancy. Shaw working in shirt sleeves was just doing what had to be done. Those that lived were set aside or moved across the street to await transportation into Lansing. To assure their removal in the fastest time possible, Lt. Lyons was placed in charge—moving them in the machines of Bath citizens until ambulances might arrive in adequate numbers.

127

The wait was not long. Immediately behind the first contingent came ambulances and speeding carloads of doctors and nurses. As quickly as injured children were rushed into an ambulance, it sped off—with an accompanying doctor or nurse, and sometimes the child's parent. In the rush for life or death treatment, some children were transported into Lansing without identification or notice to the parents. Parents unable to locate their children at the school site, rushed to Lansing in the desperate hope that the child would be found at either Sparrow or St. Lawrence Hospital. Only as the ambulance work became better organized, were lists started. The trouble was that partial lists were as good as no lists at all.

As distraught parents arrived at the school, or as the body of a dead child was added to the row of small victims, blankets were hesitantly lifted for identification. For some the inspection brought hope— for others gasps and tears. Troopers monitoring the periodic inspections were visibly shaken in empathy. Comforting arms were offered to fathers suddenly crushed by identification of a dead child. There was no hysteria—numbness, shock, defeat, cries of grief—but no hysteria.[5]

The very act of approaching the death row required every combination of emotion—courage, fear, pessimism, hopelessness —love. Some of the children were so mangled, so tortured, they required study for recognition if recognition was possible at all. Parents took turns, attempted to protect each other, to ease the pain.

When LaVere Harte was unable to locate his nine year old boy at the school he returned to his parent's farm across from the Kehoes to get his wife. Back at the school, LaVere asked his wife to wait near the street at the front sidewalk. Mrs. Harte wasn't normally all that obedient, but she knew her husband, knew the great pain of his effort, and his great concern for her. As she waited, LaVere forced himself to take the short walk to the grassy knoll. There, he focused, nodding his head as he spoke briefly to a man at his side. Their first born was dead. Forcing himself to walk back to his wife, LaVere spared his wife as best he could. He told her their boy had already been taken by the undertaker.

Local and nearby undertakers were arriving nearly as fast as medical personnel; and they were as badly needed. With their presence, it was possible for each dead child to be tagged with full identification and undertaking destination. Mercifully, for the parents, the undertakers made it possible for these youngsters to be quickly removed to the only care it was now possible to give them.

Rescue, identification, medical attention, and evacuation went on simultaneously. In the school basement men worked to clear out debris. As a worker beside Roscoe Witchell shoveled, someone warned him not to shovel anything on the child at his foot. The worker looked down, recognizing for the first time how a dead child might look covered with plaster. Stunned, the rescuer dropped his shovel, and climbed slowly but deliberately from the basement to disappear into the growing throngs of bystanders. Witchell, who had already helped remove several children from the wreckage, was later to recognize his daughter in the small row of dead children, lining the grassy knoll. The Litchfield undertaker was there and asked if Witchell was agreeable to taking the ten year old Elizabeth to his establishment. For Witchell, there was little to do but to agree, and to be thankful for the man's attentiveness.

Everyone, of course, wanted to fight death row—to deny its reality. A young father was sure he could detect a sign of life in his son—a slight pulse. Hurrying back with Doctor Shaw, he waited anxiously for the kneeling doctor to complete his examination. But the Doctor was sure. He'd been sure before. As the two stood up, tears came to the young man's eyes and he stared for a long time at the ground, torn for his son, for himself—and for his wife. Slowly, he turned around and headed back to join a rescue crew. No way was he yet able to deal this kind of blow to his wife.

In the fight against death, absolutely no sign of life, real or imagined went unnoticed. A little girl had been placed on the grassy knoll lifeless. As she lay there someone noticed that the blood from her nose was alternately forming and collapsing a bubble. If it was in fact life, however, it came too little and too late.

Nurses administered temporary first aid in one corner of the school yard while ambulances arrived and sped away; undertakers assisted parents with their dead—the work of the rescue crews went on, still hampered, however, by the fallen seemingly impenetrable roof. Until it could be removed totally, the rescue operation would remain seriously frustrated. Hand tools and axes chopped away in bits and pieces but simple and rude force could not be used from atop the roof because of the possibility of crushing children hidden under the debris. Still, many victims, dead as well as injured had already been removed from the wreckage; and the work of rescue picked up momentum. It picked up even as recognition was spreading that the devastation was a "set job."

Almost immediately following the second explosion at the school, word was being passed that the owner of the death car, whoever he was, was the one responsible. Although the body had apparently disintegrated, Kehoe's name began passing from rescuer to rescuer. A distinctive odometer attached to the front wheel was the giveaway. As far as most people knew, Kehoe was the only one in Bath township who drove a car equipped like that. Deliberate dynamiting wasn't anything that most people found easy to hear, but Kehoe's name was beginning to be relayed—by hushed and sombre voices.

129

Charles Lane, State Fire Marshall, of the Secret Service Division (Department of Public Safety) was reaching the same conclusion by independent means. Arriving on the scene about 10:30, he immediately ruled out the possibility of a high test gas explosion. No sooner had he done that than a trooper handed him two pounds of dynamite taken from the Kehoe farm. While Lane inspected the dynamite, two other law enforcement officers came upon unexploded dynamite in the coal room of the school's basement. Captain O'Brien of the Lansing Police Department and William Klock of the Ingham County Sheriff's Department made the discovery. A portion of ceiling had collapsed in the coal room, and the dynamite, encased in the eavestrough piping had fallen to the floor. The finding of dynamite was chilling enough—but this dynamite was connected with wiring—from a source not immediately visible. Klock and O'Brien wheeled and ran for the upstairs. For all anyone knew, the dynamite was connected to a timing device.

The time was just 10:45. The immediate vicinity was cleared and all rescue work was ordered halted by the state police until a search could be made. At least five men hurried into the basement. Troopers Halderman and McNaughton were joined by Lieutenant Morse of the Department's Secret Service, and by Assistant Chief Lefke of the Lansing Fire Department. With them was a radio engineer from Michigan State College, F. I. Phippeny.[6] As they examined the relatively small amount of dynamite on the basement floor they followed the wires leading to and from it. The trail of the wires was extensive—and leading to first one cache of explosives and then another. Finally, the troopers located the source, apparently the only source—two hot shot batteries and a mangled alarm clock all but destroyed by the explosion it had touched off.

Although the officers couldn't be sure, positively, that all dynamite was now removed, it was a logical conclusion. They had followed the wires; and the wires led to one point. If the wires had led to a point other than the point of detonation, the police might have thought otherwise.

Whether the firing source was found or not, the rescue work might have resumed anyway. Parents were prepared to take any risk to find and save their children. Delay was more deadly for their children than dynamite.

In all, several bushels of explosives in stick and bag form (with caps), were located, totaling 504 pounds. Several trips were required to bring it safely to the surface. As the last basketfull was brought out, the signal was given to resume rescue work. The crowd, which had been pushed back and roped away for safety, had waited silently and in awe—but impatiently. Now, parents and rescuers surged forward.

As the dynamite was being removed from the building, traffic flowed down the gravel roads leading to Bath in a steady stream. No fewer than 34 Lansing firemen were on hand as well as firemen from St. Johns and Ovid-Elsie. The Consumers Power crewmen were joined by executives and crewmen from two Lansing construction firms,[7] fully armed with wrecking bars. As news of the tragedy spread through Lansing, factories there had immediately excused anyone from the Bath area to return there for rescue work. In addition, busloads of laborers were released by Oldsmobile, Reo and Fisher Body to join in the rescue effort. Six or seven state policemen were added to the original number on the scene as well as 50 cadets from the ROTC of the agricultural college. Every available ambulance from the Lansing area was being pressed into duty, including company ambulances from Reo Motor Company.

The force was finally more than adequate to remove the last major obstacle to rescue—the ponderous and collapsed sections of the sprawling roof. As the crowd watched, workers mounted the leaning roof and chopped holes in it. A steel cable was passed into the one hole and out the other and then back to the play ground where large numbers of men gripped the cable ends. By running parallel to each other and away from the building, the cable was transformed into a giant shear. By main force, the men heaved and a large section of roof was stripped away. It may not have been awfully neat and scientific—but it worked.

With the roof cleared away, the search for the dead and injured resumed unimpeded. Although crowds were kept back by rope, the scene was still one of unbelievable grimness and confusion. Some bystanders were nauseated. Some fainted. Others were calloused beyond belief. A souvenier hunter approached the Kehoe car and deftly snipped a section of intestine from the steering column, placing it carefully in a jar of apparent alcohol.

The small son of an ambulance driver, waiting for his father to return with wounded, was overcome with the scene of horror. The panorama of people darting about, of screaming, of utter confusion, of overhanging intestines—was too much. He rolled the window down and puked—and puked—and himself became at least a temporary casualty.

The almost reverent eyes of the roped off bystanders, however, were on the excavation. Twenty one year old Nina Matson, the Latin and English teacher, was carried from the ruins by a Consumer Power lineman. Mr. Detluff met the two and carried her the rest of the way to aid. She was obviously seriously injured. No part of her pretty face and body had apparently escaped. Blanche Harte, the thirty

131

year old fifth-grade teacher, was also carried out in critical condition and rushed to a hospital.

As the crowd watched, reporters from the nearest communities joined it. Reporters from the Lansing papers, the State Journal and the Capitol News had come in barely behind the state troopers and the firemen. Staff from the weekly at St. Johns and from the Owosso Argus were not far back. With the reporters were their photographers. Working to relay the news to their own papers, they also pinch hit for the big city papers whose reporters were still on the way.

A makeshift press station was set up in the wood shed in back of the telephone office. Beside the wood piled in the corner, were a barrel, two rickety chairs, two tables, and a typewriter someone had rounded up. Some of the reporters called the place a rattle trap, but they weren't complaining. Almost as important as having a place to write was having a place to get away to.

A young woman reporter stuck it out at the school as long as she could, came back to the shed, sat down and slumped motionless over the typewriter, her hands covering her face. Presently, she sat back up, sighed, and said, "God, I need a fag." It was no easy request. There wasn't a cigarette to be bought in the village. A reporter from another paper studied her, slowly, reflectively, pulled a package from his pocket, tapped his hand until a cigarette positioned itself, then offered it to her. As he withdrew his light, the young lady took one deep inhale, held it, then forced it slowly and deliberately out. It was all she needed. She tossed the cigarette aside and started typing.[8]

As more reporters came in, the pressure on the telephone exchange became impossible. Between officials of one sort or another and the reporters, the ordinary citizen hardly had a chance. The young operator placed calls on a priority footing. Low priorities were put on a listing to be called later—after messages for help, or notifications of tragedy or safety, and after press releases. The small country exchange was literally swarming with people, but one early call had especially worried the seventeen year old operator. Her mother had actually heard the explosion as she was working in Laingsburg—ten miles away. Almost immediately she had telephoned Lenora—and blurted, "Are the children all right?" Lenora's answer was quick, instinctive, and untrue. "Yes," she said, "they are all right, Mom. They are in the building with me." Her mother was satisfied with that; and Lenora went on with her lines, trying to cope.

To help take the pressure off, workmen hurriedly installed both a telephone line and a telegraph wire in the emergency press station in the shed. Bell Telephone diverted two lines from the Owosso exchange to Bath and arranged for extra operators to arrive in the afternoon.

Down the hill at the depot, another emergency press room was rushed into service by improvising reporters. The little, pastoral frame station with the vertical exterior slats wasn't really built for anything like this, but it did the job. For a short time, the place was deserted after the agent was given permission to leave his post (to attend to his children). Reporters, finding the place empty had moved quickly to take advantage of the opportunity. Emergency telegraph apparatus was installed for their use—and they took over the waiting room. No one was going to be waiting around at the railroad station anyway. No one had use for the pot bellied stove that centered the room. Passengers who did disembark at the station (and they poured in from either direction) glanced curiously at reporters sitting on crates and boxes, using the waiting room benches for desks. Student aides from the Agricultural College Michigan State News periodically hurried to or from assignment. Normally confined to reporting on the safe beat of intramural campus events, the young student reporters suddenly found themselves in the middle of a titanic news event.

In awe of the seasoned reporters of the metropolitan dailies to whom they were assigned, they were the eager arms and legs which made many stories possible. When they were not tracking down facts or checking the list of the dead or injured, they were sent on missions to gather human interest sidelight material on the results of the blast. These were the ugly missions, the kind that even seasoned reporters preferred to sidestep—the invasion of privacy following personal tragedy, to reveal to the public one's innermost pain.

But Bath was different. The whole catastrophe. It was like the cover had been stripped from an entire community—revealing everyone naked—a public rape to be publicly endured. How could reporters invade a privacy which seemed not to exist.

Shock gave some protection, of course. It would be seen in the eyes, the manner, and the behavior of the parents, the victims— everywhere. When George Hall took a break from rescue work to scan the row of dead children, he came upon his own son. The recognition was instant, as was the rejection of his death which would not be accepted there. "Well, there's Billy," he said, and returned to his rescue work.

When Mrs. Harte was given the news of her son's death by her husband, she walked away. As she walked, she was met by Mrs. Huyck, walking in the opposite direction. Mrs. Huyck said simply, "My husband is dead."

Mrs. Harte answered just as simply, "My Robert is dead," and the two moved on their way to someway go through the rest of the day.

Mrs. Harte found herself back at the farm, feeling that she had lived a lifetime. Suddenly remembering the baby chicks, she was struck with panic. They hadn't been fed yet. As she anxiously hastened to look after them, she noticed the clock. It was not yet afternoon.

Earlier, at nearly eleven o'clock the young Prosecutor from St. Johns passed the farm enroute to Bath with his companion, Bart Fox. The unpaved road from St. Johns on south by DeWitt and then east on Clark Road was no speed way. The automobile made the trip better than horse and buggy, but not an awfully lot faster.

As usual they found the road was fairly deserted—until they reached the Gunnisonville Road, Bath's main connecting link with Lansing. There, they joined heavy traffic heading in the direction of Bath. Although the prosecutor and sheriff wondered at the devastation which had struck the Kehoe farm, they stuck with the flow of traffic which passed it without slowing.

As they reached Main Street to turn into town, road blocks were already being set up to discourage sightseers from coming into the village. No effort was made to slow the marked Sheriff's car, however, and the Sheriff drove directly to the school site. Even before they parked, the panorama of crowds and destruction told them they were in for an ordeal. Whatever had happened here was obviously much bigger than anything either of them had ever encountered.

The Sheriff was no sooner out of the car than he was intercepted by Frank Smith's wife. Only minutes earlier she had noticed what looked like a body or part of a body down in the corner of her garden. The spot was diagonally across the road from where the Kehoe machine had blown up and about seventy-five feet away. Mrs. Smith walked over to the body, studied it for a moment from the standing position, and then knelt down for a closer examination. Although she didn't recognize who it was, she noticed papers protruding from a pocket. Removing the papers gingerly, she stood back up to study them. The one was a bank book belonging to Andrew Kehoe—from the Lilley State Bank of Tecumseh. The other was an Operator's License dated February 17, 1926—made out about the time Kehoe had purchased the pickup. Sheriff Fox was on the road in front of the school when Mrs. Smith made the discovery. Seeing him there, she walked over and handed the papers to him. The two talked briefly, and Mrs. Smith pointed over at the body's location.

Mrs. Smith was the Sheriff's first contact. He hadn't had an opportunity to be filled in yet by other officials. For a split second he might have felt a little put out, a little at a disadvantage—but then the plain truth hit him. Mrs. Smith was obviously in a better position to orient him than anyone else. She had shown him Kehoe's driver's license and Kehoe's bank book; and now she was pointing out the remnants of the body to him. The sheriff sensed well enough that it was no little thing she was putting him onto. He scribbled down her name for safe keeping, thanked her, and stepped down the ditch to her garden. He inspected the body and then, with other authorities sought additional confirmation that the body did, in fact, belong to Andrew Kehoe.

The importance of a positive identification was not being overlooked by anyone. Until the body was removed, a series of Kehoe's acquaintances repeated the unpleasant task. Ernest Babcock, an eleventh grader said he knew Kehoe. He thought he had seen a body fly up at the time of the second explosion and come down through the telephone wires. A state policeman took him by the hand to try to make the identification.

Mel Kyes also came over from the school, bent down, and raised the head up to get a look at it. Then he walked back over to the school to locate Sydney Howell, the neighbor who probably knew Kehoe as well or better than anyone. When Howell returned to the spot with Kyes he went through the same motion of lifting the head up. As he did so he noticed the distinctive mark to the hair, and the perfectly intact face. As Howell stood back up, he looked at Kyes and slowly, but with certainty shook his head.

**

Bill Searl's introduction to Bath wasn't any gentler than the Sheriff's. As he reached the school grounds, he approached a state police officer, introduced himself, and asked for a briefing. He listened carefully as the officer filled him in, but his eyes took in just as carefully the unimaginable atrocity before him. It was inconceivable that anyone could purposely have done this thing, and yet, as he listened, he watched officers removing the dynamite. Half listening, and half observing, he was impressed with the utter chaos and confusion of the situation. Here he was, the chief law enforcement officer of Clinton County, late on the scene (through no fault of his own), to a disaster in his own jurisdiction, with God knows how many other enforcement agencies already on hand. With him, the Prosecutor had Sheriff Fox. Before him were the state police, the Fire Marshall, the secret police, the Lansing Police, East Lansing Police, deputies from the Ingham County Sheriff's Department, security police from the Reo Motor Works, ROTC Cadets from the Agricultural College, and firemen from Lansing, East Lansing, North Lansing, Ovid, Laingsburg and St. Johns—and probably other deputies as well. In one way or another they were probably all involved in an indescribable mixture of rescue and investigation. But investigation of what crimes exactly? Committed by whom? Investigated by whom?

Here it was, a crime or disaster of the greatest proportion, demanding a wealth of enforcement experience, of organizational application in the collection, analysis, and preparation of evidence. That was what the situation appeared to demand. What it was possibly getting in lieu of organization was a potential free for all scavenger hunt—a hunt for evidence or souveniers, however one might feel like classifying it, with the last hunter the green country prosecutor.

In the place of vast enforcement experience, Searl might have recalled his own record. (In a typical six months he could show an impressive 110 convictions out of 114 prosecutions—but the bulk would be made up of such things as six assault and battery, 39 motor vehicle violations, 34 drunk driving related, seven violations of the prohibition law, six larceny, one indecent liberties, and one profanity.) If he thought about it at all, it probably made him a little sick. Homicide and arson weren't exactly his specialty.

Searl observed and listened hurriedly. As he sized it all up, however, his biggest impression was of the carnage. Possibly, he over-estimated, but he guessed that nearly thirty child bodies could be seen. It was beyond comprehension. Death—sudden, complete, repulsive, violating the flower of life. He stared briefly at the lifeless body of what had once been a beautiful, vibrant young girl. He was aware of sobs, of a background of sobs, of a young woman fainting from the heat and the obscenity. Suddenly, he could feel it coming on—an uncontrollable anxiety attack. Abruptly, he excused himself. He needed to be away, just for a minute or two—to think, to gain control, and to make decisions.

He walked quickly away, and leaned against a nearby car, supporting himself. Reassuredly, he could feel his head clearing, and the calm returning. All he needed really was to put the thing into some perspective. He was relatively inexperienced, true, but he was also highly competent. As for preparation, he could reason that no one, absolutely no one would ever have been prepared for this. He could also dismiss any defensiveness within himself which might surface in a demand to pull rank and take charge. Any attempt to stop and reorganize this momentum and proliferation of law enforcement was doomed completely to failure. Better to have some faith in the experience at hand; let it run its course and then harvest it.

This was the way it had to be. The carnage was indescribable, and the search for more children, their rescue, was clearly not over. "Habeas Corpus"—this was where all priority had to be. Everything else was secondary.

Searl straightened himself up and breathed deeply of relief. He thought he had it now. But just to be on the safe side, he decided to give his father a ring. It didn't hurt having a judge you could turn to for a little friendly advice. Searl asked someone where the telephone office was, and headed over. Once the connection was made, he ran the whole thing by his father. The old man was shocked at the atrocity. He was shocked more that the atrocity might have been committed by his client, Andrew Kehoe. He was pleased that his son wanted to touch base with him. Resassurance, though, was all that the young man really needed. He was no dependent leaner. He was his own man. As the prosecutor left the telephone office, he was resolved to carry out the plan he had laid out. It was to include a review of his strategy with the Attorney General's office.

Returning to the school grounds, the prosecutor went about the business of preparing for the formal investigation. He watched a minute, as a giant section of the toppled and leaning roof was stripped away by main force—by a huge work force of volunteers.

As the roof was pulled free, two small boys, white with plaster dust, ran unexpectedly from the uncovered debris and darted into the surrounding crowd. Behind them, the standing interior of the north wing (what was left of it) was exposed abruptly to public view. The classrooms, of course, were completely gone, but the east wall and the upstairs hallway remained partly intact. The pegs on the wall which formed the hall cloakroom were still there, some barren, some grimly holding the coats or jackets which had been hung there just hours before. The crowd stood strangely silent—seeing in one breathtaking picture, the school section utterly destroyed, and the school alive, and just as it had been.

Once more, the prosecutor felt a slight sense of swooning—but this time he had help. Suddenly, he was beseiged by numbers of men for advice and information—and for instructions. There was no time for anything else. In rapid fire order there were briefings with Lt. Morse of the Secret Service (who was assuming charge of the criminal investigation), with Mr. Lane, the State Fire Marshall, and with Sheriff Fox. In addition, the veteran but ill prepared country coroner had arrived. And there were reporters—God, there were reporters.

Out of the briefings, one thing was certain—there was an enormous amount of work to be done in a short time. A temporary morgue needed to be set up; the dead and injured required absolute identification, the rescue work had to be continued, the investigation of crime and criminals had to be correlated and swiftly concluded. In the midst of crisis, the Prosecutor moved to bring it all together. Inpaneling a coroner's jury on the spot he scheduled an official inquest for the following morning. For help, the Prosecutor found an unexpected aide—a reporter from the Owosso Argus, who seemed as interested in helping as in reporting—in this case an infallible combination. The Prosecutor desperately needed facts and the reporter knew his facts and how to get them.

Among the facts the prosecutor wanted was a complete list of every one involved in the tragedy. With Clerk Frank and Trooper Carpenter of the State Police, (and with the reporter) the Prosecutor set out to positively identify the dead. No one expected it to be pleasant business—and it wasn't, but it carried some strange satisfaction with it during the unreal time it lasted. For parents, these identifiers became an important check point—a roll call not to be missed, a confirmation when confirmations were desperately needed that the child had existed.

Octa Harte approached the group, to report the death of his boy, Galen. "I've lost my boy," he said quietly, sadly, "but Eugene Hart has lost three of his youngers, and another badly hurt. It must be hard on Gene." He paused, and then went on, this simple and honest farmer, "Galen was a mighty fine boy, if I do say it. He seemed to be so much interested in the things I am interested in. I am certainly going to miss him. I . . . I just wanted to tell someone."[9] When he left, Henry Nichols came along, and three more names were added to the list of known dead and injured.

And that's the way it went. When all the dead who could be identified were identified, the remainder were carried by waiting ambulance to the temporary morgue which was set up in the town hall a little more than a block away. Clerk Frank and Trooper Carpenter operated the morgue under instructions from the county coroner.[10] No sooner were they set up than relatives began arriving, looking for and hoping to find their children.

High noon had come and gone with the sun beating heavily on the hot and laboring rescue workers. With the help of neighbors, Mrs. Warner had carried out Glenn Smith's last instructions. Large quantities of sandwiches and coffee were prepared and readied in the cool basement of the old Community Hall. Some men took the refreshing and filling break. Some didn't. Those that did, gulped, ate and ran—responding to both the thanks and urging they felt.

Outside, and in the countryside, rumors were spread of Mrs. Kehoe's possible fate. As soon as it was fairly well established that she had returned home with Kehoe Monday night, the Lansing Fire Department's chemical truck was dispatched to the farm. Neighbors pointed out the location of the bedroom at the rear and west side of the house. If she had been killed inside the house, the bedroom looked like the best bet. Mrs. Howell had thought instinctively of the bedroom, and it was one place, apparently, which hadn't been entered by the Consumer Power linemen who had first entered the house.

As neighbors watched, the entire contents of the chemical truck were unloaded on the smouldering inferno-like remains of the bedroom section of the house. Two chemical tanks of 60 gallons each were used to douse and saturate that particular area. No one, of course, had any hope of finding Mrs. Kehoe alive in the burned out farm house. For that matter, no one had any hope of finding her dead. If she was to be found, the search would be over. If she wasn't to be found, there would be some hope that she was still alive. With the fire out, and cooling, the firemen waited until they could look through the ashes.

The search for Mrs. Kehoe at the farm was not the only one taking place. By early afternoon, word was already out on the wireless that Andrew Kehoe was the apparent perpetrator of the tragedy. Sitting in his office, attorney Dunneback had just heard the news when three of Nellie's sisters came to him for help. The news had come like a bolt of lightening to them. They had rushed from their employment and together had decided to seek their attorney's assistance. Their first thought had been of their sister's well being—the need to cushion the shock for her in learning of the tragedy and Andrew's complicity.

For the attorney, they recalled Nellie's discharge from the hospital, her brief stay with them, and then her return to the farm. Thankfully, they were also able to recall the name of the Jackson area farm family Nellie had been left with. The sisters were confident that with the attorney's help they would be able to locate the Vost family and Nellie. They could break the news to her, if she didn't already know, and they could comfort her. They knew that without their help, the news could be devastating to Nellie.

They were right about the attorney's ability. He knew exactly how to go about locating the family. The attorney and his clients headed immediately for Jackson and the county seat. From there they drove directly to the Vosts.

Simultaneously, another search was started when the Bath Station Agent gave the alarm about the box Kehoe had expressed out just before the main explosion. The agent's record showed exactly who it had been sent to. In the morning it looked like a harmless package boxed in an empty dynamite box. After the explosion it looked more like the mailing of dynamite in a dynamite box—and the search was on. Smith, the intended receiver, clearly hadn't received the box. He had furnished the necessary bond to cover Kehoe's duties as school treasurer, but could think of absolutely no reason why Kehoe would be sending him anything.

The secret service, though, were more than a little worried. If Kehoe had gone suddenly and completely mad, there was no reason to expect that logic would be found for any of his actions. More important than that, if the contents were indeed made up as a bomb, additional murders could yet take place. After a thorough check, the police were satisfied that the box had never arrived in Lansing. The question was, "Where had it gone or where was it going?" With the help of the railroad, they began a race against the clock—running down every conceivable possibility.

**

By shortly after noon, the halls and corridors of both Lansing hospitals were jammed with cots for the injured. At the Olds Hotel a noon campaign luncheon for rebuilding or enlarging Sparrow Hospital had the air of a military campaign headquarters anxiously awaiting and receiving word on the nearby battle.[11] The two tables representing the Doctors Division of the fund drive were empty. Every available doctor was either on the scene, or tending to victims as they arrived at the hospitals.

By one o'clock, the search and rescue effort was by no means complete at the school, but, at least in part, it was moving into another, less desperate stage. The number of reporters were increasing, camera crews were on the streets, and a plane continued to circle overhead, taking pictures.

At about one o'clock, Governor Green arrived by motor car from nearby Lansing. The townspeople were appreciative of that, and of the man's genuine concern. For a time he worked alongside the other men, in shirt sleeves rolled to the elbow. He didn't stay long, but he took leave only after speaking with the Prosecutor and the state police. When he left, he was assured that everything that could be done was being done. The Governor was confident that he could do more for Bath back at the Governor's Office than he could on the scene itself.

While the governor was leaving, reinforcements were coming in. Elba Morse, a skilled disaster administrator with the Red Cross was in nearby Montcalm County when she heard of the tragedy—and she started out immediately for Bath. Doctor Shaw's old unit, the 119th Field Artillery, moved units into Bath and prepared to provide necessary cots and blankets. It also prepared to set up a field kitchen for the use of the various rescue units. Even before that, the Lawrence Baking Company of Lansing sent out a truckload of pies and sandwiches which were served by the ladies of Bath.

Still, the sombre work of relief, and excavation continued. The dead body of Miss Weatherby, the third and fourth grade teacher was not uncovered until later in the afternoon. The last teacher to be removed, rescuers reported that she was discovered in the sitting position, a dead child in each arm.

As early as two o'clock the roads into Bath became nearly impassable. For two miles out of Bath in every direction, autos were parked bumper to bumper along the roads. Emergency traffic was able to get in and out in continuing flow, but even that was not completely without mishap. A reporter for one of the press services required hospitalization when his speeding taxi went out of control on the way to Bath. A state policeman, attempting to direct traffic coming into Bath was run over by an oncoming auto, and suffered a broken arm.

At the morgue, identification after painful identification was being made. Sometimes it was too difficult to ask. A tenth grader, Arthur McFarren, was asked to go to the morgue to identify an acquaintance. Jolted by the sight of his brother instead, the youngster became aware of a mental image—his brother, loping toward the classroom, but like an old man. It was accompanied by, or perhaps slightly followed, Arthur's recollection that his parents had driven to Lansing—to search the hospital there for the boy they could not find in the wreckage.

By that time more than a dozen ambulances were lined up outside the morgue, waiting to convey the dead youngsters either to mortuaries or to their homes. The need for ambulances to convey the injured was coming to an end.

But townspeople were somehow unable to go home, until it was absolutely over—with all children accounted for. Even in the face of the greatest possible personal loss, they cared for each other. There were words, too many words like "I hope you didn't lose your boy, John," or hopefully, "Did your little girl get out all right, Mable?"

Sometimes, the answer had to be, "I don't know. I have been to the town hall, and she isn't there—but she isn't home yet, either. I just hope she's running around in the crowd somewhere."[12]

That was part of the problem. Between the explosions, and the dispersal of children, youngsters could be most anywhere. Lists were being checked against incomplete list. Until a master list could be constructed and checked against the school census the search into the wreckage had to continue. Unfortunately, school census takers had the census books elsewhere.

By late afternoon, Thelma Ewing reached home from her studies at Ypsilanti Normal. Knowing only that one of her brothers was critically injured, she had bussed from Ypsilanti to Lansing and then transferred to the train. Detraining at the Bath depot, she encountered the mobs of people which filled Main Street. As she elbowed her way up hill, her fears for her entire family increased. When she finally reached her house with its shattered windows it was unrecognizable. The living room was filled with people no one had ever seen before. Mr. Ewing, as chief officer of the township, was attempting to answer the questions of reporters, and Mrs. Ewing, who could be overheard from a back room, was on the verge of severe shock. Thelma's brother had lived only two hours after being removed from the wreckage. Doctors had recognized that the

141

badly mangled boy could not survive a trip to the hospital. Emergency efforts to save him at home never had a chance.

At the school grounds, further probing and uncovering seemed unproductive after five or six o'clock, but the searching and digging continued. The tired workmen retreated to the community hall where they were treated to sandwiches and the brew of great pots of hot coffee. By dark, further effort was pointless.

Throughout the afternoon and into the evening, the desperate work of investigation went on. At the Kehoe farmhouse, the Fire Marshall and the Lansing Firemen had waited patiently, but fruitlessly for the embers to cool. Nellie was not to be found there. Separately, but simultaneously, the hopes of Nellie's sisters were dashed. With Attorney Dunneback's help, the Vost family had been located near Jackson, but there had been no visit from Nellie and the family knew absolutely nothing of Nellie's whereabouts. Nellie's sisters had simply been duped. As they returned with Attorney Dunnebacke to Lansing, they had no hope of finding Nellie alive.

Although the authorities were finding no trace of Nellie, they were able to zero in on the scope and some of the method of Kehoe's destruction. All of the buildings of the farm, save one, had been totally and utterly destroyed by burning and explosives. Only the hen house had escaped, and only that through some malfunction in Kehoe's firing device. Farm machinery valuable enough to pay off the mortgage was wantonly destroyed by the heat of the fire. Machinery which might have survived fire alone had been carefully dynamited. The burned carcasses of Kehoe's horses lay in full view. One-eyed Kit, Kehoe's rejected gift to old man McMullen, had fallen where she burned. The legs of both horses had been wired at the feet to prevent escape.

To complete the destruction, Kehoe had carefully girdled the shade trees near the house. A swath more than an inch wide was cut around the trees only two or three inches from the ground. The grape vines were sawed off next to the ground, but were carefully replaced on their stumps to escape notice. Anything loose about the farm had been gathered up and placed in buildings which were set for burning. It was a design for complete destruction—obliteration. Kehoe's only explanation was found on a section of spared wire fence. In Kehoe's typical manner, the wooden rectangular sign had been carefully cut and just as carefully stenciled. Perfectly centered and punctuated, it read simply, "CRIMINALS ARE MADE, NOT BORN."[13]

From the chicken coop, the Lansing Police retrieved the apparent prototype of the device Kehoe had used to fire his farm buildings— an inverted bottle of gasoline set in a can, rigged with a spark plug fed from an electrical source in the house.

The state fire marshall was so impressed with the amount of care and work which had gone into the destruction that he suspected the work of one or more accomplices. The possibility was expressed to newsmen; and the drama of Bath was given a new dimension.

By late evening, there came a key break in the investigation. The mystery box which Kehoe had expressed in the morning had been located. Trainmen had apparently misread the Lansing address as an abbreviation for Laingsburg—and the parcel had gone there instead.

Lieutenant Morse and Detective Watkins of the secret service arrived in Laingsburg some time before midnight.[14] They picked up the box at the Laingsburg depot and, handling it with extreme care, drove straight to their East Lansing headquarters. As a precautionary measure the box was placed out on the police barracks parade grounds for the night—to await inspection by a federal explosives expert.

**

Inside the plain homes of Bath that night bereaving parents sought a peace that was hard to come by. Reporters and the assistants of reporters just would not give up. Some parents put the light out early hoping to gain escape. Others delayed putting the lights out at all—hoping to push back that inevitable next dawn—the nightmare of waking up to an absent child.

In other homes there was an uneasiness of fear. Rumors had spread that Kehoe and possible accomplices had survived and might still be in the vicinity. Families made their guesses as to whom the accomplices might be—and they carefully locked their doors before turning in. Some checked first for dynamite, including Mrs. Huyck.

Kehoe's own neighbors, the Harte's, had lost their grandson LaVere, and their daughter-in-law lay mortally injured in a Lansing hospital; but one of Mrs. Kehoe's sisters had come over—crushed with the inability to find any trace of the missing Nellie. When she left, the Harte's collapsed into bed—physically and emotionally exhausted.

By midnight, Mrs. Abrams, the caseworker from the Social Services Bureau completed her work—the whereabouts of every victim save one had been established. Reaching her home in Lansing, tired and starved, she was greeted by appreciative neighbors with a hot meal. In the whole Lansing area, people simply wanted to do what they could.

The prosecutor stuck it out until 1 a.m. and then he, too, headed for home. He had stuck it out through enough questioning, identifying, investigating and impanelling to last a life time—and the inquest was scheduled to start in the morning.

The day had exerted a horrible toll. Forty-three children and adults had already died in the disaster—and in Lansing, in the Sparrow and St. Lawrence Hospitals and in the Lange sanitorium forty-three lay injured (not to mention those injured who had been cared for in their homes). At least thirty-three doctors and untold nurses worked in relays all day and were still working through the night, both in operating rooms and the corridors.[15]

At the deserted school grounds a guard was posted and floodlights were strung to illuminate the area—just in case. A haunting quiet prevailed. At the edge of the sprawling, jagged hole lay a little wax doll, wide eyed, plaster dust covering her new dress. She lay precisely as she had lain throughout the day.[16] Hundreds of workmen, parents, and sightseers had trampled by her and around her. Not one had overlooked her. Not one had disturbed her. It was a phenomenon—a wish, perhaps, that the owner might return to reclaim her—a wish, perhaps, that all of the children of Bath might return to reclaim their youth.

Chapter XIX
Shock Waves And Ashes

While Bath slept or tried to, headlines were being prepared for the national and world press—headlines which would announce the disaster to communities which hadn't read it in their Wednesday afternoon editions. They were simple headlines, glaring. They brushed aside stories of preparations for Lindbergh's great solo transatlantic flight; relegated the devastating Mississippi River Floods to secondary coverage; and obliterated coverage of the apparent sex scandal which threatened the House of David religious sect.

The New York Times read, "MANIAC BLOWS UP SCHOOL." Readers of the London Times saw, "DYNAMITE OUTRAGE AT A SCHOOL." The Los Angeles Times headlined, "41 KILLED WHEN FIEND BLOWS UP SCHOOL." Even the New Orleans Times-Picayun in the flood ravaged Mississippi River published, "33 CHILDREN PERISH BY DYNAMITE BLAST PLANTED BY MANIAC." For subscribers to the New York Daily Mirror, the toll was something different. The Mirror's headlines exclaimed simply, "KILLS 50— BOMBS SCHOOL."

The stories which followed the headlines might not have been any more accurate than some of the headlines—but they told the basic story. An unparalleled atrocity had been committed. An atrocity against children. Bath had become suddenly the center of the world, a world stricken with mixtures of anger, disbelief, sadness and grief. Readers within traveling distance of Bath were drawn to the village like a magnet.

Possibly it was Wednesday's afternoon headline that attracted Special Deputies from the Saginaw County Sheriff's Department. Possibly it was the initial S-O-S which had gone out for help. In either event, two special deputies from that distant department had determined on Wednesday night to make a select search for the missing Mrs. Kehoe. Acting on the theory that it is sometimes better to search close and narrow than far and wide, they drove to Bath early Thursday morning, briefly inspected the devastated school grounds, and then drove directly to the Kehoe farm. As they had hoped, they were ahead of the crowds.

On the Kehoe land, they first inspected some still burning furniture near the remains of the Kehoe farm house. Mysteriously, the furniture which had been rescued from the farmhouse had been set ablaze during the night—but Mrs. Kehoe was not in it.

As the deputies extended their search to the outbuildings, however, they discovered her. More accurately, after very careful examination of remains found by the corn crib, they concluded that they had found her. Nothing was left of the wooden hog chute she had been carried in. Only the metal wheels and axle remained. For the very little that remained of Mrs. Kehoe, it was not surprising that hundreds might have walked by her the day before without recognizing that the charred form was human. The corpse was literally burned to a crisp, the base of the skull in contact with the ground, the lower part of the body still partially suspended and dangling from the wheels and axle. The right leg bone appeared to be broken and the left arm was broken off. A metal treasure chest lay beside the body, scorched, the lid ajar, and its contents partially scattered beside it. The deputies noticed the silverware, and watch, and guessed that a piece of silverware laying atop Mrs. Kehoe's chest had fallen out of the metal box as the box tumbled to the ground with Mrs. Kehoe. The deputies also concluded to their own satisfaction that the body had been burned the previous morning; and that it was burned exactly where they found it.

With the discovery, the deputies (Ray Cole and John Ward) walked across the road and reported the finding to Mrs. Harte. They asked permission to use the telephone and sent word immediately to

145

the Clinton County authorities. Also, they thought their finding that the body had been burned the day before might put the Harte's minds at rest. Actually, the finding did put some minds at ease. It convinced some folks, at least, that Kehoe and his possible accomplices weren't still up and about and threatening people.

The discovery, ghastly as it was, also brought the final desperate search for Nellie Kehoe to an end. For some it was a relief. Even for the Price sisters it ended the torment of not knowing.

Anticipating that the news of Mrs. Kehoe's discovery would spread quickly, the area was immediately roped off to safeguard it from sightseers. Although, the precaution itself broadcast and pinpointed the location, when Prosecutor Searl and the Fire Marshall responded to the call from the outcounty deputies, they were able to minutely examine the remains, precisely as they had been originally discovered, and just ahead of the converging crowds.

At approximately the same time that Mrs. Kehoe's body was discovered, explosive experts moved with extreme caution to open the mystery box at the parade grounds of the state police barracks. Both to their surprise and relief, they found that the dynamite box contained only the school treasurer's records—the records plus a bizarre letter Kehoe had typed to his bondsman on the previous Saturday. While officials puzzled over their discovery, they sent the word out that another episode in the tragedy had been closed.

"Dear Sir," Kehoe had written, addressing Clyde Smith, "I am leaving the school board and turning over to you all my accounts. Due to an uncashed check, the bank had 22¢ more than my books showed when I took them over. Due to an error on the part of the Secretary in order no. 118 dated November 18, 1926. He changed the figures on the order after the check had been sent to the payee—the bank gained one cent more over my books, making the bank account show 23¢ more than my books. Otherwise I am sure you will find my books exactly right.

I thank you for going my bond.
Sincerely yours,
(signed) A. P. Kehoe."[1]

As with just about everything Kehoe did, the letter was done with draftsman like precision—perfectly squared and centered, with care taken that his closing would begin precisely at the mid point of the page's width. The pride he took in being treasurer was clear. The extreme care he took for his arithmetic was equally evident, as was his need to point one more time to the flaw in the quality of Mel Kyes.

"I am leaving the school board—," Kehoe had written. It was an interesting choice of words—truth and defeat and, possibly, even indecision all in one. Kehoe perhaps leaving himself a way out up to the last minute. His signature, though, was not hesitant. It was bold and it was confident—signature to a demented letter written by an impossibly disturbed man. In taking one last parting shot at Mel Kyes, Kehoe had also attempted to show himself a man of honor, responsibility and integrity. Kehoe, the humorist might well have anticipated, too, one final last laugh on the public sent scrambling by the harmless box.

In the afternoon, however, one more severe blow was struck the community. Blanche Harte, the young fifth grade teacher, died of her injuries at a Lansing hospital. Her death brought a pause in the climbing death toll, but it punctuated the completely desperate plight of the community. The death toll was now forty-four dead, forty-four hospitalized, and more with additional injuries. The school, the central institution of the community had been destroyed, its leader dead. Half of the teaching force was dead, injured, or in shock. The village postmaster was dead. Reverend McDonald, the community's chief spiritual leader, had been rendered an impossible blow through the death of his daughter, Thelma; and Mr. Ewing, the township's chief governing official, fought to cope with the loss of his eleven year old son, Earl, and the threatened breakdown of his wife. At the same time, the governing board of the school was in shock and disarray—the mass murder and destruction being the work of one of its own members. Added to that was the greatest loss of all, the flower of the community's youth.

Those were the losses of blood, spirit, leadership and soul. The material loss of the school was a spiritual loss as well, but its dollar value loss also represented a financial catastrophe. The school had been insured all right, but for loss against fire, not dynamite. Uncovered, its loss meant that the community which had really just started paying off its debt would now be forced to add the indebtedness of a second school. Off hand, it seemed like an impossibility. Given some deliberate thought, it seemed like even more of an impossibility. The facts were that the building of the consolidated school was a hardship to begin with—even with an intact community and spirited aggressive leadership. Now, it faced a doubled tax burden, with defeated will and decimated leadership. In truth, the board was without even the money to pay off the final operating expenses of the year.

Finally, the citizens of the township were under heavy additional special tax assessment—and the village's main church had been significantly damaged by the explosions. In total, the plight of the community and its austere economy equaled disaster.

In recognition of the immensity of the crime and its aftermath, the Prosecutor postponed until Monday the beginning of the official inquest. (The postponement would have the benefit of further preparation including review with the Attorney General's Office.)

In recognition of the burden of the disaster on the community, the

147

Governor issued a statewide appeal for help to the stricken village. Reported on radio, and given prominent display in the press, the proclamation read:

It is hardly possible to imagine a more terrible catastrophe than yesterday's at Bath. There is little that we can do to lessen the grief of these stricken people. They have our boundless sympathy. While it is not given to us to assuage their grief, we can help in the material problem that confronts this community.

There has been a heavy expense cast upon them that I am sure the good people of Michigan will want to share. Besides the relief that we can give in individual cases, there is the restoration of their school house. The financial obligation on this small community of a new school house, at this time is going to be very burdensome as the district is already heavily bonded. To assist in the relief work and to help in the matter of a new school building, I have appointed a committee headed by John W. Haarer of the City National Bank, Lansing, Michigan, to solicit and receive funds for this purpose. I believe that we will all feel better if we make a contribution to these people who have been so terribly stricken.

Fred W. Green
Governor

To assist Haarer, the Governor appointed Richard Scott, President of the Reo Motor Car Company, and Schuyler Marshall of St. Johns. To administer the relief fund for Bath, a committee was appointed which was made up of the Governor as well as the chairmen of the Red Cross Chapters in Ingham and Clinton Counties (Reverend Edwin W. Bishop of Ingham, and William M. Smith of Clinton).

Haarer, who had suffered through the critical injury of a son less than a year earlier,[2] wasted no time in jumping into action. He immediately issued a follow-up appeal. The follow-up was critical because it gave instructions to the public on how and where donations were to be made. Appealing in behalf of the committee, Haarer stated:

. . . We ask that mayors of cities and supervisors of townships throughout the state, or any other accredited local agencies receive local voluntary offerings and to forward the same to the Governor's committee in Lansing.

It is understood that the regular Red Cross agencies of Clinton and Ingham Counties shall be responsible for the disbursement of the emergency relief and that the governor's committee shall hold and expend in conjunction with Bath Township authorities the balance remaining for permanent rehabilitation.

The most gruesome and pitiful tragedy that Michigan has perhaps ever experienced appeals to our sympathies and claims our aid.[3]

The proclamation from the Governor and Haarer's follow-up made the relief intentions clear; funds collected would go first to meet the emergency needs of families and individuals; the excess would go to rebuilding the school.

The need for the funds was painfully clear. Some families were near destitution to begin with. For others, the crush of hospital and funeral expenses would be unbearable. To save grave digging expenses, one destitute father had already asked permission to personally dig his child's grave in the Bath cemetery.

Possibly, the Governor's office had little doubt that Michigan citizens would be able to raise the money. Ordinarily that would have been safe conjecture, but in middle to late May, 1927, there was a possible obstacle. Michigan's citizens had already dug deep to raise funds for the victims of the catastrophic Mississippi River Floods. Each community had mounted a serious drive for that effort, and the citizens had responded from the heart and the pocketbook. They were, in fact, still in the midst of that effort. For the victims of Bath, it could have been a negative circumstance. Only the response would tell.

While the funding effort was getting under way, Bath was completing plans for the burial of its dead. On Wednesday there were reports that a group community funeral was being planned, but by Thursday, the plan of individual arrangements was confirmed. For the reading public, local and metropolitan newspapers laid out the schedule and location for each child and adult funeral. As was the custom, at least half of the funerals were scheduled for the family home. In the case of farm families, general directions to the family home were printed for the reader.

As it happened, by individual preference, the funerals were to be stretched out. Roughly, one third of the victims were to be buried on Friday, one third on Saturday, and the remainder on Sunday—the first of the funerals to commence at noon or shortly before noon on Friday. The high school graduation which had been scheduled for Thursday evening had been cancelled. A local paper reported that "commencement for eternity" had been substituted in its place.

Actually, necessity absolutely required that the funerals be stretched out. For one thing, morticians in the area were unprepared to handle such large numbers in one day. For another, Bath's children and adults needed to exchange places with each other as immediate family, as pall bearers, and as supportive friends and relatives. They needed to plan for that; and it could happen only if the funerals were held over a series of days. Lastly, Bath may simply have needed a three day memorial—the tragedy was that large, the village that small. The bond of tragedy which linked the community together in sorrow and in pain was born of poignant family grief. The greater than ordinary preparations and activities which were required of each affected family were probably a God send.

On Friday morning, the first day of burial began. The main street of the village was blocked off in readiness. Villagers and farm folk were out and about the streets early. They were dressed in their Sunday best, intent on honoring their children with the finest they had to offer.

One of the first funerals was for the small daughter of Reverend

149

and Mrs. McDonald. Following the services at the residence, the funeral procession slowly made its way some thirty miles distant for the burial in the family cemetery at Springport. At about the same time, the son of the township supervisor was buried at Perry. Superintendent Huyck was laid to rest a couple of counties away near Carson City and his childhood home. His Masonic Lodge paid him fitting tribute, of course, but many from Bath who would have wanted to attend his funeral just couldn't. As other funerals continued throughout the day, the tears flowed almost without interruption; and the tension of the immense anguish and grief found beginning release.

In DeWitt and at Bath, there were double funerals. They were news worthy; but so were all the Bath funerals. So were the child pallbearers carrying the small caskets. One of the several reporters on hand observed a double service most carefully for anything of "human interest." He scribbled in his notebook as a young mother took embarrassed and needless leave of the service with her happily gurgling infant. That was too bad, the reporter thought. How, under any circusmtances, could there be irritation toward any child of Bath? In his notes, the reporter contrasted the young mother's foolish discomfit with the boundless tolerance and tenderness for children which surely permeated Bath that day.

The reporter also took careful note of the young minister who struggled with the difficult burden of the funeral sermon. The minister was a sensitive young man. With great compassion he concluded the service. "Let," he said (he did not say, "suffer,") "Let the little children come unto me . . . for such is the Kingdom of God."[4]

Of course, all of the people in the area were not in attendance at the funerals. First on Thursday, and then on Friday, sightseers had begun mobbing the Kehoe farm—a never ending stream, seeking to see, to hear first hand, seeking, searching the ruins for souveniers. Those who couldn't make it to the scene were buying popular post card pictures of the tragedy which had been hurriedly placed on sale by Lansing and Bath storekeepers. (Buyers could choose between photos showing nurses and ambulances at rescue, Kehoe's destroyed auto with remnant intestines, Kehoe's last sign message, and the wreckage of the school.[5])

For news reporters, the whole Bath assignment may have been difficult, but it was especially difficult for them to square the behavior of the curious with the sanctity the reporters associated with Bath. Scored was the apparent morbidity of the numbers who crowded the Kehoe place seeking intimate contact with the disaster and one of its victims. Derided were those who sought photographs or the identity of photographers so that a photograph might be obtained. In a way, it was a curious derision, coming from those who depended upon such curiosity for a livlihood. Very clearly, though, many reporters saw Bath as hallowed ground—territory to which they held an honored invitation. They gave their writing great care—and much of it was inspired.

With some underestimation of the press, a great and careful attempt had been made to keep secret the location and place of two of Friday's funerals. The efforts met with only partial success. Relatives of Mrs. Kehoe had striven mightily to maintain some semblance of privacy for her services. Efforts were made not to divulge the circumstances to the news media. The Price sisters sought to give their sister simplicity and privacy, to protect her at least in death from the utter madness of the circumstances which had befallen her. But there were simply too many relatives and friends to maintain the secret. Both the time, 2:30 p.m., and the place, Lansing Resurrection Church, were printed in the press. As it happened, fewer than 100 friends and relatives attended the services, but news photographers hassled the party both in entering and leaving the church. A physical confrontation was avoided only when the photographers retreated to a second story window across the street.[6] Later, either the photographers had second thoughts about their coverage of Mrs. Kehoe's furneral, or their publishers did. The dailies gave the services very little coverage. The coverage which was given included no pictures.

The other Friday funeral was given absolutely no advance publicity. Actually, there was no funeral. The Clinton County authorities had consigned Kehoe's remains to the Clinton County morgue to await disposition. The authorities figured, quite realistically, that perhaps no one would appear for the remains. On Thursday, however, Kehoe's sister, Agnes, drove up from Battle Creek to make arrangements for burial. In appearing on this wholly difficult mission, she at least escaped the deluge of reporters which had descended on her sisters. With tears streaming down her face, she made arrangement for the body to be shipped for burial to the family plot at Clinton. In making the arrangement she clearly spoke for the Kehoe family, and for the family's apparent willingness to accept Andrew in death.

The plan aborted, however. Either the family had second thoughts itself, or the plan came into face to face conflict with one of the rules of the Catholic Church. Suicides could not be buried in sacred ground. As a result, the plans were hurriedly changed. Agnes agreed to burial in the cemetery at St. Johns. She asked for permission to view the body, but the request was denied.[7] If she sought any type of funeral service, that too was denied. As soon as the time was set for the Friday burial, she telephoned her sisters to relay the message—and left.

The burial itself was carefully prepared. Authorities had rightly

151

guessed that Kehoe's grave might well become the chief attraction of the curious, of vandals, or to frenzied relatives of victims, seeking to avenge themselves. To eliminate that possibility, an effort at concealment was carried out.

Late Thursday or Friday morning, more than one grave was dug at the St. John's cemetery in preparation for the Friday burial. Although one or two persistent and clever newsmen did learn of the intended time and place of burial, no advance public release of news was made. When the burial took place at noontime, it was performed with comparative solitude and secrecy. No pastor presided and no prayer was read. Only the undertaker and the gravediggers were present. Two newsmen watched from a short distance away. If need be, they could act as witness to the event.

The grave itself was out of the way, in the pauper's section. One of the newsmen wrote later, "The lot selected for Kehoe's last resting place was at the extreme rear of the cemetery, in the least exposed portion, where the maples are few and scraggly . . . There was not even the companion grave of his wife, for she was being buried the same day in a cemetery in Lansing."[8] To be sure he didn't miss anything, the reporter decided to stick around the site a while longer. In the two hours he waited, two autos slowly approached and paused at the graveside. The occupants were Agnes Kehoe, Andrew's sister, and Lewis Kehoe, Andrew's only brother; plus two or three Lansing friends. Aside from the limited reporting of the event which appeared in the papers, no record of the burial was made. As far as the cemetery record was concerned, Andrew Kehoe had never existed; and he never died.

As the first day of services came to a close at Bath, the township was still holding together. The first funerals had served as a beginning release of tension—but other tensions were building. The apprehension over possible accomplices had not subsided—even in the face of new disclaiming statements by investigators. When someone in the village made a statement interpreted to be sympathetic toward Kehoe—the mood became lynch ugly. Emotions, which had been allowed to give vent to sorrow were suddenly in danger of being loosed for other purposes—but the controls held and there was no incident.

Number wise, Saturday surpassed Friday for funeral services. Eighteen, possibly nineteen of Kehoe's victims were buried, including the young and the old. Glenn Smith, the heroic and youthful postmaster, was among them. He and his father-in-law Nelson McFarren were given a double service at the Methodist Church. Blanche Harte, the popular fifth grade teacher was also among the victims buried Friday. So were the Hall children, whose father had gone to the burning Kehoe home seeking to give assistance. Throughout the morning and the afternoon, funeral parties exchanged members and locations, and procession after procession found its way to the Bath village cemetery.

Far away, but during the same afternoon, Lindbergh touched down at Paris. In gambling with his life, he had eluded death—and a new era in aviation history was born. News reports ecstatically estimated 25,000 people were in the wild and cheering throngs at the airport to greet him.

Bath could hardly have cared less. While the growing number of visitors in Bath may not have approached the size of the Paris crowd, it was suggestive to the state police that special traffic precautions should be prepared for Sunday.

Actually, the police had more to go on than Saturday's numbers. Newspapers were still giving heavy coverage to Bath and its pathos. Saturday's papers gave detailed coverage to Friday's funerals—and with that coverage was a national wire service news photo—sure to tug at the heart strings. The photograph was a closeup of Mr. Ewing, the Township Supervisor whose son, Earl, had been killed in the explosion. Sharing the facial closeup was the head of the Ewing family dog, Sport. The caption under the family picture read, "Sport seems to be asking the father where Earl is."[9]

There was also very direct evidence of a probable Sunday rush. Out of towners had begun booking hotel and restaurant accommodations in Lansing at an unprecedented rate. Inquiries on directions to Bath were mounting by the hour. The combination of the catastrophe and the Governor's appeal was already generating great response. Even a benefit baseball game had been scheduled for Sunday afternoon at Bath between the Veteran's Bureau team of Fort Custer and the Lansing Oldsmobile team. By today's standards, the timing, coming as it did on the day of the last funeral, might have seemed a little premature—even grotesque. But the standards were 1927 standards and the people were 1927 people.

In short, the State Police had all the indicators of heavy traffic that they needed. On Saturday, they announced their carefully conceived plan of traffic control. Not only was the plan well conceived, but it was novel. The press release given out referred to it as a "one way road system." Its meaning was that traffic from Lansing to Bath and return could travel in one direction only on the route which was laid out. The police announcement indicated no deviations would be allowed. By Saturday night, detour signs were up pointing to and along the entire route; and the state police buttressed for action. The entire compliment of men stationed at the East Lansing Headquarters was assigned to directing Bath traffic the next day. By way of reinforcements, additional uniformed officers were called in from the outside. To complete the control plan, the northern approaches to Bath were placed under the direction of the Clinton County Sheriff's Department.

Sunday morning dawned bright and early. From the very beginning, it was clear that police estimates had been on the conservative side. Sunday was the one day in the week that practically the entire state's work force could take the day off—farm and city workers alike. It was the day of rest, of worship. It was also the day the public had chosen to memorialize the children of Bath. Like it or not, it was out of the hands of individuals and of officials; and it was also out of the hands of Bath. On Sunday, May 22, 1927, Michigan's citizens were going to attend Church in Bath, so to speak. In the process, they were going to tax police abilities, and village understanding to the limit. The problem was that not all the citizens knew how to behave in Church.

From shortly after day break, traffic commenced moving into Bath from Lansing. It moved slowly, and respectfully, but once into the Bath vicinity, many cars headed off onto the sideroads for special sightseeing. Other cars simply stopped on the route itself to observe, gawk, or contemplate. In a way, the route the police had laid out encouraged that. Starting at the corner of New York and Grand River in Lansing, the route went out the Gunnisonville Road and then right, past the Kehoe farm and into Bath—looping to several miles east of Lansing on the Park Lake Road. As the day wore on, the sun became increasingly hotter, unseasonably so. The volume of traffic on the dusty roads raised a slight haze over the entire village area. Motorists stopped, got out of their cars for a break. Some got out in Bath to peer through the windows of homes which were preparing for funerals (the three caskets in the Hart home on Main Street were a favorite). Some stared in awe there. Other visitors made straight for the homes which were marked with memorial flowers. Still others stopped to picnic on adjacent lawns, perhaps not knowing that the residence might be that of one of the victims. Supervisor Ewing's family, for one, looked out the window to see picnickers on the grass.

By noon, the double line of traffic moving into Bath was fifteen miles long and growing longer.[10] It had become a solid irresistable phalanx. It spilled into the side roads and even there moved only bumper to bumper. Whether in the Village or on side roads, police assistance was needed by families seeking to carry out funerals for their children. Other traffic was regularly brought to a complete halt as the police opened corridors through the long double lines to allow the funeral parties to proceed.

The outpouring of public sympathy even spilled over into the Lansing hospitals. The visitors wanted to see the children. Many succeeded. Many others were denied admission and pressed on to Bath.

People were curious, of course, but they wanted to do some thing. They wanted to pay homage. They wanted to show they cared. One woman, obviously embarrassed, but concerned, pressed money into the hands of a worker manning the Red Cross first aid station in Bath. (Others had bombarded the Lansing Red Cross Office with bouquets of flowers.) She was a stranger, of course, but though she said nothing, her eyes conveyed the grief and sympathy she wanted to express. It was a difficult thing for her to do—but she did it. In a single, quick and awkward motion, she turned and walked self consciously away.

Over the endless din and putt putt of idling machines the Zimmermans at St. Johns, the Hunters, Geisenhavers, Woodmans, Bergans, and Harts of Bath all laid children to rest. Two of the families had lost two children each. A third, the Harts, lost three. At nearby Howard City, a service was held for the young and tender teacher who had died with a child in each arm.

By late afternoon, the funerals and burials had been concluded. Still, the traffic came on. It did not cease until well after midnight. Every hotel room in the Lansing area had been sold out to accommodate the occasion. Restaurants were filled to overflowing. The state police reported it was the busiest day in the history of the department. Their official estimates placed 75,000 to 100,000 autos at Bath for the day. Thousands of other motorists had turned back when they glimpsed the awesome lines of traffic. In all, up to four hundred thousand citizens from Michigan, Indiana, Ohio, and Illinois passed through Bath that day. It was a memorial, a spectacular memorial which completely dwarfed the size of the Paris crowd which had shown up to meet Lindbergh the day before.

But was it a memorial crowd or was it something else? Some of Bath's citizens, and some newsmen on the scene, saw the crowds as an unbelievable obscenity—thousands of milling curious and morbid peope intent on denying the bereaved the privacy of their agony and sorrow. That is the way some saw it, and experienced it—but definitely not the majority. Most saw it as an unparalleled funeral procession, an incomparable show of sympathy for Bath, a nearly unbelievable tribute to the children of the community and their importance.

At least for the present, then, Bath's memorial services were over. The dead lay scattered in 12 area cemeteries, ushered there with the help of seventeen pastors. Large numbers of the injured remained in Lansing hospitals, and more remained at home.

Some observers saw in Bath and its decimation a victim which might never recover—victim of a plot to murder an entire community. By intent or otherwise, Kehoe had struck at the heart of Bath and its people by murder of the children. Only the future could determine if the blow to the community was truly mortal.

**

On the Friday night just past, the members of the Bath school board had met in their first official meeting since the explosions. Due to the circumstances, the board met just as in earlier times at the Town Hall. In fact, the members were just about back where they had started from. There were, however, some conspicuous changes. Each of the members present for the start of the meeting was emotionally beaten. Each member felt heavily the great loss of children and faculty which had been entrusted to the board's care. Each board member had suffered personal loss in the tragedy; and each was emotionally spent from taking part in a series of funerals and burials throughout the day.

And there were other changes. Newsmen were present for the meeting. It seemed that newsmen were present at every meeting. Could any activity ever occur again in Bath without a newsman?

As George Morris called the meeting to order, he acknowledged the presence of Mr. Searl, the young prosecutor. Searl's presence was a change, of course, an invited change—but the most conspicuous change was in the membership of the board itself. Mel Kyes was there, ready to take his secretarial notes. Bert Detluff and George Spangler had come in. The missing member was Andrew Kehoe.

The atmosphere was glum. No one at the table appeared to have a taste for the meeting, but it was something that had to be done. The first order of business was the replacement of Kehoe. Some names were mentioned. The board was in dire need of some new source of strength. With little discussion, the membership decided to turn to an early leader. J. W. Webster had been a charter member of the board, in fact, its first acting Chairman. The board, even the whole community, would have been happy with that choice. Given the call, however, Webster declined, giving the pressure of his chicken business as his reason. The newsmen present may have found Webster's decision utterly incomprehensible. For Webster, however, it was a matter of survival. The force of the explosion of the Bath school had broken 24,000 incubating eggs. For Webster and his customer farmers, it was a crisis of the first order, one that would claim his full attention for some time to come.

Faced with the rejection by Webster, the dejected board moved to offer the position to another long term reliable, Enos Peacock. When the phone call was made, Peacock accepted, and a car was sent for him. It was justice, really. Peacock was the long time community leader who Kehoe had defeated to come on the board. As he came into the room to join the meeting, Enos Peacock was a vindicated man.

With Peacock present, George Spangler made the official motion to appoint him trustee to fill the vacancy of Andrew Kehoe. Mel Kyes followed with the motion to appoint him to his old position as

Treasurer. As Mr. Peacock stood up for the swearing in, he tensed with the importance of the occasion, and shifted uneasily from foot to foot. He listened carefully as the prosecutor administered each phrase of the oath. Carefuly, slowly and precisely he repeated the words after him. With the oath completed, Mr. Peacock joined the other members of the board at the table. The circle was complete.

In getting to the other business at hand, the board acted uncertainly, and gave a sense of helplessness, and indirection. Still, it acted. A resolution of thanks was drafted for outside help. A response was penned to a sympathy telegram received from the Toronto Board of Education.

Most difficult, though, was the discussion of the school itself and the responsibility for it. The prosecutor answered some questions regarding possible liability of the board for personal and property losses. Possibly the board might wish to seek an opinion from the Attorney General's Office. The question of any responsibility for the explosion, direct or otherwise, would probably be dealt with at the inquest which was scheduled to start on Monday morning.

The news was not by any means all bad. The Governor's proclamation of Thursday meant that at least some of the financial burden of building a new school would be lightened. In addition, the Governor had received a telegram from Senator Couzens which sounded like an offer of unlimited financial assistance. The board had received nothing official. It could only conjecture on the amount and form of assistance it might receive, but the news was promising.

On the strength of that, the members speculated on the site for the new school, and appointed Mel Kyes to confer on building with the State Superintendent of Public Instruction. In the discussion that followed, most of the sentiment expressed was against rebuilding on the same site. The board owned five acres of land just to the east of the destroyed school. A rebuilt school could be located there. The suggestion was made that if the new school was located there, the site of the present school could be converted into a memorial park in honor of the innocent disaster victims. Mel Kyes spoke specifically in favor of such a plan. Kyes offered that the new school "perhaps might better be put back from the road on another lot and a monument to our dead erected on the old site." But on second thought, he backed up. "After all," he said, "we are almost in the position of beggers and whatever they say will, of course, be all right."

The tone of the meeting was captured by one of the reporters who was present. In the next edition of the Lansing Capitol News he wrote, "As the pathetic meeting drew to a close, it gave the impression of a ship without a rudder, minus any chartered course."

True, there had been some good news, but the oppressive loss of life which weighed on each member's mind paled it to insignificance. Save perhaps Peacock, each member struggled with his own responsibility for what had happened. Could any of them individually or collectively have prevented the tragedy? It was a question for each member and the entire community to ponder. The members only knew that they had been charged with the well being of the community children—and had failed.

The board's official minutes pretty well told the tale. Absolutely no direct reference was made to the catastrophic events of the 27th. Only two indirect references were made to the disaster. The first was a record of Spangler's motion to "... appoint Enos Peacock as trustee to fill the vacancy of A. P. Kehoe." The Secretary's second reference read, "Moved by G. E. Spangler we appoint Mel Kyes to confer with Mr. Coffee (State Superintendent of Public Instruction) in regards to rebuilding the school house."

Even for the typically cryptic minutes of the board, it was a masterpiece of understatement. Nothing could better have expressed the injury the board felt than this statement by nonstatement. The loss and the pain were simply too great to face.

CHAPTER XX
The Inquest

Monday morning started another difficult week for Bath. It was time to end the ceremonial mourning—time to begin the seemingly impossible job of starting life anew. Storekeepers listlessly opened their doors to business. Farmers returned to their neglected fields, and Bath began the painful process of reliving the whole experience—through inquest.

Technically, the inquest was to be a Coroner's inquest, presided over by C. E. Lamb the county coroner. Lamb, however, was admittedly more of a farmer than a coroner. He knew little of such things as formal inquests and was content to leave the preparation and the conduct of the inquest to Bill Searl, the prosecutor.

Young Searl was agreeable. He was qualified, and he was prepared. Not only was he a member of a distinguished legal family, but he was popular and recognized in his own right. A graduate of the University of Michigan, Searl was a fraternity brother of Kim Sigler, Michigan's future Governor. He had served as an officer in the infantry during the first world war, and had joined his father in law practice in 1920. In 1924 he took over the office of Clinton County Prosecuting Attorney, and in 1926 was re-elected without opposition. Those who didn't know him by reputation as Prosecutor, probably knew him for his reputation in the popular American Legion. As District Commander he held a post of considerable prestige and influence.

Finally, those in the community who knew him neither by reputation or in his capacity as lawyer and prosecutor, had gotten to know him personally in the last six days. He had come in from St. Johns as quickly as he could. He had moved right into the middle of things, and he had stuck with it.

In sum and substance, Bill Searl was a man who could be respected and trusted. Bath, on May 23, 1927 required, absolutely required a man who could be respected and trusted.

Without any doubt, whatsoever, Searl and the Coroner were aware of that coming yardstick when they had selected the jurors on the spot of the disaster during that first fateful afternoon. The jurors had been selected in the midst of the rescue chaos, but there was nothing chaotic about their selection. Ed Drumheller, Bert Wilcox, Clarence Tolman, Ishmell Everett, Wilmer Coleman, and Alton Church were all respected men of the township, and all childless. The latter fact would by no means guarantee it, but would at least encourage a more dispassionate weighing of facts.

As Monday morning rolled around, the townspeople were reeling from the disaster, three days of funerals and burials, a variety of newspaper and word of mouth versions of what had really happened, newspaper stories of accomplices, and a residual fear and compulsion to self protection. There were newspaper reports that Kehoe's school accounts were found to be in disorder, that dynamite had been stolen from a nearby construction site, that the mortgage had been foreclosed the week before causing him to go beserk, that he had bashed his wife's head in, that he had parked in his car across from the school gloating as children were hurtled from the building. Several accounts had him hurriedly stringing wire from the dynamite to his car just before the explosion. One version had the Superintendent rushing from the school in a last minute effort to stop Kehoe as he prepared to pull the switch at his car. Some accounts had the Superintendent and Kehoe engaged in a deathly wrestling match just before the explosion. Kehoe was variously reported to have triggered the last explosion by pushing a switch, by firing a revolver into the dynamite laden back end of his pickup, and by firing a rifle into the same dynamite.

Newspapers rushed photographs of Kehoe into print which acquaintances swore were not of him; alleged acquaintances were interviewed who gave varying and divergent accounts of the real

159

Kehoe and his background. One paper reported that dynamite had been found and removed from nearby homes and autos, and most carried stories of Kehoe's wanton murder of his own horse and the neighbor's dog. No newspaper conjectured that Kehoe might still live and none carried any continuing stories of conjecture about possible accomplices—but rumors of both possibilities were alive and well in the Bath area.

Technically, the inquest before Coroner Lamb started on the 19th at which time some brief informal testimony had been taken, without record, and with further inquest testimony delayed until Monday the 23rd. When the inquest was convened at the Bath community hall on the 23rd, the jurors had already been sworn in. By oath each jury member had sworn, "to inquire in behalf of the people of this state, when, in what manner, and by what means the said Emory E. Huyck came to his death." Officially, then, it was an inquest into the cause of death of the Superintendent. Practically, it would examine the time, the means, and the manner of all the deaths which had occurred in Bath during the preceding week.

Although the inquest was not a criminal investigation, it could lead to the filing of charges if the inquest concluded as it might that Kehoe and others were involved. Although a finding of no accomplices would not mean that charges could not be filed at some future time, the finding, whatever it was, would be a matter of life or death to the citizens of Bath. The inquest was vitally important in another respect. In looking at the matter of responsibility for the death, it would look beyond the question of murderers and accomplices. It would look at the matter of indirect responsibility. Specifically, was the school board or any of its employees responsible through negligence?

With the beginning of the inquest at 10:30 a.m., the pressure was clearly on the Prosecutor. Wisely, he had not thrown himself in front of the stampede of law enforcement personnel at the disaster. The inquest would reveal whether he had since been able to draw some order out of the disorganized saturation law and rescue effort which had taken place.

The pressure was also on the Prosecutor in another important respect. As the county attorney, he had some responsibility to represent the public agencies of the county, including the Bath School Board. In directing the inquest, however, he was put into the position of examining evidence of the Board's guilt or innocence.

Witnesses who had been subpoenaed began showing up for the inquest well before the 10:30 a.m. appointed time. Searl had chosen the old Community Hall as the site for the inquest. Ironically, the hall associated chiefly with Bath's good times, was to record the township's greatest agony. The historical old building had served the Bath area well since it was first dedicated in May of 1863. It was the center for social activities in the Township and, despite its name, had never been public owned or operated. Probably because of its name, reporters confused it with the Town Hall which was located across the street and which truly was the township government building.

Aside from the Consolidated School Building itself, the Community Hall was possibly the most distinctive looking building on the main street. It was a narrow, three story frame building which was basically plain, white, and homely. Like other buildings on the main street, it had the appearance of the frontier. But it was distinctive. Concrete steps dropped both to the left and to the right from the front entry which was protected by a front overhang. It was a touch of sophistication which didn't quite make it for beauty, but which also gave good, practical shelter from the weather for those waiting to be picked up by carriage or auto.

The entrance opened to the main (2nd) floor of the building. The lobby preceded a set of inner doors. A small box office was located just to the right of the lobby; and large inner double doors opened into the long dance floor or ballroom. At the far end of the floor was the small elevated and primitive stage. Wooden steps led up to the well worn stage from the left and the right. A large roll curtain was suspended from center stage.

For the hearing, wooden benches were placed along side either wall for spectators. There was probably capacity for upwards of 100 people. In front of the stage were placed two large tables. The jurors sat at the one table. The witnesses sat at the other with the Court Reporter, Glen Whitman. For the most part, Mr. Searl remained standing.

The day was probably bright enough to illuminate the room through the opposing sets of narrow windows, but four bare light bulbs which were suspended from the ceiling over the length and center of the floor provided additional light. In spite of quality wainscoting on either side of the room, the plain wooden floor added to the overall impression of barrenness for the hearing.

Throughout the days of the inquest, the double doors leading into the room were kept open, and spectators dropped in or out at their leisure. At the beginning of the inquest, several reporters were on hand, as well as waiting witnesses.

The Prosecutor was dressed in a business suit and tie, and looked properly formal. The slightly aquiline nose, and the striking red hair gave him an appearance one could remember. The atmosphere was emotionally charged, but the Prosecutor's affect was effective in controlling it. As he led witness after witness through testimony, his demeanor was purposefully calm and casual. Some thought he seemed almost bored.

From a parade of witnesses, from Kehoe's friends and foes alike,

161

and from the law enforcement agencies, the Prosecutor developed the story of the Bath Disaster.

The evidence, some direct, some circumstancial, pointed incontrovertibly to Kehoe as the murderer. He had made substantial preparations for the destruction of the school and his own home, had rehearsed the destruction of the school, and had the opportunity. The evidence also established that he had legal access to large quantities of explosives—would have had no need to obtain it by theft, and that he was a skilled explosives farmer.

A parade of witnesses testified they had absolutely identified Kehoe's corpse—had actually recognized his facial features. The testimony put the end to the developing myth that Kehoe had survived the explosion and was still in the area.

A smaller number of witnesses testified to identifying Superintendent Huyck. Those witnesses testified that they made identification through the Masonic ring and by the distinctive checkered coat he was wearing. For the record, the testimony was sufficient to establish that the Superintendent was indeed dead.

The testimony also brought out facts relating to motive—Kehoe's strong dislike for Huyck and the consolidated school, the relationship between Kehoe and Kyes described as "a little grudge", and Kyes possible distrust of Kehoe in the latter's volunteer work for the school. (Detluff's testimony that Kehoe had repaired the school generator in the summer months was disputed by Kyes. Said Kyes, "Barker Fowler did the repair work on the generator wiring. *At least that is what their bills show."* There was just the hint that somehow Kehoe 'might' have gotton ahold of some Barker Fowler billing forms.) Considerable testimony was also taken on the possible effect of mortgage proceedings on Kehoe. However, the true motive remained clouded.

When Mr. Howell, Kehoe's friend was questioned, he answered, "Yes, I have heard him talk about Mr. Huyck."[1]

Q: And about the consolidated school?

A. Yes, to a certain extent.

Q: What do you mean, to a certain extent?

A: Well, he wasn't so very rabid about it if that is what you mean.

Q: You have heard others in the township complain about it?

A: I certainly have. . . .

Howell's continuing belief and trust in Kehoe was demonstrated elsewhere in his testimony. He testified as to his belief that Mrs. Kehoe's body had been burned accidentally by the heat from the adjoining building. Howell guessed that Kehoe had carried the body to that location after she was dead, thinking the neighbors would find it. He testified he had seen no sign of gasoline, kerosene, or oil on the remains to the hog chute.

162

In response to a question from the Prosecutor, Howell then offered a theory on the destruction of the school:

Q: Do you think he meant it to go off the night before?
A: That was my idea.
Q: There was a PTA meeting there the night before?
A: Yes, sir.
Q: Why?. . .
A: Because he had no enmity toward the children, and I thought possibly he might have toward the people. In fact, I never knew him to have any hatred, be invective. But after the thing was blowed up, I made up my mind, must have had a hatred. Thought possibly. . .he was fond of children, as far as I knew. He didn't have children of his own.

Regardless of how much Howell might have wanted to believe in Kehoe, his theory was not supported by the other evidence presented. For Howell's friends and neighbors, and for relatives of the victims, his testimony rankled. At a time when the community was being very alert to the possibility of suspected accomplices, any testimony which sounded supportive of Kehoe was dangerous, indeed.

The longest testimony taken at the inquest did deal with possible motive, and it was taken from Joseph Dunnebacke, the Attorney for Julia Price and the Price estate. It was testimony taken not so much in search of motive as it was testimony offered in denial of motive. Dunnebacke had apparently volunteered to testify in order to set a misleading record straight—at least, he considered the record to be misleading.

Dunnebacke prefaced his remarks by stating that news reports about Julia Price were unjust, if not libelous. He referred particularly to a news article in the May 18th State Journal which read in part, "Foreclosure of mortgage on Kehoe's farm by Mrs. Lawrence Price of Lansing, his wife's aunt, is believed to have crazed the man and caused him to seek revenge on the community." Referring to that and other statements, Dunnebacke said, "There is but one deduction to be drawn from those statements and that is that Mrs. Price, or if you will please, the executors of the estate, had crowded Kehoe to the point where he had become desperate with the resultant atrocious happenings."

Dunnebacke proceeded to give a detailed accounting and chronology of the estate's great patience in dealing with Kehoe's indebtedness. According to Dunnebacke, even the initiation of foreclosure proceedings in chancery had been undertaken without any intent of dispossessing Kehoe of the farm. Said Dunnebacke, leaning forward with great emotional emphasis, "From the beginning to the end the record is that we were patient, helpful, and I repeat again was

163

solicitous of his comfort and his wife's comfort. . . . Whatever may have influenced him to this dastardly happening couldn't have been by reason of any fear that he was going to be dispossessed of that farm." It was a dramatic moment—everything on the line as the Attorney sought to clear the Price Family, the executors, and himself of any suggestion that they were somehow responsible for the most despicable of all American crimes.

However, the most authoritative testimony regarding Mrs. Kehoe's death was presented by the state fire marshall. He described the condition of Mrs. Kehoe's body in minute detail; gave evidence which appeared to make it clear that Kehoe had indeed intended to set the torch to his wife and the box of valuables which had been placed atop her. However, his testimony also dashed the popular newspaper version that she had been found with her skull bashed in:

Q: Did you find anything to indicate that she had been struck upon the head before the fire?

A: There was a slight crack in the skull, in the forehead, although not indicating that the same had come from a blow, as there was no indentation. (He explained that such cracks were generally found in bodies which had been exposed to intense heat—caused by formation of interior gas from the brain.)

Q: So that (the crack) might have been there and might occur without a blow upon the head of any kind?

A: Yes

Q: . . .The body might have been cut or shot in any way and you would not have been able to discover that?

A: Yes

Testifying that the body was burned where found, (It disintegrated when an attempt was made to move it.) the fire marshall also divulged the contents of the metal box found beside Mrs. Kehoe: a roll of what might have been currency or possibly Liberty Bonds; a Macabeen Pin; a lady's gold watch, Gruen no. 1407459 Case 96852 with inner case name R. S. Lockhart, Jackson; a dozen teaspoons marked with a K on the handles; a KC pin, a broach and chain, an opal ring, a diamond ring, a pair of earrings, an Ingham County marriage license, statements and bills from St. Lawrence and Ford Hospitals, and a compartment of silverware with setting for six.

Although the fire marshall swore that the body was not wired to the cart in any way, he did not rule out the possibility that she could have been tied to the cart in other ways. It left the door open for one more gruesome possibility.

In many ways the testimony given throughout the three days was free of conflict—each piece of testimony contributing to the full picture. The two main exceptions were regarding the sequence of fire and exposion, and the precise nature of Kehoe's final murderous and suicidal act.

As to the former, witnesses appeared evenly divided. Some were sure that Kehoe had fired the farm before the explosion at the school. Others saw it just the opposite. Each version was vehemently supported and with some impatience toward witnesses who saw it otherwise. The listening jurors had to be confused. If they could have concluded anything, it would have been that the two events were simply too close to call.

Regarding the final murderous onslaught, several eye-witnesses came forward, but each appeared to have been witness to something different. Young Orville Knight testified first. As he recalled the incident, the Superintendent was leaning against a Ford delivery truck talking to someone at the time of the explosion which killed him.

Old man DeBar also gave eye witness testimony (the strange old gentleman, whose home had been riddled by the second explosion). Under questioning he testified that he had seen Kehoe coming from the school house, and that he hadn't seen him coming from the school house. He testified that Kehoe had called to him after the cars were all afire and that he had called over the Post Master and Nelson McFarren. His testimony was so confusing and self contradictory that the Prosecutor, searching for an answer said in dismay, "Do you hear me all right?"

As the old gentleman left the room, there was no hint of derision from those present. Long before the tragedy the old man had won a place for himself in the community, and that wasn't about to change now. But one other thing was clear from his testimony. He was undoubtedly the source of some newspaper versions of what had happened in Bath on the 18th.

Another possible source was a witness who testified he saw Huyck and Kehoe at Kehoe's machine fighting for control of a gun just before the explosion.

According to the witness, Kehoe was on his knees during the struggle, knees in the seat, back against the steering wheel. The struggle lasted only momentarily and then the explosion.

The Prosecutor was skeptical:

Q: You couldn't be mistaken about these things could you?

A: No, sir.

The Prosecutor's skepticism was probably most aroused by the witness' repeated testimony that he had seen no other activity or people in the school yard at the time. The place had been a veritable beehive of activity.

While testimony under oath was being taken at the inquest, the Detroit Times was proposing that there was only one eye witness to

165

the tragedy. Their candidate was a newspaperman's dream: Anna Perrone, the young mother whose eye had been ripped out by schrapnel coming from the exploding car. In an article of the 22nd, the Times reported, "If she does live, she will be the most important witness at the inquest." The article went on to report an interview scoop with Mrs. Perrone, who, scarcely able to talk, spoke only in halting words: "A man in the auto waved to the Superintendent. . . The Superintendent went to the car. The man at the wheel leaned back and suddenly the ground shook and I felt something strike my head." The article went on to say that Mrs. Perrone did not know the man, but said it was not Kehoe! Few if any of the other papers had picked up the story. If their reporters had been able to get by hospital personnel to talk with Mrs. Perrone, they would have learned that her mastery of the English language was just about non-existent.

But there were other telling witnesses and some of them were at the inquest. The most impressive were the linemen from Consumer's Power. Curtis, Lang, and Snively reported it just as they had experienced it that day.

If the jury needed to look for substantiation, it needed to look no further than the testimony given by Cassie McFarren. In the end, it was the testimony which the jury bought.

Of course, the question on the minds of a great many people was the question of accomplices—of possible continued danger to the community. Harry Barnard's testimony reflected the community's continuing growing fear: In direct answer to a question, he referred to the final death explosion as "the last explosion," but then added, "or we hope it is the last one."

It was a question so horrible to contemplate that some might have chosen to repress it, but it had to be faced; and the Prosecutor confronted it head on. Repeatedly he solicited direct testimony on the question.

Monty Ellsworth was one who suggested that no one else was involved. "Kehoe," he said, "was always by himself. He seemed to be a man with himself always. I had that impression. . . . While he was awfully friendly, there was something about him—you didn't feel right close to him."

Jay Pope echoed that sentiment. He testified, "I don't think there was a man in Bath that he would take into his confidence."

A possibly clinching opinion, though, seemed to come from the Sheriff. The Prosecutor had asked:

Q: Have you any reason to believe anyone else was in this besides Kehoe?

A: I have not. . . . . It wouldn't seem possible to me that any man capable of planning a crime of this kind would take anybody into his confidence if he expected to carry it out.

The only possible testimony which could have raised continuing doubts was offered by Ida Hall, the grandmother who lived next to the school. Under oath, she recalled the time she had seen a second car in apparent company of a first as the driver of the first deposited unidentified contents into the front entry of the school at 2:00 a.m. in the morning. It wasn't much, but it was probably enough to heighten suspicion in the minds of at least some of the local residents.

Of course, direct complicity wasn't the only kind of guilt the Prosecutor needed to consider. As great a question, perhaps, one which might weight more heavily on the minds of the board members and community, was the question of indirect responsibility through possible negligence. The Prosecutor absolutely needed to determine if Kehoe's behavior was so obviously aberrant in the days, weeks, and months before the explosion that it was noticeable to people in the community? The Prosecutor also needed to determine if a normally prudent staff at the school would have been able to detect evidence of the preparations which were going on under their very feet?

To provide the answers, the Prosecutor asked witness after witness if any evidence of insanity had ever been detected in Andrew Kehoe. With only one exception the answer was invariably, "No." The exception was provided by old man McMullen, the reluctant recipient of Kehoe's gift horse. The Prosecutor had asked:

Q: . . .did you ever see anything to indicate he was insane in any way?
A: Well, I couldn't say that I did. . .
Q: And yet, you surmised that he might have hung himself that morning (the morning McMullen awoke Kehoe to tell him he could not keep the horse).
A: Yes. I thought possibly something did happen. It was in my mind why he should give me that horse, when not under any obligation to me at all. . . .

Other than that, even those who had seen and talked with Kehoe early in the fatal morning had detected nothing wrong.

As to why suspicions of school personnel hadn't been aroused, a possible but not necessarily acceptable explanation was offered in Kehoe's ready access to the school. Testimony indicated that had Kehoe been observed actually crawling out of one of the basement trap doors, no one would have questioned it.

Testimony at the inquest was finally concluded on Wednesday, the 25th with Lieutenant Lyle Morse under oath. Morse, the Assistant Chief of the Secret Service Division, was the law enforcement officer who had been placed officially in charge of the investigation.

According to the lieutenant, the explosives, including the 504 lbs which were recovered from the building, were so well concealed that they could have been detected only by someone searching in the

167

sub basement with a flashlight. He admitted that the explosives could have been placed when the school was built—but pointed out that no eavestroughing would have been necessary at that time. Finally, the Lieutenant testified that electrical experts were of the opinion that the complete charges did not explode because the load was way too heavy for the juice.

With excusing the Lieutenant, the Prosecutor turned to the jury and addressed the members, "Gentlemen, we have no other witnesses here, and we expect to close the inquest unless there is some other questions you want answered, or unless you know of some other witness, or unless there are some other witnesses in the room that know about this." He waited a moment, scanning both the jury and the auditorium, and then went on, "I think this is all then, Gentlemen, I think you can go down in the basement to deliberate on this."

As the jurors and coroner filed out of the room and down the stairway to the kitchen and dining area in the basement, the Prosecutor could sit down and do a little reflecting himself. He had chosen not to call any of Nellie's sisters to testify. He might have liked to, to throw some light on the nature of Kehoe, as only family members might know it. As the Prosecutor reflected on it, however, he was satisfied that he had done the right thing in sparing them. Throughout the entire inquest, he had avoided the lure of irrelevant side roads into Kehoe's character and private life. He had stuck instead to determining the deaths and the means by which they had been brought about.

In the days of testimony, the Prosecutor had solicited and received a remarkably detailed and coherent record of tragedy. Not all the witnesses had come forward, but enough had—at least for the purposes of the inquest. In all, 55 witnesses had been heard as to when and how Emory Huyck met his death.

The Prosecutor didn't need to wait long. The typing of the verdict took about as long as the deliberation. Emory Huyck, the jury found, had been murdered "about 9:10 AM Central Standard Time, on May 18, 1927 by Andrew P. Kehoe." They also found that the deaths of the children and teachers "hereinafter set forth as having been caused by the collapse of said school building, resulted from a premeditated and deliberate plan laid by Andrew P. Kehoe." The jury confessed ignorance as to how long the explosives had been concealed.

As to Nellie, the jury made no attempt to conclude how Andrew had killed her. It concluded only that he had killed her sometime between the evening of May 16 and 8:45 on May 18th.

According to the jury, Kehoe had committed suicide when he deliberately exploded his car causing the deaths of Emory Huyck, Glenn Smith and Nelson McFarren who were "standing near his car." The explosion was preceded by Kehoe's entry into the village at a "high rate of speed." The jury had obviously opted for the testimony given by the linemen from Consumer's Power.

The jury also agreed with the testimony of the state police in concluding that Kehoe had ignited his farm buildings, and had failed to blow up the entire school because of an over load.

For the community, the most important findings of the jury were two-fold: all the deaths and destruction were attributed to Kehoe and no one else. (The jury did not specifically rule out accomplices—but it did find that murder had been committed, murder by Kehoe.) Secondly, the jury decided, "We find that the said Andrew P. Kehoe was sane at all times, and so conducted himself and concealed his operations that there was no cause to suspicion any of the above acts; and we further find that the school board, and Frank Smith, Janitor of said school building, were not negligent in and about their duties, and were not guilty of any negligence in not discovering said plan."

On the surface, the finding that Kehoe "was sane at all times" looked insane itself. That is probably the way outsiders would have seen it, possibly even some of the locals in their lay opinion. Within the meaning of the Prosecutor and the jury, however, it was the only logical finding. It meant simply that to all outward appearances Kehoe had appeared sane. The purpose of the finding was not so much to judge Kehoe as it was to judge the Board. If testimony had been presented of outwardly aberrant behavior, the Board and Frank Smith would have been found wanting. Civil legal action could have been invited against them.

With the Jury's verdict in, the question was now the community's.[2] Would it accept the findings of peers, or would it continue to search for responsibility, for accomplices? With the jury's verdict, official looking back was over. For the community, however, looking back had just begun.

Chapter XXI
Attempt at Revival

No inquest had been ordered yet into the death of Bath itself— even though death had been pronounced as accomplished or imminent by some of the media. The pronouncement was probably not the product of fanciful exaggeration. More likely, it grew out of the nature of the crime, and its immensity. The crime had all the appearances of an attempt to murder an entire community through its children.

As the weekend beginning the official inquest had started, the Bath community still lived, but it was desperately hurt and struggling. The people of Bath were in pain. They were dazed and in shock—but they were not alone.

The Red Cross, which had been on the scene almost from the start, carried out an extensive inventory of need over the weekend. In cooperation with other social agencies nearly every family in Bath and the countryside was surveyed to determine the need for medical or other attention. Riding running board over a route cleared by the police, Principal Huggett led nurses about the countryside in search of children needing tetanus shots. Other task forces were set up to administer food and bedding, to provide hospital visitation and to do case investigations to determine the need for financial assistance. As early as May 23rd, the midwestern branch of the American Red Cross reported that the local chapters had the situation in hand "as far as material relief is concerned."[1]

The unbelievable crowds of the weekend were only one indication of the sympathy and compassion which swept the nation and the corners of the earth. The response to the Governor's appeal for funds was spontaneous and enthusiastic. Lodges, unions, communities, fraternities, sororities, prison bodies passed the hat. Individuals who didn't give money presented new fund raising ideas or spearheaded new fund raising efforts.

A suggestion received by the Governor which was not acted upon was a request that the Mississippi flood victims drive be frozen to enable money to be raised for Bath. A companion suggestion was that each Michigan school teacher be instructed to collect 2¢ from each student to rebuild the Bath school structure. One writer to the Governor proposed that there be a one day canvas of Michigan, during which 25 cents would be collected from each Michigan resident for the rebuilding of the school.[2]

School children from Italy wrote to the Bath school board to say that their sorrow was too great to bear. Wrote one 5th grade class, "...Even if we are small, we understand all the sorrow and misfortune that has struck on our dear brothers, and in the name of our teacher we are urging your school board, to tell them that we give our sympathy to the families of dead and injured children, and to all the village, and the sentiment of our affection to the small classmates."

A 3rd grade teacher from the same country wrote with her students, "...we are praying to God to give to the unfortunate mothers and fathers, the strength to bear the great sorrow that has descent on them, we are near to you in spirit, and with affection we

170

are the school mates of 3D grade of Sammarcelle Kesi, Sammarcelle. . ."[3]

From New York, prize fight promoter, Tom Bigger wired the Michigan Governor, "FLOYD FITZSIMMONS WANTS TO GIVE TWENTY FIVE PERCENT OF PROFITS ON MCGRAW—CLARK FIGHT FOR BATH FUND."[4]

Closer to home, the struggling Fund Drive for Lansing's Sparrow Hospital suddenly had new life. The clincher came with the announcement that a Bath memorial ward would be built. The Sparrow Memorial Fund was announced on the 19th—over subscriptions to the main drive were to be diverted to the memorial.[5]

While Lansing was soliciting greater hospital resources, health personnel from Michigan and surrounding states were leaving to join swelling relief forces converging on the Mississippi floodlands. Still, the beleaguered delta country had time for Bath. From Holy Cross College in New Orleans, H. J. Alderton (Brother Isidor) wrote, "I just want you to know that hearts in the Southland are sorrowing with you this day. . . .Therefore, I say that we in our sorrow pause and give thought to you this day. Our hearts are with you, our prayers are for you. May God strengthen and comfort all. . ."

Other citizens were inspired to write in a different way—with poetry. The quality varied, some was said to be spiritually guided, but it all came from fellow citizens who had been deeply moved by the Bath experience. A common theme, was that the children had merely preceded their parents to Heaven. An epic written by Mrs. W. H. Blount, for instance, followed a Bath child from her home to class and the fatal explosion. It started,
"Mother, there's the school bell ringing
    I believe our clock is slow."
And the mother sighed and answered,
    "Yes, it's time for you to go."
Down the path, across the foot bridge,
    Where the yellow cowslips grew,
"Ah! The purple Johnny Jump-Ups,
    For my teacher, just a few."
and finished:
"Forty Children and their teachers,
    Knelt before the Savior King.
In his loving arms He clasped them,
    As the last bell ceased to ring."[6]

It was poetry of the times and for the time. When it was absolutely essential that tears flow, it helped them flow, and it was comforting. It was also characteristic. People were giving what they could best give.

For most, though, it was easiest to give money—*a little money.* The rush was on. The question was, "Would the rush be big enough,

171

long enough" to take care of Bath's emergency and rehabilitation needs? The responsibility to see that it did was in the hands of the Governor's general relief fund, namely John Haarer, its chairman. What neither Haarer nor anyone else anticipated was the wish of Senator James Couzens to join the rush.

First news of the Bath disaster had reached the Senator in Washington. Later, when he read the Governor's proclamation for help, he acted immediately and characteristically. The telegram reached the Governor's office on Friday the 20th. It read: MY SINCERE SYMPATHIES GO OUT TO THE PEOPLE OF BATH IN THEIR GREAT TROUBLE AND THROUGH YOU I OFFER ANY FINANCIAL ASSISTANCE THAT YOU DESIRE WHETHER IN THE INTERESTS OF THE PARENTS OF THE CHILDREN WHO LOST THEIR LOVED ONES OR IN THE REBUILDING OF THE SCHOOL.

JAMES COUZENS

The wire undoubtedly caught the Governor's staff by surprise. Normally, communications regarding the Relief Fund would simply have been routed to Mr.Haarer. This one was brought immediately to the Governor's personal attention. The staff well knew who Jim Couzens was, and so did the Governor.

On Saturday, the Governor sent out a reply telegram. It was a telegram which had been done and redone with great care. In its original unsent form the telegram started: YOUR GENEROSITY IN OFFERING FINANCIAL ASSISTANCE INCIDENT TO CATAS-TROPHE AT BATH IS TYPICAL OF YOU. I AM REFERRING YOUR WIRE TO COMMITTEE IN CHARGE WHO WILL COMMUNICATE WITH YOU.[7]

After considerable reworking, the Governor sent a critically different telegram. In its entirety it read: YOUR SYMPATHY AND GENEROSITY IN OFFERING FINANCIAL ASSISTANCE INCI-DENT TO CATASTROPHE AT BATH IS GREATLY APPRECIATED BY ALL THE PEOPLE OF MICHIGAN. YOU HAVE DONE A FINE THING AND WE ARE PROUD OF YOU.

FRED W. GREEN

The reworked telegram was obviously warmer and more enthusiastic—no trace of the coolness which could have been interpreted from the first. More importantly, it bowed to Couzen's power and stature. Apparently, the Senator was not going to be referred to the committee in charge after all. Communication on the matter of Bath was going to be directly with the Governor. Initially, as his telegram indicated, the Senator expressed an intent that his offer be used according to the Governor's wishes. Governor Green, however, in backing off from applying the committee's rules to the Senator, was already making room for the more characteristic Couzens he knew.

Jim Couzens wasn't one to be overly impressed with the rules of the day, anyway. One of the wealthiest men in the country, Couzens was a United States Senator with a remarkable history. If Kehoe's intent had been to destroy Bath, he could hardly have stirred up a more worthy adversary.

In back ground and attitudes, Couzens and Kehoe had some things strangely in common. In others, they departed drastically. Both Couzens and Kehoe had broken with the church, both had severe problems with accepting the authority of others. They shared wrathful tempers and each was plagued with self doubt and difficulties in personal relationships. They were private persons and they were compulsively orderly.

Like Kehoe, Couzens had been born in 1872 of immigrant, highly religious parents. In Couzen's case, the parents had migrated to Chatham, Canada from England. The father was a tyrant to the boy and so saturated the home with Presbyterian dogma that Couzens rejected religion and confronted power his entire life.

In appearance, Couzens had a ruddish, well scrubbed look. His face was distinguished by white hair, a round face, somewhat pug nose, and glasses. There was a no nonsense, take charge air about him. Great orderliness and neatness were traits as was the quality of aloofness. Those who knew him best didn't feel they really knew the inner man. He was a loner.

By nature, he was aggressive, combatant, and to the point. An acquaintance once recalled when Couzens (as a grade schooler) was "Invited to attend an entertainment program at the McKeough (not Kehoe) school. . . .he proceeded to jump from one desk to another. His idea was to get for himself the choice seat and he took the most direct way."[8] Couzens had proceeded to jump from one desk to another ever since.

By most anyone's standards, Couzens was a successful, self made man. As a young man he had come across to Detroit from Canada to seek his fortune. Earning employment as a bookkeeper and office manager, he gained a reputation that placed him in the circle of Detroit inventors and business adventurers who dreamed of making fortunes from the automobile.

In 1903 he scraped together every penny he could muster and became a key charter stockholder in the newly formed Ford Motor Incorporated. In practice, he and Henry Ford became partners in operating the organization which was to revolutionize American Industry.

Couzens became the driving force in the early years of the new company. He was given the multiple responsibilities of Treasurer,

173

Vice President, and General Manager. His role was said to have been as decisive as Ford's and, in the public mind, one man was as important to the company as the other.

With Ford's approval, Couzens sponsored the $5 day. It was a landmark action which heralded a new day for both labor and management. He pushed the concept that labor was entitled to a fair share of corporate earnings. He not only argued that corporations had social responsibility, he introduced programs at Ford to carry out that responsibility (to the point that workers sometimes cried out for a little privacy from their too caring Ford Big Daddy).

Ford and Couzens made a great team while they lasted, but neither was really cut out to be a team member for long. In 1915 the two broke. For Ford, the final straw was Couzens' censor of a Ford "Peace" article from the Company magazine. Couzen's left, though as an immensely wealthy man, retired early as one of the Nation's most successful industrialists.

When, in 1916, Couzens came out of retirement and into public life, he made no attempt to start easy. He took on the very sticky and messy job as Detroit Police Commissioner. Critics laughed early, but Couzens laughed last. On the strength of his success as Police Commissioner, Couzens was elected to become Detroit's first "strong mayor." (Here, Couzens' background is remarkably similar to that of Nellie Kehoe's uncle, Lawrence Price. Price was auto maker, Police Chief, and chief of county government. Like Price, Couzens had been tempted to enter the 1916 Senate race, but on the Republican side—when he backed off, he served as campaign treasurer to Price's opponent.) As mayor, Jim Couzens had an outstanding record, and was appointed to the United States Senate in 1922.

In spite of a record which was probably already unique in American business and public life, Couzens was a restless and somehow unfulfilled man. As Detroit's Mayor he once remarked to newspaper companions, "Peace of mind, yes, that is it and I'm damned if I will ever know it. I'm the biggest failure in life I have ever known."[9]

In the Senate, Couzens' independence, even from his Republican Party, became legendary. Almost single handedly he fought the elements within the party which aimed to make it the party of wealth and privilege. Unlike Kehoe who thought he was owed more than he owned, Couzens felt that time and chance contributed to his own wealth. He saw wealth as a trust to be used responsibly for others. He was absolutely insistent, too, on responsible government and was willing to clash with both Harding and Coolidge to get it. A liberal in a party of conservatives, he had said, "The few who dare, must speak, and speak again, to right the wrongs of many."[10] By similar actions, he managed to ruffle so many feathers that in the

174

1924 election he was opposed by the Manufacturers' Association, the Anti Saloon League, the KKK, and the Chamber of Commerce. He had become, though, a champion of the little guy and he won in a landslide.

Besides assertiveness of conviction and his sense of public responsibility, the Couzens' quality which was decisive for Bath was compassion—but it was a gift that was strangely wrapped. Couzens was an extremely compassionate man, but with an inability to express that compassion personally and intimately. It was an inability which had been sorely tested before Bath.

Couzens had married a Catholic girl and had agreed to raise any children Catholic. The first child had died shortly after birth. The second child, a handsome boy, was named Homer. His birth had signaled the happiest phase in Couzens' life. When the boy's fourteenth birthday came, Jim Couzens presented him with his own brand new Model T.

Shortly after, tragedy struck. The car was spotted overturned on a road nearby the Couzens' residence, and Couzens was notified. When Couzens and his wife rushed to the scene, they found their boy dead beneath the car. A great light in Couzens' life had gone out—but the tears never came. He could only repeat then and later, "What a fine big boy he was." At a later date, his biographer was to say of this tough, brusque man, "He suffered actual pain at the sight of a crippled child, or even if he merely read about such a child.[11]

Clearly, the news of the murder and mangling of the children of Bath stirred something very deep and personal in Jim Couzens. He responded spontaneously and from the heart. His telegram to the Governor showed an early inclination to simply turn his money over to the Governor and run. As a matter of fact, though, Jim Couzens never was one to simply put up his money and run. The chances of it happening this time were primarily in the hands of the Governor and the Bath school board.

As the first news of the Couzens' telegram hit the press, it was heavily overshadowed by headlines announcing the spontaneous response to the Governor's appeal. Within one day several thousands of dollars were reported to have been raised. Chairman Haarer announced that there was already sufficient money to guarantee payment of hospital and funeral expenses for families unable to meet those expenses themselves. According to the jubilant chairman, telephone and telegraph messages were coming in from all over the state announcing mounting contributions.

The Chairman's obvious and well deserved pleasure, however, was captured before he received news of the Couzens' offer. Once Couzens' telegram was in hand, the anxiety began to rise. First of all, Mr. Haarer had set in motion a vast fund raising machine which was geared to collect sums from large numbers of people. Somehow, the

175

Couzens' offer seemed competitive at the same time that it appeared to offer instant success. It was like being caught between a fluff and a soft place.

At the same time there was possibly some real reason to sweat. Almost immediately there were indications that the original avalanche of contributions would drop and possibly halt as word of the Senator's telegram spread. Without confirmation of the Senator's intent, the results could be calamitous.

Asked for details at his Washington office, Couzens said, "My telegram speaks for itself, I was informed that the Governor had appealed for help for the people of Bath and I expressed a desire to contribute whatever was required, leaving it to the Governor to say how much was needed."[12]

In his own public comment, (before sending an official telegram in reply to Couzens) the Governor anticipated receiving the Senators gift through the committee but "to use it according to the Senators desires." By the time the Governor actually sent off his reply telegram, he was interpreting the Senator as underwriting the success of the drive. At the same time the Governor and Haarer both attempted to keep the original drive going. Said the Governor, "We have found a way to express our sympathy and I believe we all should contribute and not leave everything for Senator Couzens to do."[13]

Haarers comment however reflected his growing annoyance, "Senator Couzens," he said, "has never said that he would shoulder the entire load."

Even if he did, ". . .it would be a gesture of very poor grace to assume that because he would be able to do this, if necessary, that therefore, he should be allowed to do so."[14]

As the days went by it became ever clearer that the Senator's offer was otherwise bringing the Governor's drive to a near standstill. It was also definite that the Senator's gift was not going to go through the normal channels of the Haarer committee. More than that, Mr. Haarer never could bring himself to accept that the Couzens' contribution signaled the drive's success rather than its failure. On June 9th, the Clinton County Republican reported, "The premature and unauthenticated publicity given Senator Couzens' offer to help has cost the Bath Relief Fund many thousands of dollars in Mr. Haarers opinion."

In the end, the Senator gave more than his money. He had strong opinions on the rebuilding of the school and he gave them. he wanted the school rebuilt on the same site. To do otherwise would leave a gap, a vacant ground which would be a constant reminder of the terrible tragedy.[15] These were his views and he clearly made no secret about them.

The Senator's precise views on the rebuilding of the school, and his aversion to a memorial were cryptically clear in the instructional letter he sent to his architect on June 9th. He wrote, "I am at this writing disposed to have the school rebuilt so that it will be the same as it was before the catastrophe—certainly I do not want any memorial vestibule or other appurtenances that did not exist before the catastrophe——"

The Governor, also, was against the idea of a memorial. In rejecting the idea of a Children's Memorial State Park proposed for the nearby Looking Glass River, he said, "I think it best that the terrible incident be forgotten as soon as possible." He had agreed with sentiments expressed by board members that the school should be built on a new site—but for a different reason. The Governor said, "We want to rebuild the school in such a way as to make it wholly different from the one that can now be only a monument to Kehoe's madness."[16] Only the board, apparently, wanted a memorial.

Mr. Haarer had once indicated that the relief committee was only concerned with the financial end—that the planning and building of the school would be left to the Bath Board of Education. Now, however, even the board appeared to be out of it.

On June 16th Senator Couzens and the Governor visited the Bath children and adults still hospitalized at Lansing. He also visited Bath itself, inspecting the ruins, meeting with townspeople and officials there. For Bath, and the children of Bath it was a big day, one they had been preparing for during the past two weeks. The Senator looked at three different sets of plans which had been prepared for the new school. He also clarified his intent to pay for the new school. He would shoulder that burden, but retirement of the old debt would be up to the taxpayers.

On June 23rd, the Bath School Board officially accepted the $75,000 Couzens' offer. Speaking for the Board, Mel Kyes said that it was the unanimous opinion of the board that the school should be built on the old site. (The Couzens' offer had been restated in the form of a telegram to the Board. It was an offer to "rebuild the school the same as it was.")[17] Said Kyes, referring to Couzens, "We are only too grateful to leave everything to the builders."[18] It was an indication of confidence not only in the Senator, but in Couzens' chosen architect, Warren Holmes, designer of the now demolished school.

In truth, the Board had received a great and wonderful gift. In truth, the board and the community were still in grief. Unable yet to function independently as a board, the members needed desperately to lean on someone. In Couzens, the board found itself a Big Daddy willing to make the decisions. In the floundering community, the Senator found his lost child.

**

177

While the Governor's appeal and the Couzens' offer dominated the relief news, other drives were mounted. In response to a request from a former principal, the Bath Board granted approval for a special memorial drive. The former principal was L. L. Tyler, Superintendent of schools at Muskegon. Buoyed with the approval of the Bath Board, Mr. Tyler sent letters of appeal to the State's 500 school districts. The letters went out on May 27th and suggested that each of Michigan's school children might want to contribute a few pennies to purchase a memorial tablet to be placed in the auditorium of the new school. The appeal took—and the pennies began coming in almost faster than they could be counted.

Community response to another drive was also enthusiastic, even with one key misgiving. On May 25th a drive was mounted by the Methodist Church to raise $5,000 to restore the structure which had been damaged in the explosion. The drive was mounted by the district Superintendent, apparently without the knowledge of the beleaguered Bath Minister. Reverend McDonald opposed the request as an unnecessary opportunistic adventure. He found the drive an embarrassment. The good Superintendent, though, was probably as swept up in the public compassion as anyone. He may also have been sensitive to the young minister's needs. In grief himself, Reverend McDonald was faced with the almost impossible job of increasing his ministrations to a sorely needy congregation. After the tragedy and after the death of his child, Reverend McDonald had written the congregation, "The duties of my office have increased a hundred fold and my abilities have decreased in a similar ratio. . . . . I beg you to be charitable. I do not know a person more anxious to help always and more dreadful of being a hindrance, than Mrs. McDonald. She is so shattered and fearfully nervous that our efforts to help others have been pitifully hindered. . . . .my how we would like to be in your homes more often. We most surely need each other. . . ."[19]   The Reverend's plight, as he pointed out, was not unique. The Bath first aid headquarters which was maintained to dress the wounds of physically injured children was augmented by a Red Cross Social Worker. The stricken families required expert attention to their shock and grief—and symptoms of mental disorder were being detected in several of the children. It was a finding supported by the social service bureau in Lansing. Some of the parents were simply too shocked or broken to act in their own behalf. The trouble was that compassion, which often isn't enough, was about the only kind of treatment available to children or adults.

Still, the assistance which poured in on Bath in one form or another was plentiful. The work of the reporting charities was impressive. The Red Cross was serving 91 "disaster cases"—family and property damage cases affecting 413 persons. Vast stores of donations in the form of sheets, pillowcases and what have you, were distributed freely, sometimes over the protests of recipient families. In addition wealthy benefactors from the nearby area sometimes singled out particular hospitalized children for special unpublicized interest.

Public charity on the other hand was not something to be freely given or received in 1927. As a class, the poor, for whatever reason they were poor were a hated class. Community "welfare" was regularly placed in the control of men who outdid themselves in creating new ways to humiliate those so helpless as to require relief. Self shame was so rampant and so inbred that only the most desperate applied for help—and then often too late to avoid injury to body or mind. Families destitute enough for the standard fare of 4 pounds of rolled oats, or 25 pounds of flour passed a fairly simple means test—the investigator simply searched the home and the cupboard to be sure it was bare. Under rare conditions such families might be fortunate enough to qualify for unsanitary meat coming from a garbage disposal community piggery.

The psychology of giving and receiving was one of benevolence toward the "deserving." There was no concept of "right" to assistance. "Beggars can't be choosers." Every gift carried an implied obligation to the giver. If the receiver was grateful enough, and the gift was critical enough, like survival, the receiver might even assume the identification of his benefactor. Gratitude, though, was an absolute requirement. So, was maximum self help.

This was the background to the charity freely given to Bath. To the giving outside community, "Disaster" was the magic word. To the Bath community, and its resident recipients, a lifetime of brainwashing could not be so easily shaken off.

Cast in the position of being a charity case itself, Bath did not succumb to the temptation to lay back and let it all roll in. The township people and their officials attempted as best they could to apply the rules to themselves.

On May 24th, the Lansing School Board communicated an offer to the Bath School Board. The Lansing Board offered to educate the Bath High School students free of charge during the coming school year. The Lansing Board confined the offer to the high school students reasoning that the parents of Bath would want to keep the younger students closer to home. It was an offer that Lansing figured the Bath Board wouldn't want to refuse, might not be able to refuse. Bath, however, even without a school building, refused the offer!

Immediately after the first rush of the disaster, Bath also began administering the relief monies itself, through the regular channels. Welfare, such as it was in 1927, was administered through the Township Supervisor. The idea was that the Township Supervisor

179

was the single person who knew best the status of the township coffers and the true financial circumstances of the residents. To be absolutely sure that none of the bounteous funds were mis-spent on those who might be undeserving, relief monies were turned over to Mr. Ewing for distribution. In no way was Bath going to allow the money to be just given away.

The school board was even more exacting in its giving. Estimates had been made that compensation to families of the faculty might run in the neighborhood of $15,000. In an advised but seemingly heartless move, the Board went through the motions of keeping that amount as close to zero as possible.

When Mrs. Huyck, wife of the slain Superintendent, claimed compensation under the state workmen's compensation law, the Bath School Board sought an opinion from the State Attorney General. The Board was not going to pay unless it was liable.

The Attorney General answered with one of the stranger opinions issued from a gross of strange opinions.[21] Sensibly enough, Attorney General Potter found that the question of liability hinged on whether the school Superintendent was killed in the course of his employment. But the Attorney General couldn't leave well enough alone. He went on to explain,

"If Kehoe made this assault solely to gratify his feeling of hatred and anger toward the Superintendent, then the injury resulted solely from the voluntary act of Kehoe and did not arise directly out of the employment or as an incident to it."

To save himself from possible lynching, however, the Attorney General went on:

"If, however, the sole reason for the assault was Kehoe's hatred for the deceased because of his being Superintendent of Schools and caused by some of the things he had said and done in the performance of his duties as such Superintendent, then the board might find he received the injury out of and in the course of his employment."

Although no one had ever established that Kehoe had called the Superintendent over to his car, the Attorney General noted that it was the Superintendent's "duty" to respond to that request. Incidentally, the Attorney General found that the Board was not liable for the Superintendent's salary for any period after his death. In concluding, the Attorney General decided to play it perfectly safe. He said,

"It is my opinion whether or not your district is liable for compensation depends upon findings of fact and circumstances as made by the Industrial Accident Board."

With the opinion in hand, the School Board moved ahead from a position of liability. With Mrs. Huyck it started a Summer long negotiation process for a compensation figure of $3,570. When

Roscoe Harte (Blanche's husband) also put in a bid for compensation, it started the same process. The Board minutes read,

"Moved by Roy Reasoner that Enos Peacock see how much money he can find available to pay Roscoe Harte compensation and then call Roscoe Harte before the board and see if we can make a lump sum settlement."

Clearly, whether it was its own money or someone else's, the Board was going to be as tight fisted as a responsible board had to be. In Harte's case, as in Mrs. Huyck's, the Board's conservatism was difficult. Roscoe Harte was a disabled War Veteran, technically dependent on his wife's earnings. When Harte was finally awarded $3,000 he turned it right back to the community in the form of a $3,000 trust fund for loans to further the education of needy Bath graduates.

And there were other examples. Senator Couzens and the Governor's appeal notwithstanding, Bath was taking on the looks of picking itself up by its own bootstraps. Work bees were scheduled to clear the school grounds of wreckage and debris. The object was to salvage as much as possible—to save on the cost of rebuilding.

The work bees, in fact, made the first in a series of sombre discoveries. Ernest Babcock's father may have made the first discovery—an intact sack of "cement." With Ernest looking on, the father ripped into the sack with a knife. After carrying the sack down a country road, the elder Babcock put a lighted match to its contents. It burned all right. Flashing powder, they called it.

That was just the first of the discoveries. On June first, State Police received a report that there was additional dynamite at the site. Troopers searched the entire morning but could find nothing. On July 21st, workers discovered a sack of dynamite.[23] That wasn't all. In a ventilator was found excelsior and a kerosene soaked rug. On July 26th, an additional 25 pounds of Pyrotol was located.[24] The findings were especially ominous in view of the builder's intent to reuse as much of the remaining school structure as possible. Strangely, none of these findings was apparently followed by any all out attempt to dismatle the entire remains, brick by brick.

The findings came amidst continuing, sometimes growing tensions. The rumours and suspicions of remaining accomplices had been allayed by the inquest but not eliminated. Young couples used to courting and petting in parking places as remote from all others as possible, now sought common parking places. Couples came together, parked together, and left together. No one wanted to take unnecessary chances.

And the crowds of sightseers kept coming. As late as a month after the disaster, police were still needed to direct traffic. On Sundays the Kehoe place was practically inundated with the autos of curious tourists. It was unnerving, but it kept police in the area.

Late in June, Kehoe's staunchest friend noticed the crowd, and went on down to join them. Speaking to the crowd of his knowledge of Kehoe, he said, "Mr. Kehoe was such a fine man he never would have done what he did unless he had been insane." To victims' relatives who happened to be in the crowd, it sounded like someone was extolling Kehoe's virtues. The father of an injured boy grabbed Howell by the throat. It was more than he could tolerate. Fortunately, Howell escaped injury. When the Clinton County Republican picked up the story on the 23rd of June, it stated that the underlying question was, "How far can free speech go?" Actually, the confrontation simply confirmed that the rift with the community had grown irreconcilable. In little more than a year, Mr. Howell was killed when his machine struck the rear end of a fast passenger train at the crossing just down the road from Kehoe's. Some time after that, the family moved away, its ties with many old friends in the community long since severed.

The agitation which continued at Bath wasn't eased any by the Ku Klux Klan. Never one to be a calming influence, the Klan put out a special edition on the Bath Disaster. With a claim of five million copies in the first edition, its headlines read, "Roman Catholic dynamites Bath Public Schools." The Klan described the disaster as "The greatest premeditated murder of children since the St. Bartholomew Massacre murdering 30,000 French Protestants." The edition alleged that newspapers had suppressed the truth about Kehoe's Catholic background, and that Kehoe was a zealous Catholic. The gist of the publication was that Kehoe, acting as a tool of the Catholic Church, had plotted the destruction of the public school and its children.

In the Klan's view (prompted by alleged whispering campaigns that Kehoe was a Methodist and a Mason), Kehoe was an ardent Catholic who had fought to retain an unqualified teacher, Ruth Babcock, simply because she was Catholic—and he had vowed to the Protestant Superintendent that he would bring other Catholic teachers into the system. It alleged that since the explosion, a Roman Catholic had stated, "Don't be surprised if this is duplicated in a short time." The Klan paper concluded its review of Catholic actions and plottings by asking, "How long, O Lord, how long?"

The Klan paper was short on facts (Kehoe had long since ceased being a practicing Catholic, Ruth Babcock was known only to be a Protestant) but long on inciting. The suggestion that the disaster might be repeated in a short time, could bring taut nerves to the breaking point. It also could raise a question: Could a misjudging Klan have singled Kehoe out in the past for harrassment?

Against this background an even more incredulous dynamite discovery was made on a Sunday afternoon in the Fall (October 2nd).[25] A woman tourist inspecting the residual building noticed

182

some objects which were visible in the exposed cutaway of the subflooring. To her, the objects looked like sticks of dynamite. Fordney Cushman and his father were on the grounds, and she approached them for an opinion. They made a closer examination and then went for the constable. Mr. Harrington, it seemed, wasn't through with his rescue work after all. While he removed the dynamite, a call was put into the State Police. Trooper McNaughton, who had assisted in removing the original find on May 18th, was dispatched to pick up the latest discovery.

In all, 244 more sticks of dynamite weighing approximately 208 pounds were removed. They had been well and neatly wrapped, and secreted in workmanlike fashion in the floor partition.

The latest discovery created some shock waves. Bath residents who had been opposed to rebuilding on the same site anyway were more than agitated. They were insistent that no rebuilding commence until the old structure was completely razed. Their argument was unwittingly reinforced by the chief architect. Warren Holmes confided to the State Journal that it would be necessary to remove all the ceilings of the part of the building being remodeled to assure safety. According to the State Journal, it was Mr. Holmes opinion "that although large quantities of explosives have been removed from the school there is no doubt some left in the south wing of the structure and great care will be taken to locate the deadly plants." Amazing! Several months of repeated discovery had gone by—and there still was no plan to raze the structure. Residents could only be assured that "great care" would be taken to locate whatever remained.[26] On October 6th, however, it was reported in the Clinton Republican that the architect and Senator Couzens had decided to erect an entirely new building. Incredulously, the need for economy apparently prevailed against this reported decision. The south wing and the original east section were saved for restoration rather than replacement!

That announcement still didn't ease things completely. After all, the last discovery had raised a troublesome question. If the last cache had been resting there since the explosion, why hadn't it been noticed by the workmen who had been laboring with the floor partition? How could a cursory examination by a bystander reveal what had remained hidden to them? If the possibility of new plantings was openly expressed, however, it was repressed just as quickly—perhaps for the same reason the inquest had disallowed the possibilities of accomplices. The prospect was too horrible to be possible.

Possibly the same belief was controlling over a later State Police investigation. When the State Police received reports that a Bath resident was making threats against the new school, an investigator was sent out. The officer's investigation consisted of questioning a bank employee about the character of the person making the threats. When the Bank employee assured the officer that the individual was harmless the investigation was closed! Given the background of the recent mass murder, this casual disposition was unbelievable. It was all unbelievable. Incredibly sloppy search and investigatory work, stubborn niggardly insistence on salvaging building structure—the first in the face of potentially great danger, the second in accompaniment to great charity. Somehow, Bath seemed to accept it all. If there was an explanation to be had, community shock was a good candidate.

**

Through the shock, Kehoe continued to take his toll. On August 23rd the last obvious victim of the Bath disaster was claimed. Ten year old Beatrice Gibbs died at St. Lawrence Hospital of an infected limb. A victim of compound fractures of both arms and legs, one fracture refused to heal properly and developed an infection. An article in the Journal read, "For twelve weeks the fair haired mite fought her losing fight with courage and with cheerfulness. Her strength ebbed slowly and Monday afternoon she faded into the beyond." Some of Beatrice's classmates who were injured were more fortunate. Some were but beginning months and even years of repeated surgical and plastic repair.

For many of Bath's adults the pain of remaining in Bath was too great. Families pulled up stakes and moved out. Some adults who stayed in the township did so only at a price. They could not bring themselves to enter the village.

If the toll went on, though, so did the healing process. The Summer of '27 saw two major efforts underway—one initiated by the official leaders of the community, one initiated and carried through by an individual.

Monty Ellsworth, Kehoe's 39 year old neighbor, probably never thought of himself as a healer. As it turned out, though, he was one. Ellsworth was a big and jovial sort who had moved into Bath from Lansing some eight years before. He was a businessman who had tried his hand at first one thing and then another. He had some personal problems—a shaky marriage, a drinking problem traceable to his years as a saloonkeeper in Lansing, and an asthmatic condition that made friends worry about his sometimes awesome wheezing attacks.

What with all that, and attempting to be a father to his grade school age stepson, Ellsworth just about had his hands full. But Ellsworth always had more on his mind—or maybe that is why he had more on his mind. Basically, Ellsworth was a dreamer of schemes to make

184

money—an opportunist constantly scanning the horizon for something new. When the Bath disaster hit, he didn't need to look nearly as far as the horizon. All he had to do was look out his front window; for the unending lines of traffic added up to one thing—a souvenier market of unlimited potential.

Besides his business scheming, another quality in Ellsworth may have been decisive in determining that the souvenier would be a small book, written about the disaster, itself. That quality was his innate sensitivity.

Although, Ellsworth had no experience as a writer, himself, he may well have been the only person in the area or the country capable of undertaking such a sensitive assignment. Certainly, he was the only one who tried. His Bath background, moreover, made him uniquely qualified for the task.

As a merchant of various sorts in Bath, he'd done everything from operating a general store to buying and selling poultry, to butchering wholesale. With some little assistance from Kehoe he was ready to venture into the gas station business at the time of the tragedy. His was the kind of varying activity that brought him into contact with just about every man, woman, and child in the township. Although he wasn't one of the official leaders of the community, never having run for public office, he was one of the best known men in Bath, and one of the most popular. He was also one of the sharper. He knew, for instance that a man running a marginal business better stay away from political contests. Most critical of all, Ellsworth was himself in the heart of the disaster. His step child had been in the explosion and Ellsworth was as prominent in the rescue effort as anyone in Bath.

Ellsworth had one other unique asset. From an objective standpoint he probably knew Andrew Kehoe better than anyone in Bath.

Ellsworth's one weakness was that he had no experience in writing, taking notes, and organizing them. Ellsworth attempted to correct that deficiency by picking his niece to assist him. She was a Bath teenager. She too had been through the disaster; and she had been schooled in the proper use of words.

Intuitively, Ellsworth knew that he had to get his book written and to print in a hurry. He knew the market was there—but it might not last. He also was pretty sure that he knew what the public wanted. They wanted something readable, short, graphic and authentic. People wanted to know about the disaster, and they wanted to know about Andrew Kehoe. Ellsworth was confident he could meet all these requirements.

Putting his other work aside, Ellsworth put all his energies into developing his book. It was a massive, breakneck assignment—especially the way Ellsworth conceived of developing it. Throughout the Summer he interviewed, gathered photographs, and wrote.

Before he was done, he had visited practically every child who had been injured in the explosion. Beyond that, he talked with every available parent of both the dead and injured children. The parents had confidence in Monty Ellsworth and they talked. They spoke of their crushing anguish, their dashed hopes, their fears—and the future. They also offered Ellsworth their most treasured photographs and snapshots for publication in the book.

In addition to presenting a unique eye witness view of the disaster, Ellsworth also succeeded where the probing journalists had failed. He dug deeper into Kehoe's childhood than anyone had—and he came up with some fascinating information. Some of that, under later light, would never survive the test of accuracy—but it would become central to a Kehoe legend which may never die.

When Ellsworth published his book, it was in brown paperback. He named it *The Bath School Disaster*. If the book seemed grisly in spots, it was because Ellsworth tried to report the disaster as he experienced it and as it was reported to him. It was a simple and honest book—and it was beautifully sensitive. Ellsworth captured Bath just the way it was in 1927. He captured the quality of the people, the love for their children, and the great pride of the community in the school and the teachers.

The book was no great polished work of prose—but in its way it was a classic. Ellsworth had written it, published it, put his heart and soul in it—but it was more than a one man production. Every Bath family had contributed with love, and reverence. And it was haunting. For eternity, the children of Bath smiled out from its pages.

Ellsworth had captured the community experience. In doing so he experienced the disaster a hundred times. In the end, he succeeded in producing a work which may not have been his original intention. Possibly it was going to be a best seller, and possibly not. But definitely it was a memorial. In almost yearbook form, Ellsworth and the community had created the memorial both the Governor and the Senator would have denied them. It was as inevitable and as necessary as the wind.

Chapter XXII
Challenge to Greatness

For the school board the Summer months were to be as intense and as decisive as they were for Ellsworth. Big, likeable Albert Detluff, whose friendship toward Kehoe had been betrayed, tendered his resignation in June. He had taken a job with a Lansing automaker. Continuation on the board was no longer feasible.

In July the annual school meeting and board elections offered a test of public confidence in the Board. The inquest had found the Board blameless for the disaster—but the inquest had been decided by a small group of jurors whose deliberations were confined to reviewing "evidence." In July, the question would be one of broad public sentiment.

As it turned out, the elections left no doubt. The board's choice of Peacock was confirmed on the first ballot. Spangler was reelected; and the only newcomer was Roy Reasoner who had given Kehoe his last defeat at the polls. When the officers were elected, it was the old lineup—but with renewed public confidence. Morris, President; Kyes, Secretary; Peacock again, Treasurer. The verdict was now conclusive, or, at least, it appeared to be. The inquest held the Board blameless, the Board members considered themselves blameless, and now the public held it blameless. More importantly, through its vote the Bath public was revealing that it held itself without responsibility for what had happened. The future of Bath might ride on whether that expression was a genuine gut expression, or a repression of the unacceptable.

With the elections out of the way, the Board went about its business. In order to reject the offer of the Lansing School District to educate Bath children, the Board needed an acceptable alternative —one which could carry it until the new school would be ready a year later. The Board also needed a bit of collusion from high places—and it got it.

First off, in an astounding piece of benign neglect, the U of M accreditation team set the stage. In an accreditation decision dated two weeks after the disaster, it conveniently omitted all mention of the destruction of the school![1] Based upon pre-disaster inspection of April 27th and on a follow up letter of Máy 9th, it gave the school generally excellent ratings and granted one year accreditation until June 30, 1928. Apparently, Bath had a year of grace to make do as best it could.

The Board, with a new Superintendent but without a script, decided to improvise. The three floors of the Community Hall were made available to the Board without charge—the Board would put in new flooring and equipment. In addition to housing the third, fourth, fifth and sixth grades, the Hall would provide special classrooms for high school students.

Besides, the Community Hall, the town hall across the road was also made available without charge. The town hall would house the second graders under Thelma Ewing, daughter of the township supervisor. In addition, Hinckly's vacant store building was rented to make room for the high school classes and the home room. The Board also rented out Menzer Church's building, as well as two rooms in back of Crum's Pharmacy. The rooms at Crums were to house the administrative offices and the Kindergarten and First grades.

For H. H. Brandt, the Superintendent, and for Wayne Van Riper, the new principal—the plan had all the earmarkings of an administrative nightmare—or of a rare educational challenge. They, and the community took it as a challenge. A very grateful community was to welcome three teachers back, but the rest, the dead, the incapacitated, and the others needed to be replaced.

When school opened on the first Monday in September, though, Ward Kyes was back on hand once more to drive the kids in on Bus Route Number 5. For a change, there'd been no hassle over his contract. So there he was, back in the driver's seat, earning a paycheck Kehoe had said he'd never see. The Lansing State Journal was on hand to witness the occasion. Ted Christie wrote in his covering article, "Scarcely had its (the school bell) echoes died away before the consolidated school buses rumbled up and deposited their burdens of youthful potentiality upon the sun baked streets of this sleepy little town. Laughing and chatting and gesticulating they tumbled from their high seated perches and spread themselves in every direction." To Christie the scene was much like that of a college campus with youngsters moving back and forth across the street as their schedule required. He did note, ". . . there was a limp here, and a rigid arm there. Yonder was a cherub with a ragged scar and over there was a lad with a missing finger." There were also missing children—the dead, the still hospitalized, and the children whose families had decided to leave Bath.

But to all appearances, the girls in their starched bright gingham, and the freshly scrubbed boys "might have been the boys and girls of any country school." What Christie saw was "no tragedy here. Only gaiety and health and a certain anticipation of the days to come . . ."[2] Apparently, Kehoe had accomplished, if only temporarily, a complete reversal of his goal. The opposing factions of Bath had become unified for consolidation and for their children.

And Christie's observations did seem right. The Superintendent, the Board, the parents launched into the new year determined to make a bright new start. Bath school news, never reported in area papers, suddenly became a regular feature. Cheerfulness was the common quality—restored pride was the obvious goal.

Actually, there was a lot to write about. Brandt was determined to shed the school of its insular quality, to branch out, and to become competitive. Under Huyck, football had been strictly taboo. Other athletics were suspect. Under Brandt, Bath's first football team took the field—and preparations were made for the basketball season. If people were going to look for a new overprotection at Bath, they were not going to find it.

Typically, other activities were organized. A newly formed debate team worked out with the experienced high school team from East Lansing, and prepared for competition. Glee clubs and an orchestra were formed. Said the Clinton Republican News, "The Superintendent reports the orchestra boys will soon be able to provide all the music the town can handle."[3] Bath was trying hard, it seemed. It was making the effort to come back. Even the untimely death of the Superintendent's wife did not stop the effort.[4]

By the first Tuesday in November, construction at the new school was ready for the laying of the cornerstone. At the morning ceremonies, "Only a scant few assembled at the school grounds—and some of them, unable to bear the memories left before the program was over—members of the Industrial School Band furnished music and filed to their places on the newly laid first floor—then came in the school trustees and the Superintendent. Then, a sudden hush fell over the assembly as the school children of Bath Community marching from their make-shift schoolrooms down the street, reached the edge of the school yard and then halted. Soon they started again and crossed the yard to the new building. First came the high school students bearings between them the flag and flowers. Following the upper classmen came the smaller children from whose ranks such a horrible toll had been taken." Reverend McDonald offered a prayer followed by the band's America.

It was a signal occasion, demanding greatness—and the main speaker complied. John Phelan, Dean of Michigan State College was the speaker, and what he gave was surely Education's counterpart to the Gettysburg address. He said, "We are gathered here today to lay the cornerstone of one of the greatest institutions that a community, small or large, may have—a public school. We are, I trust, at the same time laying the cornerstone of a great resolution: that this school may be a place of light and joy and happiness where both young and old may gather, and on these gatherings no shadow fall—"

Phelan paused, and then pressed on, "To the community (also)

189

this school is a place where young d old may gather to meet together to talk with each other, to be of service to one another. This common gathering of the people is a social need old as society itself—. No greater tragedy, no greater grief could have come to any community than came to you—. To individuals and sometimes to communities there come great tests of life. The test of a great sorrow and a great tragedy has been yours. You met it with a great courage." Phelan paused once more, struggling for composure and, possibly, for emphasis. Then, he concluded with one line, a challenge to his audience and to Bath. "The test of the future," he said "is that you will make this school a great school."[5] For that day and at that time, no one in the audience doubted that Bath would meet that challenge.

For the time being, the challenge was great enough of controlling a campus which was scattered up and down Main Street. Teachers found supplies and equipment hard to come by. Students sometimes found a bit too much stimulation in the excitement and looseness of the arrangement, and in the presence of new staff and administrators. When one morning the principal accused his class of seniors of being an ignorant bunch, he got a smart reply. Anson McNatt, the class president, answered. "No, sir, we are just like a mirror. We reflect whatever is in front of us." The remark was answered by a round house right from the principal which sent Anson sprawling. The message to Anson was clear enough—but under the old administration, Anson would have mirrored a much tighter discipline.

The improvised school also offered real security problems. The danger of fire was no fantasy. Teachers kept pails of sand or water handy to douse floors which might become overheated from the pot bellied stoves. The all frame community hall looked especially hazardous. To increase security, the Board paid for an extra fireman to cover the downtown nights and Sundays. Still, if people intent on injury or sabotage were yet around, the buildings and even the children presented an exposed target. It was not the arrangement one would prescribe for an overprotective society. Beneath a facade of gaity, there was underlying tension, however, and when workmen dropped a ladder on the roof over the Hinckly classrooms—children and teachers shot from the premises in a lightening reflex evacuation.

Parents, understandably anxious, looked to the new school—and preparations went on. But preparing for a new school wasn't easy— to some it wasn't even proper. Even to live sometimes didn't seem proper. The struggle was there. Possibly for all parents it was there. It was an internal struggle, but one which had to be externalized. In Bath, even the ambivalence became externalized. As preparations

190

for the new building went on, the Board voted to close school on the anniversary of the tragedy. Then, under protest, the Board rescinded its order and turned the question over to the PTA. It was more proper, it seemed, to let the parents of the living settle it.

At the annual meeting, an even stronger motion was made by relatives of children who had lost their lives. The motion was made to make May 18th a memorial day for all time! In the subsequent vote, however, the motion was voted down by the townspeople in a decision that may have looked cruel and callous. But that is not the way the decision was presented or intended. It was a matter of out-look, of symbolism—the need not to fixate on the past—the need to best serve the dead by serving the living. No one was really against memorial; it was just a question of how.

The question was also one of identification. At the same annual meeting, by a vote of all the eligible townspeople Bath voted in effect to change its identity! If the Senator consented, the new school was to be named Couzens Agricultural School! The vote was one of childlike gratitude, and it was a vote born of grief.

The naming was timely enough. The building was fast nearing completion and seemingly, about all it lacked was a name. As school facilities went, the new building looked like the best that money could buy. Senator Couzens had relented a bit from his early insistence that the school be a complete replica of its predecessor. For the purpose of more fully meeting the needs of the community, kitchen and eating facilities had been added as had a gymnasium auditorium with stage which was without peer in agricultural Michigan.

The Board had also backed off a bit from its earlier position that it would leave the building of the school completely in the hands of the Senator and his architect. Whether the Senator approved or not, the Board had given Professor Tyler the go ahead on his memorial drive among Michigan's school children. This was a drive which was close to the Board's heart. It watched over that development very carefully.

With the thousands of pennies which had been collected from the school children of Michigan, Professor Tyler arranged for the sculpting of a memorial statue by Carleton W. Angell, a renown sculptor and artist for the University of Michigan Museum System. Although museum scientists may have had some initial trouble understanding exactly why the museum needed an artist, Angell's work at the University was self explanatory. Angell was absolutely devoted to life and its reproduction. He was a family man, a great fan of Norman Rockwell's and a master of texture. From life he could capture what the scientist would not see. For the sculpting of a memorial statue, Angell was the perfect selection. The statue, "Girl

191

with a Cat", was the product of his work—born of his discussions with Tyler, the townspeople of Bath, and his compassion. In a child, Angell saw Bath's past and he saw its future.

Fittingly, the preparation for installation of the statue became the focal point of the Board's interest in the new building. The members were insistent that the architect adhere to the letter to their specifications for location and visibility. When the builders attempted to make some modifications, the Board was adamant. With dedication ready, the statue was placed precisely where the Board wanted it—in an alcove, just inside the entrance.

The school was ready enough, ready, in fact, in a way that Emory Huyck had only dreamed of. Through a nice bit of side stepping, manipulation, and continued 'benign neglect', the University had granted the Bath school its long sought 2 year accreditation. Actually, the whole thing had the aroma of irregularity, but no one around would have detected anything but the scent of roses.

Until the Spring, the University had continued to avoid any acknowledgement that the old school no longer existed. Its accreditation investigator avoided the make-shift campus like the plague. Only when inspection couldn't be put off any longer did he make the trip. When the trip was made, Bath was conveniently off on Spring vacation. With that excuse, the inspector ignored the store front classrooms and inspected the excellent facilities of the new building instead. The accreditation, based on that inspection, gave Bath a clean bill of health—not a single recommendation for improvement was made.

Once again no reference was made to the dynamited school— with one exception. The exception consisted of a notation that the previous year's inspection report was destroyed in the explosion. It was not immediately clear whether the reference was to point up the seriousness of the explosion or to give a rather strange explanation for the school's failure to carry out recommendations which had become irrelevant.

No one would have been interested in alleging collusion, but it was surely there. The University, in its need to protect, had done its job. A destroyed educational system had its credibility extended— and a village trying with difficulty to pick itself up was given a hand.

The University had nevertheless missed a unique opportunity to study, observe, and learn from a truly rare and exciting educational experience—the complete integration of classes into the commercial existence of the village. It was an opportunity which might not again be duplicated.

Even as the builder prepared the school for completion, the Board decided to turn dedication ceremonies over to the Town Council (in keeping with the community school theme). The Council, in turn, went full steam ahead, in keeping with a theme of celebration.

The day of dedication was planned as a gala festive occasion. Advance notices indicated that Senator Couzens would give a short address. Even the Governor might be there. Activities were planned for the whole day. There were going to be tours of the new school, a formal dedication program, sports and athletic events, horse races, refreshment stands and from the new stage a home talent play, "A Woman's Honor." There was also going to be the formal unveiling of "Girl With A Cat," the memorial statue made possible by pennies contributed by Michigan's school children.

Shortly before the event, Couzens begged off, asking for pardon from the 'embarrassing ordeal.' For a man who was never known to back away from a challenge, it seemed strange, off hand. It shouldn't have. The man who had always needed to repress his strongest personal emotions simply couldn't take the chance. For the people of Bath, the Couzens decision was a severe disappointment—but, coming from the gentleman who had given them so much, it was a decision they could both understand and accept.

Other than that, the day went off exactly as planned. Doctor Pitman from Michigan Normal spelled Couzens and he continued the momentum which had already been started in Bath. "Let your prayers be no longer for the dead," he said, "but for the living youth to whom this building is dedicated."—and then the celebration began.

The throngs of visitors found the 1,500 souvenier programs to be in short supply, but they found a truly excellent school/community facility. The handwriting was on the wall for the old community hall.

A reporter for a national wire service wrote, "Bath bid today for a little space in the papers; not for the screaming black headlines which a year ago told the world that 44 lives, mostly small children, had been lost in the dynamiting of a school house; it asked only for a few inches of type, back among the advertisements, maybe, to tell the world the sequel to that other tragic event."[6]

The work of Kehoe that could be undone, had been undone. Among other things, Bath was now in the hands of its own collective community conscience—a conscience in which Kehoe and disaster were an imbedded part. It was a fact that made the community's image of Kehoe critical.

Chapter XXIII
Kehoe

The headlines had names for him—"Madman," "Fiend," "Maniac," "Diabolical Pied Piper of Hamlin," "Demented Farmer." These were at one the headlines and the bottom line. The question was, "How did Andrew Kehoe get that way?"

Immediately following the disaster there was a scramble to find out. It was a scramble of the media, of the press—and a greater scramble was predicted. The Detroit Free Press suggested, logically enough that, "Modern science. . .will undertake to analyze his impulse and his attitude with considerable precision."[1]

Strangely, the Free Press prediction never materialized; and the scramble among the press corp, while desperate, was short lived and fell short of the mark. The media effort, which otherwise might have been intensive, persistent, and successful, probably fell victim to the Lindbergh mania which swept the country.

While the scramble lasted, it produced information, most of which found its way to the printed pages of the newspapers or to rumor mills. Unfortunately, a great deal of the information printed about Kehoe's past was (and is) suspect—first because of the propensity of the 1927 press to invent news, and next because of the obvious propensity of the news sources to invent relationships with Kehoe which never existed, or to extend the limits of that which was truly known about Kehoe into the unknown.

Fabrications and exaggerations were probably encouraged by the fact that those who knew Kehoe best were not in a mood to talk or share information. The Price sisters gave absolutely no information to the press. Kehoe's brother in Lenawee County and his sisters in Battle Creek withdrew from the press, after giving very limited information during the initial shock of learning of the catastrophe. How strongly the wall of privacy was attacked is not known. What is known is that the wall withstood the prying efforts of the news media almost undisturbed. The wall cracked a bit under the more persistent effort of Monty Ellsworth, but it still stood.

Faced with limited acess to reliable information about Kehoe, the press passed on whatever information it was able to pick up. Widely circulated was the report, attributed to Kehoe, himself, that he was an honor student and graduate in engineering from Michigan State Agricultural College. According to the press he was also discovered to be a graduate of Tecumseh High School. There were reports that he worked for a time in a creamery in Bath. (No one in Bath could seem to recall that.) His sister, Catherine, recalled that he had

194

attended electrical school in St. Louis, Missouri 15 or 16 years before the disaster. Other press reports had him working in the lumber camps near Clare, and as a coal miner or explosives expert in the coal fields of Pennsylvania and West Virginia. (This alleged occupation was associated with the reported murder of a nonexistent brother there—in addition its not likely that the compulsively clean Andrew Kehoe would even have sought employment in a coal mine.) One newspaper account had him serving in the World War as a dynamite expert. In addition, gossip had it that Kehoe was a mine setter during the War.

While the most consistent reports about Kehoe were of his stubborness and mechanical genius, even as a school boy, the report which has become legendary is the report of Kehoe's boyhood which was compiled by Ellsworth. In *The Bath School Disaster,* Ellsworth presented a Kehoe who, as a fourteen year old boy, had likely murdered his hated stepmother. For Bath it was an important finding; Kehoe was a killer who had killed before. If the criminal had been made, he had not been made in Bath.

As Kehoe's murderous orgy had made painfully clear, the true Kehoe was unknown to any of his acquaintances. He had revealed very little of his inner self, and he had revealed very little of his past. Still, a picture of the young Kehoe does emerge from information consistencies found in newspaper reports, from members of his family, other reliable acquaintances, and various documents.

Andrew was one of eleven children (fathered by Philip Kehoe.) through three wives. Philip, with his father and mother, and six brothers had come to this country, probably in the 1840's, as part of the large Irish influx of the time. They were staunch Catholic, hailed from County Wexford, and Philip's father prided himself in being of pure Celtic blood.[2] Like their Irish brethren, they saw in America a land of promise, a land which would offer relief from the famine, hardship, and religious strife of the old country.

On arriving in America, the family settled briefly in Howard County, Maryland. It was a setting close by the Bay, and the ocean—reminiscent of the ocean bays of their County Wexford homeland. However, in the 30's and 40's and 50's new land was being settled in Michigan; and Easteners all up and down the coastal area were heading for it. Philip Kehoe, the first son, caught the fever and headed West.

Philip, was a big, tall and strapping young man—barely 22 when he preceded the rest of the family to Michigan in 1855. In an area between Tecumseh and Clinton he purchased 490 acres of excellent farmland for himself and sent for the rest of the Kehoe family to follow him.

It promised to be a good life. The Michigan country was strange land to be sure, but a good land for pioneers, and one being settled by many other Irish immigrants as well. (The nearby Irish Hills were even named after these Irish settlers.) The one key difference between Philip Kehoe and many of the other Irish settlers was a difference in religion and politics. Philip Kehoe was Catholic and a staunch Democrat.

With the security and promise which the new land offered, Philip was ready to become a family man. For his bride, Philip chose Mary Malone, a proud girl his same age who had been reared by an Irish Catholic Priest.

Mary Malone was of distinctive heritage to be sure; and from the very beginning, the Church was to be central to the family's existence. Elizabeth (Lydia), the first born, came in 1860, and Mary was born 16 months later. A week following the baby's birth, Mary Malone Kehoe died, probably of complications related to the birth. In pioneer life such death was not an uncommon occurrence. Mary Malone's marriage had not been a long one but her devotion to her God was to remain permanently imprinted in the Kehoe family life.

Philip remarried within the year, taking a second Mary for wife. Mary McGovern had come into the vicinity with her parents from New York State and was two years her husband's junior. Mary McGovern was honored to find for husband such a reputable young widower. She was also challenged to equal or exceed the standard of love for family and God which Philip's first wife had helped establish. In all, eight children were born to the couple.[3] Four girls were born first: Agnes in 1862, Catherine in 1867, Frances in 1868 and Martha in 1870, and with the birth of each, Philip's disappointment grew. The all important first son had not yet been born to this Irish American family.

In nearly all other ways, Philip Kehoe could judge himself a successful man. He was an acknowledged leader in the vicinity, a model farmer and successful cattle breeder. He was being elected to fill various township posts and probably only his identification with the minority party prevented a political career. Perhaps, even more important for Philip, he had become a tower of strength to the young Catholic Church in nearby Clinton.

Andrew's birth on February 1, 1872 ended one frustration for his father, but it may have begun another. Philip Kehoe was a man's man. Men have sons. Men have sons who are men. There was no doubt about it. Philip Kehoe was very proud, and he was going to be just as demanding. A genial man, he was known even among his strict and stern neighbors, however, as a strict and stern father. Andrew, of course, if he just knew it, had it made. All he had to do was cooperate.

Andrew had arrived on the scene with 12, 11, 10, 4, 3 and 1 year old sisters waiting for him. Within the next five years, two more sisters and a brother joined him. (Patrick, Margaret, and Helle were born in

196

rapid fire order.) Before Andrew reached his fifth birthday, he had two younger sisters and a brother. Suddenly, however, the child bearing stopped just as dramatically as it had occurred. Andrew's mother was at the end of her child bearing years.

When the childbearing ended, Andrew found himself in the center of the ten children Philip and Mary were attempting to raise. All of the children were more or less wedged into the comparatively small but comfortable plain white frame Kehoe homestead. Consequently, life in the well scrubbed farmhouse was both hectic and orderly—orderly as a prerequisite to survival—orderly because the authority of the house laid it out that way. Privacy might be cherished in such a home, but it could be attained only with difficulty—unless one chose to mentally shut the others out.

For Andrew, the existence held unique experiences. As the long sought first son, he was probably both adored and resented by his older sisters. The parents undoubtedly enthroned him, but subjected him to the rule of order and left much of his direct care to his older sisters. Between the enormity of chores to be done about the pioneer farm home, and the constant demands of pregnancy and infant care, the mother had little opportunity to satisfy a craving youngster.

Possibly, the farm life was no different than that experienced by a thousand other large early Michigan farm families. It was a demanding life, a severe life and a simple one—but with opportunity for the most complex of relationships. It was also a life of bounty, and of opportunity for the special pleasures which can come from large family life. It was a life with great opportunity for learning the give and take of life—or for only learning the take, if somehow the twig was bent that way.

If the pre-school Andrew did yearn for an elusive mother's love which he though was rightfully his, more comforting days might have been ahead. With the end of child bearing, his mother could, for the first time, sit back and enjoy her children. That is what might have been anticipated. For Andrew, and for the other children, though, it didn't happen that way.

Sometime between Helle's birth late in 1876 and 1882 Mrs. Kehoe became noticeably and seriously ill. The onset may have occurred as early as late 1876 or it could have been later. By 1882 she was definitely an invalid—suffering from an illness diagnosed as a "disease of the nervious system."[4] It was a progressive illness, one which would reduce Mary Kehoe to "childlike helplessness" in her last few years. Her death was probably predictable, but she never complained. By those who knew her best she was described as a "charitable and sympathetic neighbor as well as a generous and cheerful giver, no stranger being ever known to leave her door hungry or empty handed."[5] It was a quiet quality of tenderness more hungered for by her own children than by strangers, but it was short lived. Andrew and his brother and sisters saw her undergo what for them also must have been an unbearably painful change. From the omnipotent mother who nurtured, protected and gave them love, she became even more helpless and childlike than they.

At the same time, Kehoe developed his school boy fascination and talent for the scientific world of magic. Early on, he applied his inventiveness and mechanical genius to tinkering about the farm. (He did not take to the real guts of farming—a fact which, in spite of the labor saving devices he invented, could not have been taken too well by his father.)

Certainly, as the alert child of a socially conscious parent, Andrew was undoubtedly aware of and influenced by some of the important goings on in the world about. Tom Edison from just across the Ohio line had invented the first practical light bulb. The wireless had been invented; and the whole southeast Michigan area around Monroe led the country in disbelief and shock at the defeat at Little Big Horn of their very own General George Custer.

Andrew learned, though, that life in the Kehoe homestead went on just the same. Even as the mother was dying, practices she had earlier set in motion were accentuated. The Sabbath was observed just as religiously and more soberly than ever before. Philip Kehoe became an even stronger leader of the small Catholic congregation in Clinton. The smaller Kehoe children trudged up the road and around the corner to the little white schoolhouse known as the Culbertson School. The children in high school walked, rode horseback, or took the buggy into the high school at nearby Tecumseh.

Aside from formal schooling, pioneer farmers like the Kehoes had to make do for most socialization and self improvement themselves. They formed social/educational organizations made up of neighbors. Social clubs they were called, forerunners and side runners of the Grange. Each farm family took turns hosting its club; and the meetings were usually held once a month.

The meetings were carefully planned in advance, with each member family assigned its part of the program. A typical social club evening was so full of such a variety of activities that there was literally something of interest for every man, woman, and child attending. The evenings also offered plenty of opportunity for talents to be developed or displayed. During the long winter months, the club evening was looked forward to with excitement. With horses and buggies hitched up outside the host farmhouse, fires roared inside in pot bellied stoves, and one event went on after another in the crowded parlors and living rooms.

On the program there was invariably a political/economic discussion of an issue critical to farm prosperity—but after that, the discussions and entertainment were light. Typically, there would be a skit, songs, charades, instrumental solo's, duets or other musical presentations, recitations, and possibly literary discussions. Refreshments were served including baskets of hot homemade "chips," a delicacy from the old country made possible by the Irish potatoes.

The Kehoe's had been mainsprings in the Farmers Social Club while Mary McGovern was healthy. Philip Kehoe saw to it that the family remained no less active in the Club while his wife was an invalid. The club meetings furnished a needed strength to the family and gave the children opportunity to practice and develop talents Philip Kehoe thought important. Perhaps, more importantly, the club meetings gave Philip Kehoe a respectful audience of neighborhood farmers while he expounded on the economic problems of the American farmer.

On these occasions, Andrew Kehoe undoubtedly listened to his father very carefully. He absorbed his father's knowledge; and he absorbed his father's biases. A repeated theme and concern was overproduction. Philip presented or led discussions on questions like, "Farm Waste;" or, "What financial question would do most to benefit the farmer?" or "Is Over-production the cause of our present hard times?" It was the lesson of maintaining farm prices by controlling production, restricting the flow of goods to the market. Emotionally charged, it was to become firmly imbedded in Andrew Kehoe's whole farm philosophy. It made sense but it could also feed a paranoic aversion to sharing one's farm production discoveries with anyone. It was also a philosophy which could support the variety of farming life which Andrew Kehoe liked best—the life of the gentleman farmer.

In fact, the social club discussions appear to have played an important part in preparing Andrew Kehoe for most of the decisive positions he took. Papers were prepared on country taxation, the public school system, township and county government. Questions were covered such as: "What proportion of all the funds for the county is paid for salaries? Used for schools? How are township and county officers chosen? What are their respective duties? How are taxes levied? What is done with the money?" Even the idea of a "Unit School" (possible prototype of a consolidted school) was discussed.

Probably Kehoe also derived from his father his mixed respect and distain for college education, at least in the vocational area. Following an agricultural institute (which brought the Agricultural College and other such matters to the members for thought) organized by area social clubs, the *Tecumseh Herald* reported on Philip Kehoe's review of the Institute at the next social club meeting: "Mr. Kehoe thinks the institute a success, but perhaps no better than the one held last year. He thinks at the college they are better at teaching and preaching than practicing—yet he thinks we may learn from them. . ." Only the practicing farmer could ". . .think and observe and prove whether their theories and experiments are true. They also teach us that experiments are usually expensive and the State Farm could not pay expenses and exist if they did not have the state to back them."[6] The latter might even have included a double message, a warning to Andrew that his inclination to experimentation required certain limits. (The writeup in the Herald concluded by noting that music for the Social Club meeting had been furnished by the "Misses Kehoe.")

In the eyes of the elder Kehoe, education was a very important matter to be judiciously used and evaluated. The children, without exception, were gifted and ripe for learning but their education was to be selected according to their needs. To Philip Kehoe, advanced formal education of the girls seemed more important than for the boys; and he provided for it. If the girls were inclined to higher learning, he would see that they had the opportunity to get it. This could mean attending the high school in Tecumseh, or even the nunnery in Monroe. It could even mean college. As for the boys, they could depend on the farm.

By 1888, one older sister, Mary, had already joined the convent in Monroe. It was a move in the finest Irish Catholic tradition; and it made Philip Kehoe justly proud.

Also, in 1888, under "High School Happenings" in the Tecumseh Herald, the class reporter wrote, "We are pleased to welcome to the Senior Class Miss Frances Kehoe. She has attended but one year (out of four), but has made up several studies outside of school, and as she is talented and determined we feel confident that she will go through with the class."[7] Little more than six months later she graduated with her class, one of fourteen graduates out of the forty nine who had started four years earlier. Frances, who was three to four years older than Andrew, was obviously a brilliant girl.

Although Frances was not a class officer, she was given the honor and responsibility of writing and reading the class poem. The commencement exercises were held at the Tecumseh Opera House on a hot evening less than a week away from the Fourth of July. There's little doubt that Andrew was there with the rest of the Kehoes and the townspeople, all anxious to honor the graduates. According to the Tecumseh News, "The audience at the Opera House. . .were subjected to great annoyance by the very disagreeable manner in which the lights acted. They were not lighted until nearly dark, and then flickered only a few minutes and went out. Several times this was repeated and when the class filed in and took their seats on the stage, they were almost invisible to the audience. Had it not been for two kerosene lamps, the first part of the program would have had to be given in Stygian darkness. All this was disagreeable to the audience and extremely mortifying to the class. We would respectfully suggest to the management that a little previous attention to the lighting apparatus might obviate the oft repeated trouble and save a vast amount of just complaint on the part of the public. By the way, what an improvement the electric light would be."[8]

In spite of the lighting trouble fixed upon by the News, it ultimately cleared well enough for all the class presentations to be made. As Andrew sat in the audience, he too, may have fantasized about the miracle of electricity. He was probably already fascinated by it. (Edison had invented the first practical light bulb ten years before, but its general application was still a ways off, awaiting the interest of young men like Andrew Kehoe.)

If seventeen year old Andrew Kehoe was daydreaming about electric lights, he may also have become perplexed, at least momentarily, that it was his sister on the stage instead of him. Andrew had always gotten along well in school. Classmates described him as "smart without trying to be clever." He was studious in matters that interested him; and he was at the head of his physics class. Probably, though, Andrew Kehoe was never a serious candidate for high school graduation. Contrary to published reports there is no record that he ever graduated from Tecumseh High School.

The basic reason for Andrew's not attending high school was probably to be found in the commencement exercises which took place the following summer. As part of the commencement, a debate was held on the position: "Resolved that a boy should be taught only those things which he is likely to need in practical life." The positive team included Andrew's sister, Margaret. Taking the tack that since "knowledge has no end but goodness," the positive team argued against an advanced, classical and liberal education. "Rather," they said, "let him give his whole and undivided attention to his particular calling, which when thoroughly mastered, will be a source of pleasure and profit not only for himself, but for society in general."[9] Andrew's calling by heritage was to be a farmer. By inclination it was something else. It presented a frustration for him probably not experienced by his less studious younger brother.

On November 5th, 1890, Mary McGovern Kehoe finally died in a state of paralysis—55 years of age. In the obituary the family wrote, "Though we who have been left behind sadly mourn her loss, yet we feel thankful to our Heavenly Father for his mercies toward us in removing her so slowly and gently from our midst and making it less hard to say, "Thy Will be done." Frances, with her talent for verse, possibly wrote the poem which was affixed:

A precious one from us has gone
A voice we loved is still
A place is vacant in our home
Which never can be filled
God in his wisdom has recalled
The boon his love had given
And though the body slumbers here
The soul is safe in Heaven.[10]

So it was over. The death had come long after the mourning, perhaps long after the initial repression of pain. For eighteen year old Andrew Kehoe it probably also came long after repression of the feeling of being cheated and of the thought that even a most loved one cannot be trusted. It was a thought, however, that would not remain subdued. The vacancy which the mother's illness and death had created was in Andrew himself. Probably, as Andrew's investment in his mother retreated with her health, he turned more to himself and his own private world. Acquaintances knew him as quiet and reserved, and all those things that incline people to describe others as "peculiar." By no means had he withdrawn from people, but even as a boy, people sensed when they should back off from Andrew Kehoe. He somehow transmitted a sense of temper that was better left untampered with.

Young Kehoe had also developed another trait of character which can be traced directly to the long nature of his mother's death—a death seemingly without dying. In the absence of a true episode of grief, unrequited mourning may well have taken over. It displayed itself in the pronounced tendency of the young man to brood over troubles and to carry that brooding insistently within himself.

While turning inward was possibly a part of Andrew Kehoe's adjustment to his mother's dying years, he probably turned outward to at least one individual—his father.

Philip Kehoe, through sheer strength of will power had carried the family through the years of crisis. To the outside world, Philip Kehoe may not have been an awesome individual but for his family he made it all happen. While he was no longer breeding children, he increased his successes at breeding cattle and took special pride in his prize bulls. The farm prospered and held even through hard times for farmers. Most important, he had held the family together as one. He had seen to the children's educational, shelter, musical, and vocational needs—and he had not neglected their social well being. It was an accomplishment of strength.

As was expected of Andrew, he elected to remain with his father following the mother's death (Lewis was initially there too, but Lewis was inclined toward the wild side in his young days.). It wasn't something Andrew appeared particularly suited to but he had elected to stake his future with the farm and his father. While some of his sisters moved out to pursue careers outside the home, Andrew stayed on. It promised to be a good and satisfying life for him— Philip Kehoe and Son.

The Farmer's Social Club continued to be just as active as it ever had, but Andrew now became a regular and featured performer of skits—a particular variety labeled "Dialogues." A common program item up to his twenty fourth year was, "Dialogue—Andrew Kehoe and Others." The performances were undoubtedly satisfying to Andrew. They gave him the center of the stage, a chance to display his wit, and some obvious appreciation and acclamation. A note in the Tecumseh Herald of January 31st, 1896 summarized the most recent meeting of the Farmer's Social Club. It included, ". . .Andrew Kehoe, assisted by a friend, presented a very comical dialogue."

Andrew's increasing participation also complemented well his father's continuing dominance in the more sober aspects of the Club's programming. Andrew listened to his father's continuing presentations on farm economics and politics, but kept his own participation at a level more fitting for younger men.

But then, the nice idyllic existence with his father ended. It probably ended before Andrew was ready for it. It clearly ended in a way Andrew would not have chosen. Philip Kehoe, at more than sixty years of age, took on his third wife—a comparatively young widow from Adrian. Frances Wilder, with her own offspring comfortably raised, was still young enough to be Philip Kehoe's daughter, and young enough to bear him more children. It was a marriage that probably none of the Kehoe children could have found very acceptable, least of all Andrew. As the first son, Andrew could very well see his inheritance flying out the window. Almost certainly, Philip Kehoe would be outlived by his healthy young wife; and Andrew and the other Kehoe children would be left out in the cold.

The father probably infuriated the family further by presenting his new bride with a brand new brick farmhome. It was a labor of love for the old man who obviously spared no expense in building the distinctive home. For Philip, the remarkable residence was also a symbol of his own success in life, a crowning achievement made possible by his acquired wealth. Its very location presented clear and unmistakable visible evidence of his success. Located directly across the road from the old homestead which was suddenly humble in comparison, the residence was castle and yardstick all rolled into one.

Predictably, Andrew Kehoe did not take to his father's new bride and he moved out. If rift was the basic cause of it, however, it may not have been the pretext.

There have been a variety of reports about Kehoe's whereabouts over the next eight years. Most likely, Kehoe took the occasion of his father's marriage to follow up on his inventive and mechanical inclinations. The country's enchantment with the electric light was

203

little more than beginning 20 years after Edison's discovery, but it was definitely beginning and underway. In 1896, the Tecumseh High School physics class began studying electricity. Farm Social Clubs began looking at the history of artificial light; and here and there specialized courses in electrical application were being offered.

Electricity was, in fact, a natural for Kehoe. It was magical, it was clean, it was useful and powerful, and it could be destructive. Although the precise timing is not known, he enrolled at an electrical school in St. Louis, Missouri. (According to a sister he suffered a bad fall there and was in a state of semi-consciousness for several weeks.)[11] Reportedly, he then worked as an electrician for a large St. Louis Park; and then became employed as a lineman in Iowa. (The latter employment was confirmed by Kehoe.)

The whereabouts of Kehoe for the remainder of his absence from the Tecumseh area is unknown. There are unconfirmed reports that he had taken short courses at Michigan State College, but the timing of those courses if they existed at all was probably following his return to the Tecumseh area. When he did return, neighbors were under the impression that he had attended several colleges. It was an illusion that Kehoe somehow needed to create himself.

The reason for his return is similarly unclear, but he did return to his home about 1905. Whether some failure, or some injury might have precipitated abandonment of his absence is unknown. To a major extent, the entire eight year absence is a black mystery box.

In all probability, he returned because his father needed him and asked for him, or because he reasoned with good cause that his father required his help. Philip Kehoe was no longer the strong, towering old man. He was simply old; and he had become crippled with arthritis. It was no longer possible for Philip Kehoe to manage the farm.

No one, however, was pronouncing the end of the old man's manhood. In 1902, another daughter, Irene, had been born—and she had quickly come to be adored by her father. To Philip Kehoe's previous children, she was hardly a welcome new sister. She was the unwelcome outsider.

When Andrew returned home around 1905, he took up residence in the old homestead, and worked the farm. He took meals in his father's place across the road, but he maintained his distance from both his young step sister and her mother.

Sometime before 1911 and possibly sooner, Andrew Kehoe apparently did take some agricultural short courses at Michigan State. He could well have met Nellie there as she enrolled for a similar course or as she brushed up on needed education courses for her teaching—or they could have met through the Church. (A post disaster news account, highly suspect because of glaring inaccuracies, pictured Andrew so enrolled from 1897–1900. An

204

alleged college acquaintance described him as a great mixer, life of the party, who loved to play practical jokes. As an example, the acquaintance cited the case of a young naive minister roommate who was repeatedly tricked by Andrew and a girl acquaintance into thinking that a desirable young girl wished to rendevois with him. At least two elements seemed to ring true in the story—Andrew did have a certain social presence—hardly hail fellow, well met, though, and he was accomplished in the art of deception.)[12]

In contrast to media accounts, however, the college has absolutely no record of either Andrew or Nellie Kehoe attending there; but Andrew, himself, claimed he attended the college, and other reports of Andrew's attendance were so persistent that unrecorded short agricultural courses offer the best explanation.

In actually managing his father's farm, Kehoe kept true to his ingrained farm philosophy. He converted more and more of the acreage to pastureland; and, encouraged by the presence of the Clinton woolen mill, became a serious sheep herder. At the same time, he and his neighbors were plagued by maurauding killer dogs—so much so that he received payment from the Clinton County authorities in recompense for his sheep losses.[13]

The stories which circulated later to the effect that Kehoe never did know how to farm appear to be completely unfounded. He managed his father's farm, continued its prosperity, and adjusted its methods and its products to the times. As part of that methodology, he introduced the use of explosives for clearing the land. Where he learned how, no one knows for sure, but he adopted the technique as a new toy. It was an experience in destruction, harmless destruction, perhaps, but he loved it.

He did not love his step mother. Even neighbors could tell there was tension between the two. Possibly, some of Andrew's hostility toward her was reflected to the daughter. As a nine year old, Irene knew her half brother hardly at all. He was unsociable, in fact, showed no outward affection or interest toward her at all—with one glaring and tell tale exception and possibly another.

The glaring exception was found in Kehoe's dislike of cats. Irene had a pet cat and Kehoe killed it. That's all that is known of the incident. He may have killed the cat simply because it was an annoyance to him, or he may have killed the cat because it was Irene's. A simlar occurrence later in Bath supports a preference for the former, the first overt but unrecognized symptom of an ominous character trait. The other possible exception bore not so much on Irene as on her mother. The incident, as reported by Ellsworth, has become legendary, but Ellsworth's report of the tragedy was in error.

The day was September 17th, 1911 —a beautiful sunny Sunday fall day.[14] Irene and her mother had been out gathering hickory nuts in the woods just to the rear of the Kehoe farm home. With lunch time approaching, Mrs. Kehoe returned to the house to prepare lunch while Irene remained in the woods gathering nuts. The day was warm enough to allow the use of the summer kitchen in the rear. It was one of the luxuries of the remarkable house Philip had built for her. As she moved to start her preparations, she was probably quite aware of the others in the house. Philip, who could move about now only with the aid of canes was probably seated in his favorite location on the front porch. Andrew was in the house; and Andrew's younger sister Margaret, who was staying with her father for a time, was probably in an upstairs bedroom.

Standing on a rug in front of the gasoline stove, Mrs. Kehoe attempted with a burning match to light the burner. There had been talk about this particular stove before—some sort of trouble with its lighting. It was an early variety with an overhead tank.

Suddenly, there was a flash explosion, and agonizing screams rended the entire house and outdoors. Irene raced for the kitchen just in time to see her mother's head engulfed in flames, her hair afire. The old man was there too. In a frantic and futile effort to reach his younger wife, he had thrown his canes aside and struggled desperately into the kitchen. Andrew, too, was there. Although Mrs. Kehoe was standing on a rug, no one had the sense to attempt to wrap her in it. Instead, Andrew mistakenly doused her with water—an act which only aggravated the burning. Quickly, however, the fire was subdued, and Mrs. Kehoe was carried to bed in her bedroom.

Irene and Andrew then ran the short distances down the road to the Murphys who owned one of the few phones in the area. It was about noon when the Murphy's young daughter-in-law, Hettie, heard a knock at the front porch door. It caught her preparing dinner for the rest of her family which was temporarily absent from the home. As Hettie reached the front porch door Andrew was standing there. He was not puffing and didn't give the appearance of excitement—but he asked, "Would you call Dr. Tuttle?" Hettie was concerned. "Is someone sick?" she asked.

Andrew replied simply, "No, Fannie got burned." Almost as an afterthought he added, "Would you call the priest, too?" He also asked his young neighbor if she would be able to come up to the Kehoe house to help. Hettie Murphy was pregnant at the time and she had her hands full with her own dinner being prepared on the stove; but as soon as she was free she threw away her apron and ran for Philip Kehoe's. In the excitement, she wasn't sure when she first noticed Irene. She noticed only that the pail filled with hickory nuts was still clenched tightly in the little girl's hand. (The shaking child had recovered, however, and having returned to her house with Kehoe, bravely helped remove the high boots and full length corset from her prostrate and agonizing mother.)

When Hettie Matthews reached the Kehoe residence she was quickly ushered into her older friend's bedroom. As she entered the room, Philip's wife was lying on her back, eyes wide open facing the door—a picture of intense suffering. As she saw Hettie she lifted both arms and extended them toward her. All she could say was "Hettie, Hettie!" In her pathetic condition she was incapable of saying anything else. Her skin was completely blackened from the burning, her clothing had been burned off and, even as she gestured to Hettie, burned and lifeless skin dropped from her extended arms.

Hettie Murphy was completely stunned by what she saw but gave her such moral comfort as she could. At roughly the same time both the Catholic priest and the doctor arrived. They had come from Clinton as quickly as horse and buggy could get them there. Only a glancing examination was needed, however, to determine that the condition of Frances Wilder Kehoe was more a condition for the priest than the doctor. Under intense pain, she remained conscious for a time, while the family collie kept a moaning vigil under her bedroom window. A few hours later, she died.[15]

Years later, and only after the Bath disaster, did other versions of this tragedy appear. These versions were undocumented and without any eye witness support. However, they could have contained a kernel of truth. A composite of such versions would run essentially like this:

While Philip Kehoe and his wife were away from their home (in town or at church), Andrew walked across the road from his home in the old homestead and tampered with the kitchen oil stove. When Mrs. Kehoe returned to fix dinner, it exploded, Andrew watched her burn for awhile and then threw water on her. Before Frances died she indicated that Andrew Kehoe was responsible. People around had their suspicions about Andrew, but nothing could ever be proved.

That was the composite version, and Monty Ellsworth's account was simply a variation. His reporting it was logical enough. It was undoubtedly gossipy conjecture that the Bath Disaster had stimulated or reawakened in the Tecumseh area. However, Ellsworth mistakenly reported Andrew's age as 14 when the step mother was killed. He was actually forty. Ellsworth either misheard "40" as "14" or he misread his notes. However, the gossip reported to him was clearly uninformed about the facts of the matter: the stove had been troublesome before; Philip Kehoe had never left for church—he had stopped attending years earlier because of his condition; Mrs. Kehoe would not have been the only person possibly using the stove—36 year old Margaret Kehoe was staying at the home at the time; Kehoe did not stand idly by—he tried to help, but stupidly, apparently, made the mistake of using water on his burning step mother; and Kehoe's stature within the family was apparently not questioned. One other thing—had Frances Kehoe indicated in her deathbed that anyone was responsible, such evidence would have stood in court.

Gossip and fact did rely on common truth, however. There was ill will toward the stepmother, possible hatred. Kehoe was there, reacted seemingly calmly and dispassionately after putting out the fire, and he witnessed the grotesque results of a woman consumed by fire.

All the evidence pointed to accidental death for Mrs. Kehoe. The other possibility exists in retrospect because of possible motive and apparent capability—but the possibility is so remote, given the full circumstances, that it should be dismissed. In covering the tragedy in its September 19th edition (1911), the Tecumseh Herald reported that the explosion was due to some defect in the stove. Of the family, the article stated, "A large family of step children mourn the loss of a faithful friend and mother."

With the death of the step mother, a new life loomed for Andrew as well as the remainder of the Kehoe family. Andrew moved across to his father's house but carried on his very serious courtship of Nellie Price of Lansing. The two apparently had very much in common. They were interested in education. Each came from strong Roman Catholic families which had migrated from Ireland. (County Tipperary, the Price home county, was hardly more than a stone's throw away from County Wexford, home of the Kehoe's.) Each was apparently strongly rooted in agriculture. Each was of mature years where neither might be expecting children. Both families were directly or indirectly in touch with relative wealth. Andrew was the oldest boy of his family and Nellie was the oldest daughter in hers. They had experienced the pressures of high family demands and expectations. Nellie's mother had died when she was eighteen, just as had Andrew's. Each had led rather private, inconspicuous lives, and each family was headed by strong, achieving father figures.

As a wedding gift, probably, the old man gave Andrew use of the homestead and the 25 acres it stood on. Andrew put the old homestead back to shape, refurnished and equipped it, and proudly awaited his wedding day. Strangely, none of the Tecumseh area papers carried any mention of the event (May 14, 1912), and only brief mention of it was carried in the Lansing papers. If Andrew was in any way enamoured of Nellie's relationship to her famous uncle, his use of the media absolutely didn't show it. Nor was there any mention in the Tecumseh press when the new Mrs. and Mr. Kehoe took up housekeeping at the homestead after their short honeymoon.

The warm and attractive Nellie was an immediate hit not only with the neighbors, but with the family as well. Toward the child, Irene, she was friendly and affectionate. Toward the neighbors she was sociable. Rather abruptly, however, something of a change took place, something of a withdrawal. It may have been related to Andrew's growing if not sudden break with the church.

A version of that break was that Andrew was assessed $400 to help pay for the building of a new church—that he refused and dropped out of the church, never allowing his wife to attend either. Actually, the family parish in Clinton never did build a new church. A first Catholic church was build in neighboring Tecumseh and money could have conceivably been solicited for that church. More probably, a heavy contribution was solicited from Philip Kehoe whose residence was on the Tecumseh side of Allen Road—for some affiliation with the Tecumseh Church did take place for other members of Philip's family. What is undoubtedly true is that Andrew Kehoe would have been angered at either or both solicitations and that the occasion could have been the rationale for a break that must have been more deep seated. However, the immediate net result was that Andrew stopped attending church. His wife, however, regularly continued her Sunday horse and buggy excursions into the Clinton Church—alone.

The very late break with a church which was of utmost importance to his father, to his brother and sisters, and to his wife was an outstanding incident in an emerging pattern of probably paranoic behavior. It was behavior which seemed to coincide with other critical changes in the core Kehoe family and Andrew Kehoe's relationship to it.

Philip Kehoe's indulgence and concern toward his adoring youngest daughter naturally increased with the death of his younger wife. It increased with the worsening condition of his arthritis; and he took steps to put his affairs in order.

Less than a year after his wife's death, and three months following Andrew's marriage, he wrote his will. It was a detailed and typewritten will signed in a clear but shaky hand by the old gentleman. The time was August 14th, 1912 and Irene was by then ten years of age.

In the will, Philip Kehoe took steps to provide for each of his children and his two grandchildren. For a wealthy Irish immigrant, steeped in the old world tradition of leaving the entire estate to the first son, it was an interesting if not a strange will.

The will, in its original form named Andrew as Executor. It was a decision which clearly showed continuing confidence in Andrew. However, to the typewritten designation was added the scribbled name of a second executor, Charles Marr of Wyandotte. It was almost as though Philip didn't have complete confidence in Andrew.

In the bequeaths, the Kehoe real estate was divided primarily between Andrew and Lewis, but with Philip's second homestead forty going to Margaret, Agnes and Irene as a home until Irene was

209

to reach her 21st birthday, at which time it was to be sold, share and share alike. However, the key properties bequeathed to Andrew and Lewis were given only on condition that (1) Andrew deliver mortgages for his new 160 acres to his four sisters, Catherine, Margaret, Mary and Martha payable in fourteen annual installments, and (2) that Louis deliver similar mortgages to his sisters, Agnes and Frances. In effect, the brothers were given the choice of complying or selling the land and dividing the proceeds among the girls for amounts stipulated in the will and keeping the balance if any remained. What Andrew was given was the chance to buy his inheritance from his sisters! In addition, the will provided for a large cash inheritance to Irene, and a smaller one to Philip's now motherless grandsons.

In addition, Margaret, who with Agnes was living at home at the time, was recommended to be Irene's guardian. Finally, the will included a warning:

> In case any of the beneficiaries in this my last will and testament shall dispute or contest the legality or validity of this will, or the competency of myself to make and execute this will, or any manner interfere with the proof, establishment and execution of this will, then and in such case, all provisions herein made for such beneficiary are hereby revoked. . .

It was as though Philip was very much aware of stated or unstated attacks upon the competency behind his latest marriage and child, of his indulgence in the girl. So being, he had taken steps to be sure that if those attacks were legally mounted and renewed after his death, they would not succeed.

Philip also made one other stipulation which might have been particularly nauseous to Andrew. For reasons of "greater security" he instructed that the 25 acre homestead already in Andrew's name be offered as additional collateral for payment he was to make to two of his sisters.

A year later, Philip modified the will to facilitate a change in planning for Irene. Upon his death, his homestead was to be sold immediately. In addition, he specified that furniture of his last marriage was to go to Irene, while the remainder of the furniture was to be divided among the four daughters who were not in the nunnery. Apparently, Philip's stock and farm equipment had already been given to Andrew or had been divided with his brother. Finally, Philip bequeathed his iron safe to Irene. On the surface, at least, Irene looked like a surprising choice for the safe. Symbolically, the safe could have stood for many things, but most explicitly, it symbolized the head of the house.[16]

Between the time that the original will and its modification were written, Philip Kehoe had slipped noticeably. At the time of the modification in 1913, he could no longer sign his name. He could produce his mark, but that was all. Even the canes were no longer able to support him, and his crippled but massive body was reduced to moving by wheelchair. His favorite spot on his front porch became more difficult for him to reach. Still, when the weather was nice, he wheeled himself out to sit and look. He could see up and down the road, unimpeded. Across was the pastoral view of the old homestead. Even without trying, he seemed to be keeping an eye on his eldest son.

The elder Kehoe had a substitute pasttime favorite when the weather wasn't so nice—at least when Irene was home from school., With a lap full of papers he had selected from his safe, the old gentleman would roll his wheel chair into Irene's room—anxious to familiarize her with them. Since his wife's death he had become even more loving and protective of the child than before. She was more than simply a loving child, she symbolized the wife he had loved— and she symbolized the last hurrah of his manhood. As the old man prepared for his inevitable death, his planning for Irene with Irene became a satisfying experience of love, to be repeated over and over again.

In his sensitivity and alertness to his adult children, he may have recognized that, after his death, Irene's future might be better protected by a concerned relative on her mother's side of the family. Margaret who gave Irene what mothering she received, understood that this was her father's wish.

On January 8th, 1915 the titan of the Kehoe clan passed away. Margaret, in keeping with her father's wishes, was appointed guardian of Irene. Also, as her father wished, Margaret moved with her young half sister to another state—for the fine education and the second family Philip had wanted for the girl.

Andrew, in the meantime, dutifully, perhaps, but begrudgingly, commenced carrying out his father's instructions as executor of the estate. The responsibility he had been given was no small one. It meant new duties which had to be sandwiched in between the regular responsibilities of running the farm. Under the circumstances the shared pleasure of executor stature was mixed with the unpleasantness of distributing an inheritance which could (by the Irish tradition of primo geniture) have been his alone.

It was hardly by chance that neighbors began to notice a change in Nellie. She was no longer as friendly and outgoing as she had been. She kept more and more to herself. Possibly, Nellie was homesick for her own family. Possibly she was concerned with the health of her now aging father. But there was also a difference in Andrew. The suspicious, and brooding side of his personality came to the surface, at least temporarily. He became materially convinced that a neighbor who sold him a quantity of sheep had somehow defrauded him. A hint of depression had begun to mark the quality of the Kehoe marriage.

When Lawrence Price died in early 1917, it opened up a whole new

211

world of possibilities. His estate included the old Price homestead—the farm in Bath Township which had been so much a part of Nellie's childhood. It also included 80 acres of excellent farmland, with superior farm buildings—as well as a farmhouse which was equipped with the latest conveniences. For both Nellie and Andrew it looked like the chance for a dream come true. Nellie could be back home, so to speak, close by the sisters she'd spent a near lifetime with. Andrew, on the other hand, saw the chance for a new start, a challenge. When Nellie approached her aunt with the wish to buy the Price Farm, the property was set aside.

Andrew then took steps to dispose of the old Kehoe homestead. By early 1919, Andrew had arranged to sell the property to the Allens, old acquaintances of the Kehoes and one of the pioneer families of the area. To the young Allen wife, Kehoe displayed high spirits over the impending move to Bath. It was going to be a good move. The land was excellent and the buildings were extensive; and they were a definite improvement over the ones he had.

In the further discussions Mrs. Allen had with Andrew Kehoe, two things stood out. She was impressed with the sensitivity he showed when he learned she had injured her leg because of defective flooring in an upstairs bedroom. Tears had come to his eyes as she pointed the floor defect out to him.

Mrs. Allen's other impression was of the one unkind remark she had ever heard Andrew Kehoe make. In speaking of his father's family he said, "My father married three times and had brats by each wife." It wasn't so much what he said as the way he said it. Mrs. Allen found the remark uncomfortably chilling and pushed it to the back of her mind.

Neither the Allens nor anyone else saw much of the Kehoes after they moved. Andrew still needed to be around on estate business somewhat until 1921—and he came back once for a reunion at the Culbertson School, but that was about all. From relatives they knew Andrew was on the Bath school board, that he led a farm bureau recruiting drive, and that he was serving as a township clerk. Andrew Kehoe, they guessed, was making a name for himself.

**

Andrew was not the only Kehoe offspring making a name for himself. The fact is that Philip Kehoe left behind a truly remarkable family.[17] He had fathered nine daughters and two sons through three different marriages. Of the nine daughters only four married. Of his two sons only Patrick Lewis had off spring (a single son). Three of the daughters chose careers of caring for children in one way or another.

212

Agnes, nine years older than Andrew, became a nurse for children. Martha, a year older than Andrew, and Mary, eleven years older lived outstanding lives of public service as Nuns, teachers in the Catholic Church. Frances, the brilliant sister who completed her high school education in two years, became a practicing attorney. For the turn of the century, it was a rare accomplishment. Andrew's sister, Martha (Sister Clementine) had joined the Catholic order in 1892, to continue a distinguished career in teaching. Before Sister Clementine's career ended, she taught in schools all over lower Michigan. She was an excellent typist and seamstress. For classes she drew her own maps and architectural models. Those who knew her best described her as prayerful, exact and enduring—with a quiet and retiring spirit. However, she was unflinching in the face of difficulty. "Occasionally she would be hurt but never would she show the slightest degree of retaliation, or answer sharply, but always meekly endure."[18] Definitely, the traces were there of the same upbringing experienced by Andrew—but not of the same trauma.

Andrew's older half sister, Mary joined the order at St. Marys when Andrew was fourteen in 1886. Before leaving her home, Mary (Sister Christine) had ample opportunity to watch this eldest boy as he faced and reacted to the expectations of his birthright, and to the devastation of a mother who could no longer respond in her drift toward infantility and death. Sister Christina's extraordinary insights in working with boys may well have been gained from empathies she experienced with Andrew. Her inclination to sneak cakes to boys being punished in the school cloak room was well recognized. It was said that Sister Christina was endowed by God with a natural sympathy and understanding of the character of the boy! In 25 years at St. Vincents' facility for boys, she helped shape countless boys to manhood and even toward Priesthood. Her long career of service ended in 1924; and she was spared the knowledge and the trauma of her brother's tragedy.

Commenting on her life, Father Frank Hardy said, "Only the recording angel can measure the scope of Sister Christina's influence in that one parish alone upon the boys of the past who are the men of today..."[19] From a single family source, apparently, great forces for both good and evil had been loosed.

Professional opinion on Kehoe which was offered at the time of the disaster, lacked information on Kehoe's background, but spoke to the symptoms. To one expert, Kehoe was unmoral rather than immoral—the result of some childhood trauma which later festered.[20]

Doctor Dobson of the Veteran's Hospital in Battle Creek referred to Kehoe as a paranoic, "the most dangerous of all patients." He suggested that the condition comes about "when a person deliberates over a real or fancied wrong and finally arrives at a state of mind in which he imagines a persecution out of all proportion to the basis."[21]

A psychiatric discussion in the Detroit News also concluded that Kehoe's actions were paranoic.[22] The suggestion was also made that Kehoe, because of his mental state, might not have considered the children or their fate at all. Such a person, it was noted might appear completely sane in all areas unrelated to the persecutory delusion.

At the same time, ten physicians in Owosso, marshalled perhaps by the reporter who had aided the Clinton County Prosecutor, reached a concensus that Kehoe was a manic depressive. They ruled out paranoia on the belief that a paranoic would not take his own life.[23]

All in all, the professional opinion was consistent. Most simplistically, they saw in Kehoe a man suffering from the hallucination that the school had caused his financial ruin. The blowing up of the school was the one logical way he could manifest his displeasure at it's existence and at the same time get even with those who were responsible for it.[24]

Of course, the precise dynamics of pathology which led to Kehoe's murderous climax remains clouded. With all that is known of Kehoe, too little is known. From the time Kehoe left home in 1897 until his return around 1905 practically nothing is known—other than that he attended electrical school, and worked as an electrical lineman. While so employed, he may have suffered the head injury described by his sister immediately after the Bath Disaster (or she may have invented a less stigmatized reason for his maniacal behavior). That incident (plus another scalp wound described by the sister) at least raised the possibility of brain damage or brain tumor. The brain tumor possibility can probably be discounted because of the long number of years which lapsed between the alleged fall and Kehoe's assault. The possibility of more recent brain damage can be discounted because of the long history of irrational behavior exhibited by the man.

As to heredity, there appears to be nothing in the Kehoe family background to substantiate any allegation of psychosis any more serious than senility. Allegations that Andrew and his brother and sisters were "queer ducks" seem to be based primarily on a retrospective assessment of Andrew, which stimulated unfounded opinions about the other children (one youngster's wildness had been noted; and a sister had supposedly been caught sniffing chloroform on an occasion). The record is overwhelming that the other children in the family grew up to live unusually productive lives.

By eliminating heredity, the path leads to psycho-social factors as the major if not the sole cause of Kehoe's unparalleled attack on a community, its children and himself. The dynamics, in fact, may be fairly simple.

As the first son after a long line of girls in this strong Irish family, Andrew was subjected to great pampering, switching off, and periodic comparable neglect. From his towering, stern and successful father, there were unusually great pressures for performance, for compliance and for submission (the prominent traits of orderliness in the girls were augmented by traits of stubborness in the boys, and by acting and artfulness in Andrew to avoid the perceived wrath of a loving but demanding father).

The development of conscious was undoubtedly accompanied by destructive fantasies toward both his mother, his father, and his brother and sisters. However, for young Andrew, the child nightmares of a dying mother were to become more than nightmares—they became reality. The mother's condition encouraged predisposition in the child to a private world, a make believe world, to magical thinking which could wipe out death, or to humor which could make light of it. Somehow, the prevasive morbidity of the home had to be handled. For the child, all the love and all the anger ever directed at the mother had to produce the complete range of emotion: guilt for past conduct and evil wishes; great grief and sadness; unconscious hatred for a mother bent on abandonment; suspicion of a God who would allow it, and of a father who would accept it. The long death of Kehoe's mother probably robbed him of any opportunity to resolve the conflicts with parents and peers which adolescence provides. In Kehoe's case, his conflicts were sharply heightened and repressed: the lingering death of the mother stimulated a characteristic quality of brooding in the son. Her actual death was preceded by grief in the son which could never fully vent itself and by severe and unacceptable anger at the dying mother. The groundwork was laid for a severely persecuting conscience.

The slow departure of his mother robbed him of a buffer in relating to the father and triggered an especially close tie to him.[25] Kehoe became very identified with his home and with his father's political and farm philosophies. Quite likely, he also developed the strongest of ties with the one room school he attended. His sister not only taught at the school, but it is likely that his father served on the controlling board of the country school—one of the "minor" governmental positions he was later described as holding. It was not uncommon at the time for the daughters of school board members to be favored for such teaching positions. Perhaps most important, however, was the emotional nurturing the country school gave Andrew Kehoe. As Alma Mater, (foster mother) replacing a dying mother, it became supercharged with emotion for Kehoe.

The actual death of Kehoe's mother undoubtedly reawakened all the feelings Andrew held toward her, and, because of the nature of a

215

death delayed probably brought on more self persecution—for being able to accept the death too well.

After her death, Kehoe stayed on at the farm as a dutiful son should. The old man kept the farm family and the farm life going; and Andrew was very much a complementary part of it. In carrying out the political and social responsibilities through the Farm Social Club, Andrew was the sought after performer with his clever and comical "dialogues." And he continued to honor, respect, and even idolize much that he saw in his father.

The bubble of apparently happy farm life burst for Andrew when Philip Kehoe remarried—and Andrew left. At least temporarily, he could not tolerate the father's erection of a new brick edifice in preference over the family cottage and all it had meant to the family.

When Kehoe returned to assist his father, he came back with his electrical schooling and experience, but perhaps little else to show for nearly eight years. His stories of impressive educational experiences may have been contrived and, probably, his life away hadn't been one of success or plesure to him. Possibly for the first time, the elements of destructive impulses and paranoic thought were brought together. The victimizing last wife of his father was burned to death, however accidentally. The pet kitten of Kehoe's small half sister was killed by him; and his love and expertise for dynamiting began to assert itself. Following his step mother's death, Kehoe shortly married a woman whose own family remarkably mirrored his own—a woman who carried the mother role when her own mother died. With the death of his father, Kehoe became the executor of an estate which he may have thought was rightfully his. With at least underlying anger, he then decided to give up the Kehoe homestead and all it had stood for. Using the money he received from selling his father's property, he exuberantly made his down payment on the old Lawrence Price place (the Price Homestead). With that action Kehoe appeared to be setting out to make it on his own, to be the man his father was—but the way was set by renunciation he could not tolerate of values which had been important to him. The stage was set for tragedy.

Guilt occasioned by giving up his father's estate (and reflected in fears that he didn't get the money it was worth) was transferred to the estate he bought into. Almost immediately he became plagued by the idea that he had been gypped—that he had paid too big a price. For Kehoe, the delusion became so overriding that he rejected making any further payment to the authority of the estate once his responsibilities as executor of his father's estate were concluded in 1921. Undoubtedly, in the confusing distortion taking place in Kehoe's subconscious, he was rejecting the payment for property which was rightly his by inheritance. The Price estate and the Kehoe estate were becoming as one.

For a time, Kehoe's battle with the estate of his wife's family remained isolated—overshadowed by the brilliance of his fresh new start in Bath. He was the pioneering farmer with fresh ideas. Through his wife, he was welcomed as a returning family, eager to restore old ties.

And then came the consolidated red brick school. In appearance, symbolism and economics it was destined from the start to be a natural Kehoe enemy. It was headed by an authoritarian figure; and replaced the old "homestead" country schools by consolidation. It was the consolidated family, Kehoe had grown to despise. It was also supported by a strong father type, Kyes, who consistently favored and fought for his own son.

Kehoe's initial attack on the school took clearly rational and legitimate form. He entered the political arena—became the leader in the fight against high spending and won important initial victories. With coincidental appointment to the important township post he was on the verge, if he had not already surpassed, of surpassing his father in accomplishment—of becoming the success the first son of this outstanding family was expected to be.

But then it started coming apart. Kehoe, overwhelmed with authority problems, himself, didn't know how to handle the authority he had won on the school board. Partly, this may have been due to his own frustration. On the board, all he could do was cut pennies. His basic aim of going back, of eliminating the consolidated school was impossible.

When the voters turned against Kehoe he felt betrayed. He had worked unremittingly for economies in their behalf and still they were turning against him. The conspiracy he sensed, was broadening. Then as Kehoe's delusions increased, his wife's health began to suffer. The past was irrevocably on a collision course with the future.

When Kehoe experienced very definite defeat at the polls from his peers, it was accompanied by his wife's increasing absence due to ill health. The fantasy of a deserting and needed mother increased, and the repressed anger surfaced. The great success which was demanded and expected of him had slipped from his grasp. His world was in a shambles and he sought revenge. (The unconscious wish to destroy the consolidated school became conscious.)

In the end, past and present blurred into one. Working under the intimate foundation of the school, he planted his explosive devices which would destroy everything the school stood for. It was unwanted authority, as was its Superintendent. It was his father, the side he hated. It was his father's new house—and it was the children he had come to hate.   The Price estate was his estate, the estate which should have been given to him. His wife was his mother, was his step mother—and he determined to utterly destroy his world.

217

Strangely, until nearly the very end, he maintained the facade and deception of sanity. Until nearly the very end he was able to distinguish between friend and imagined foe. The love he felt for his father was separated out, transferred if only temporarily to arthritic old Mr. McMullen. "You made a mistake," he said when the old man could not accept his gift. He was even able to warn his "friends" to stay away from a house which was about to become an exploding inferno.

Before his final act, he wrote his own epitaph—"Criminals are made and not born." Without remorse, it was at once a feeble recognition and a condemnation. He recognized that he had become a "criminal." It was, perhaps, the feeblest description used to describe his terrible cruelty. But he also cast the blame, not on himself alone, but on a nameless world—a world which in untold times and untold ways had made Andrew Kehoe a victim.

In Kehoe's last act of his desperate orgy of consuming hatred, he killed himself. The precise time, place, and manner seemed almost accidental—but it must have happened almost precisely where and how he planned it. With the toppled school, and maimed and murdered children in the background; Kehoe joined them. In loosing the final lethal explosion, at the Superintendent and himself, Kehoe achieved a common destiny. The hated father who had demanded too much and shared too little was dead. The loving, hating, vengeful and penetent son lay sacrificed and broken at his feet.

Kehoe's self pronounced failure as a man had produced the fatal sense of persecution (by his father). He retaliated in destruction against it—and then was himself destroyed in a heightened persecution of guilt by a final suicidal act.

One of the great tragedies of the world had been triggered by a skilled and gifted man, who conceived of himself as a totally rejected failure. Only time would tell the extent and completeness of the tragedy he meant to accomplish.

Chapter XXIV
Return to the Village

Couzens

No one can go back to Bath, really, without going back to Couzens. What Bath was, is, and will be is tied up in its identification with the man. What Couzens was and became was no less tied up with the identification he formed with Bath.

With no doubt at all, Couzens had become a champion of the underdog long before Bath. His biographer traced his history of giving to crippled children back to 1915 when he visited a facility for handicapped children. In 1918 he was instrumental in creating Detroit's forerunner of the Community Chest.

However, the establishment of his greatest charity was not to come until following his intimate experience with the Bath Disaster. Bath undoubtedly sharpened the Senator's almost painful concern for crippled children, and placed that concern in a statewide perspective that included rural Michigan. The signal importance of Bath among the multitude of his concerns is revealed by an apparent oversight by his biographer. In the biography, Barnard emphasized Couzen's characteristic rejection of so called "vanity trusts." Throughout his life the Senator attached a condition of maximum activity and minimum building to his giving. He sought, "Not monuments to himself, but effective activity for children . . ."[1] He was supposedly furious when he learned that the Nurses' residence at the University of Michigan was named after him. The rejection of the use of his name was, according to his biographer, a principle he always held to. The prime and possibly only exception was the permission he gave Bath to rename the school "Couzens Agricultural School."

With Bath still fresh in his mind, the Senator created, ". . . for the era, one of the nation's most important philanthropies, the Children's Fund of Michigan."[2] While the Fund supported some activities of already existing agencies, it initiated critical activity in neglected fields of health and child welfare. A condition of county eligibility for funds was the creation of health districts. Crippled children's clinics were estabished at Marquette[3] and Traverse City, and prototypes for the state's child guidance clinics were set up in Detroit and Lansing.

Couzens had stipulated, in setting up the fund, that all monies were to be expended within twenty five years of its creation. The final accounting showed that Couzens had spent more than eighteen million dollars on this charity alone. In the end, possibly a million or more Michigan children received treatment, hope, and a chance at happiness that might otherwise never have come. In establishing his Centers for Maladjusted Children, Couzens might just possibly have had a young Andrew Kehoe in mind.

While Couzens gave great attention and energy to his fund, he remained primarily absorbed in his work at the Congress. Already the renown enemy of irresponsible wealth, the Great Depression was the last straw. His attacks on suspect industrial magnates became unrelenting. As a Republican Senator, his attacks on Republican business leaders became an embarrassment for the Party. His opposition to some of the economic policies and actions of the Republican Presidents was more than an embarrassment. It stretched the definition of "Republican" almost to the breaking point.

By 1936, with the country still struggling, Couzens was convinced that he could no longer support the Republican Presidential candidate. He was equally convinced that Franklin Roosevelt was the true champion of the people. Apparently compelled by his never failing honesty, Couzens announced publicly his intention to support FDR. Couzens surely knew that the announcement would doom him politically—and he was right. The Party organization which had squirmed through his inquisition of the House of Morgan could tolerate no more.

In the primary, the party regulars ran Wilbur Brucker, former Governor of Michigan, against Couzens; and the Senator went down to defeat. The defeat was solid and consistent. Even Clinton County (home of Bath) voted against the Senator by a margin of more than two to one. But Clinton County did it without Bath Township. Bath, loyal to its beloved Senator, never flinched in his support. The vote was 85 to 48 in favor of the Senator. Clearly, the Senator had bought himself some votes nine years earlier—not with his money, but with the compelling compassion which shoved him to the front of the line of helpers.

The editors of the Clinton Republican saw Couzens' defeat as a matter of simple justice. The man who had broken ranks far too often to fight for the poor and laboring classes "had it coming." Couzens, of course, was used to attacks on his independent character. He could have taken that. His rejection by the voters, by the man in the street and by the little guy was something else. It was something he could understand, even intellectually anticipate that he was going to provoke—but it was not something he could accept.

Three days after the defeat, Roosevelt offered him the Chairman-ship of the United States Maritime Commission. It was a post that required the toughness and insights of Couzens; and it was an honor. For Couzens, though, it was little solace. A week after the election the Senator was ordered to the hospital for jaundice, diabetes, and other complications. A month later, he died.

With his death, friends and enemies alike eulogized the man who ". . . had made himself a symbol of opposition to arrogant wealth and a champion of those who lacked any wealth at all."[4] Said Roosevelt, ". . . it is a great loss to the multitude of Americans whose needs and problems were always in the forefront of his thoughts and actions."[5] At Bath, the children spontaneously contributed pennies for a floral tribute.

In restrospect, Couzens was undoubtedly one of the great Americans. His life touched and was touched by Bath. He was a fiercely independent man who fought for the rights of others, but didn't always nourish their independence with his methods. Sometimes, they needed a little protection from Couzens himself. His intervention in Bath was typical and unhesitating. It was also strangely controversal. Some might argue that if he had stood back, the other funds rushing into Bath might never have stopped. The suggestion is spurious. Bath needed Couzens' help—and it needed Couzens. Still, his intervention in Bath contributed to the question, "Did Couzens' action help to save Bath or did he help to kill the staggering township by killing it with kindness?" The answer was to be found in what Bath did with the gift.

Monty Ellsworth

Monty Ellsworth left Bath with a pickup truck, a rifle, and a box full of IOU's. The dreams and schemes of the small town speculator had reached the end of the line.

Maybe his drinking contributed to it, maynot not—but for Ellsworth, personal and business problems hit like an avalanche. His marriage collapsed. His business flopped; and his book, "The Bath School Disaster," never really took hold.

Try as he had, Ellsworth got the book into production too late for the public's meteoric interest in Bath. Ellsworth had probably correctly guessed that a market for the book would be short lived. That is probably why he didn't follow up on his initial action to have his publication rights protected. With a flash market, he could be into production and out before any possible competitors could rub the sleep from their eyes. The problem was that even Ellsworth overestimated the duration of the potential market.

There is the possibility, of course, that the book simply wasn't marketed properly. Ellsworth apparently figured that sales appeal would be restricted to the local area. He made little if any effort to hawk it on a national scale.

The more likely reason for its failure, though, was something else. The public was still heavy into its hero psychology—the fantasy of a world of good times guarded from every threat by the hero of the hour. With Lindbergh, the psychology peaked and the public psyche sought to have the binge continue forever. The Bath disaster, somehow, just didn't fit in. The great heroism which the disaster brought forth was lost in the immensity of the tragedy.

When Ellsworth pulled up stakes to move up North, he left his boxes of unsold publications behind in storage. No real demand for the books ever did materialize. Mostly, the rats got into the storage, chewing the editions up for the glue. When that happened, the bulk of the remaining copies were sold for their paper weight to the junk dealer.

The copies that were left were safeguarded. Recently, demand for copies has picked up a little, mainly around anniversary time. More than fifty years after the disaster, there are only a few copies left of the original unsold hundreds. If they are not already collector's items they soon will be.

Apparently, there is no question but that Ellsworth lost money on his venture. Ironically, the book is probably the most successful failure ever produced. Not because its losses were small, but because of the degree to which it is treasured by those who own copies.

A good many of the copies around were actually donated by Ellsworth. He made a point of giving a copy to each family he interviewed—each family with a dead or injured child. But whether given by Ellsworth or purchased, it doesn't make much difference. Before any reminiscences about Bath get very far, the "book" is brought out for reference or for pride—and always with love. The copies are old in appearance, most of them. They've been used, and used, and used again—a vehicle for a trip back, to a lost child, a remembered classmate, a revered teacher, another time. The bindings are loose from wear now, the pages yellowed and tattered, and mended with scotch tape. For the survivors of Bath's explosion, and their elderly parents, this is the only book that could ever be written about the tragedy.

As an ex saloon keeper, butcher, merchant, and small town business speculator, Monty Ellsworth was an unlikely hero. Still, in a day when psychiatric treatment for disaster trauma was practically unheard of, he provided a tonic. In his saturation interviewing for the book, in his photographs and highlights of each child, and in his publication, he provided shock and grief therapy. If Bath was to survive the disaster emotionally, Ellsworth's efforts would certainly have to be a key.

Ellsworth, of course, was not rewarded with a best seller, but he didn't die a failure either. When he left Bath, he headed for the undeveloped properties of the shores of Houghton Lake. The story

222

is that he acquired a sandsucker and turned practically worthless shoreline into valuable beach property. He also pulled himself together personally in order to win a new wife. When Ellsworth died a few years ago, he died as a resident of Florida, apparently well off. As far as is known, he never tried writing anything else.

Ruth Babcock

The chubby and fiesty young home economics teacher had left Bath nearly a year before the disaster. During that year it is unlikely that she stilled her tongue over her experience there. She was sure that she was right in her battle with the Superintendent; and she could point to Mr. Kehoe's support to prove her point. Characteristically, if Ruth Babcock thought she was right one never heard the end of it. If she thought she was wrong, well, she may never have agreed that she was in that condition—unless—

Ruth's parents were publishers and editors of the Alma Record. They were learned individuals; and Ruth's verbal abilities were obviously honestly come by. The Alma Record was an excellent weekly serving the mid-Michigan area. Its readers avidly looked forward to each Thursday edition. On the editorial pages, the Babcocks held forth on just about every topic of local and worldwide interest that concerned them. Through their daughter, the Babcocks had an inside track on the coverage of the Bath Disaster, an inside track which no other state or national paper had claim to. Ruth Babcock through her alliance with Kehoe, probably knew the murderer better than almost anyone around. At least, she had a unique exposure to him.

On this particular occasion, however, the Alma Record decided to forfeit its advantage. At the time of the disaster, Ruth's parents carefully forewent disclosure of any direct connection to Bath. Instead, they chose to make use of their editorial pages to lecture their errant daughter. The lecture was by no means by name or direct, but, hidden between the lines it was definitely there in the form of two editorials.

A week after the tragedy, an editorial appeared called, "The Tragedy of Crooked Thinking." Crooked thinking, the editorial alleged, was at the center of most of life's troubles. It was behind Kehoe's demise and was, "The end result of allowing evil thoughts to gain a foothold in our minds."[6]

Three weeks later, came an editorial entitled, "The Purpose of College." College, the editors said, was a place "where young folks are supposed to learn to think straight, to learn the use of the chart and compass that they may sail their ship safely on life's tempestuous sea."[7] Instead, the editors lamented, a lot of crooked thinking was too often the result. The admonition to their daughter

223

seemed clear enough. The message was, "Get your head on straight and put this incident behind you." Apparently, it was one lesson that Ruth Babcock learned very well.

After Bath, the headstrong young teacher continued in teaching. She taught in Saranac for a while; and then moved on to Muir. She wore her hair in a short cropped masculine style which was strange for the time. Her personality didn't improve greatly; and she appeared to be heading for the life of a spinster—but then she met William Douglass. This time, though, Ruth Babcock was very, very careful in the man with whom she chose to ally herself.

Douglass and the Village of Muir were practically synonymous. Like the cider mill he operated, Douglass was a Muir landmark. He was also a wealthy man, the town philanthropist. His money was Muir's money; and he didn't hesitate to use it. Thanks to Douglass, Muir had the first paved streets for a village its size anywhere in Michigan.

Yes, Ruth Babcock had indeed learned her lesson well. From a brief association with a community destroyer, she had moved to a permanent relationship with a community builder, the pillar of the community.

Ruth Babcock and William Douglass shared a love for good and difficult literature; and they both liked woodworking. They were also very staunch, argumentative and hot headed Democrats. After the two were married, the cider mill was a frequent site of political arguments between the Douglasses and their Republican custo-mers, some of whom found themselves physically ejected from the premises.

Ruth Babcock remained a fixture in Muir until the day she died, late in the sixty's. Her short arms, top heavy figure, and boyish hairdo had been a familiar sight on Muir streets for more than twenty years. Ruth's gruffness probably disguised a softer heart but except for the motherly interest she took in the young boy who helped at the Mill, she never appeared to go out of her way to be friends with anyone. Her hatred for Masons and her other like biases remained with her to the end—and her mouth never faltered.

In one respect, and apparently in one respect only, did she control that mouth. Never, in all the years after the Bath tragedy did she reveal to anyone a connection with the Village of Bath or what happened there.

The Couzens School

By the early 1930's the still bright and shining Couzens School stood out in sharp relief against the depression which hit Bath and the rest of the country. In rapid fire order the village and the surrounding countryside were hit with one disaster on top of the other. In the small business district, stores were abandoned, and the Peoples Bank failed. Business and residential mortgages were foreclosed. Families from the city who were turned out of their homes sought refuge in the abandoned cottages and store buildings of the village. People almost literally crawled in out of the cold. Whether it was Bath or nearby Park Lake, the result was the same; and it was lasting.

The failure of the local bank was probably ruinous for everyone; but among the victims was probably the trust fund set up by Blanche Harte's husband. His noble sacrifice for education became sacrificed itself—just when the needy students of Bath would have most depended on it for a college education.

In the frantic effort to cope which was common of most schools, Bath cut its operating expenses to the bone. Maintenance and teaching costs were slashed—women teachers without families to support were discharged. Board salaries were reduced. Perhaps, most seriously, adequate depreciation costs were not built into the budget. It was a forced "Penny wise" economy.

Inside the classrooms, however, education pretty much went on as normal. The tragedy, of course, was not forgotten. The children who had survived the disaster made yearly memorial treks to the cemetaries to decorate the graves of dead classmates. After 1937 (when the last survivors graduated) a yearly memorial tree planting was substituted as a new tradition.

The high school also sought to obtain a nickname for its athletics. In a special contest for the nickname, Dominick Perrone, the teen-age son of Bath's section hand won out. The athletes from Bath became the "Bees" named for the indomitable swarms that regularly pestered his father's railroad gang. Somehow there seemed to be some real justice in the selection. Indirectly, Anna Perrone, whose eye had been so cruelly shattered by Kehoe's last explosion, had resurrected Bath's bees for eternity. The bees Kehoe had destroyed were back.

By the fifty's, growing school enrollment required the building of a new elementary school. By the early nineteen sixties, the Couzens' building was relegated to Junior High School status; and a new high school building was built to its rear. It was bad news for the Couzens building, but not necessarily for Bath.

Bath was experiencing one of those great and rare bursts of enthusiasm and exuberance which come from a small town championship basketball team. Bath's 1960 team was crowned State Champion in Class D; and the community which some feared had lost its will was ecstatic. It was a new generation in school, a new identity. In the process, some of the old identity was being restored.

Regrettably, everything was not going so well with the Couzens Building. The great pride which Bath originally had in the school was giving way with the changing use to comparative neglect. The school board, beleaguered by an every growing school population

225

turned to Michigan State University for direction—and the University quite naturally responded with a study.

The Michigan State Study, released in February of 1967[8] attempted to give the school district new life and direction—but it was bad news for the Couzens building. First of all, the study gave background to the district's dilemma—an equalized valuation so low as to neutralize otherwise good millage efforts—a teaching staff averaging only twenty six years of age—and dilapidated plant and equipment at Couzens.

The study noted, "The response to the tragedy helped unify the citizens of the township in support of the district educational system in the years that followed. This building stands as a symbol of this community's interest in promoting quality education within the limited resources at its disposal. However, with the passage of time, this building had become obsolete and outdated. . ." The study noted the building's lack of hot water, of adequate heating and ventilation. The building's total rating put it in the "To be abandoned category," and the study urged cessation of its use at the "earliest opportunity."

Understandably, the report outraged many of the citizens of Bath. To the survivors of the disaster, it was incomprehensible that this revered building could have been allowed to come to such a state. It was also incomprehensible that learned men could recommend the abandonment of any "symbol" of what is best in a community. In fact, neither Bath's temperament nor its resources were ready for the recommendation. "Abandonment at the earliest opportunity," would have to wait, but the old school was doomed.

In truth, and from the very beginning, there had been mixed feelings about building Couzens on the old site. In addition, children attending the school were not always of the same mind. While some of the children might have been inspired by its background and its sanctity, other found the place to be eerie. Youngsters could imagine themselves to be sitting at the very desk site of a murdered predecessor. No one ever dropped out of school because of it, but to a certain extent the feeling, the imagination, the fantasy had to be there.

The building hung on for awhile before being abandoned. Even then, some of the citizens sought to have the building saved as a community center. There may have been even some suspicion that the authorities were purposely contributing to the building's rapid deterioration by overloading the floors with storage, and by use of other unnamed devices. The board, however, stuck to its guns, holding that renovation would be as costly as a new building.

In 1975 the board contracted with the Cannon Wrecking Company to have the building removed. As the name of the wrecking company suggested, "removal" meant demolition. Born in

226

demolition, the old Couzens building died in demolition. Its life had come full circle. Insensitively, or rather unknowlingly, the wrecking crew first blasted the same North end which had received Kehoe's wrath. More than one inhabitant of Bath turned instinctively away from the sight.

**

By 1977, Andrew Kehoe's half sister, Irene, was the sole survivor of the once proud and large clan which gathered around Philip Kehoe. As a young girl she had left Bath after her father's death—to pursue the fine education her father had wanted for her. The news of the Bath disaster had jolted her as a young woman of twenty five. She reacted by sweeping the news under the rug and out of her life.

As the years went by she married, raised a family, and saw a grandson go off to war. Through it all she had maintained a complete silence about her relationship to her half brother, or toward his relationship with the disaster.[9] It was a benevolent and protective secret, but it required a determined and continuing effort. Her offspring could be protected from the news only by breaking ties with the past. Contacts with relatives or acquaintances could be too revealing. It was, perhaps, a difficult price to pay. She had dearly loved her father—and Margaret had substituted for her dead mother. The protection of her own family made the price clearly worth it. As an old lady now seventy five, Irene wished only to be left in peace— that she could guarantee that peace for her immediate family.

Irene's reaction to the tragedy was basically no different from that of the other Kehoes. With one exception, the pattern understandably seems to have been to repress the happening from existence. Andrew's brother apparently kept Andrew's history a complete secret from his son. The son's children learned accidentally of the connection later on. Neither was mention of Andrew kept among the personal effects maintained by his sisters at the nunnery. Silence was the rule.

A nephew was the exception. Now grown elderly, the nephew had discussed Kehoe within his own family and staunchly held onto his memory of a kindly, sensitive uncle. With outsiders, however, he could talk of Andrew and the disaster only with considerable emotion.[10] Even fifty years after the tragedy it was painfully real for this gentleman. He had accepted long since that Andrew had blown up the school, but was convinced that only through a flaw in timing were the children killed. He reasoned that when Andrew learned of the children's deaths, he killed himself. It was a truth, the old man felt, which even fifty years later neither Bath nor the public could accept.

It was a truth, even, which other members of the Kehoe family might not be able to accept. The fine and artistic gentleman had maintained his faith in his uncle through the years, but the ties with other relatives in the family had not been encouraged and had lapsed. The drive to unification which sometimes take place in the face of adversity, was apparently overwhelmed by the immensity of the adversity, itself. In one way or another, Andrew Kehoe's atrocity had succeeded in dispersing a once proud family. Most clearly, Kehoe's act of destruction had devastating effect on the relatives he left behind him. Understandably, those relatives turned to repression to deal with their dilemma. In the process, recovery from the wound has taken place—but slowly, and with difficulty, and with the hope that attrition of surviving members would safeguard the upcoming family members completely.

In some respects, however, Kehoe's effort to utterly destroy his wife and humble the Price family and estate fell short of the mark. Nellie's sisters somehow survived the tragedy and went on with their lives in Lansing. A year after the disaster, the Price and Fisher families, royalty of the automotive empire, were linked in one of the big weddings of Lansing's history.[11]

Even Kehoe's destruction of the farm was certainly not a major setback for the Price estate. Ironically, Kehoe's last official act turned out to be one last payment on his detested mortgage. It happened when money held in the Price estate for his wife was probated to Andrew after her murder. In settling the Kehoe estate, the Judge applied the money to his unpaid debt to the Price estate.

Still, the grief inflicted by Andrew Kehoe has continued to influence the descendents of the immediate members of the Price family. Perhaps, it's the loss of a beloved Aunt (Nellie) fifty years ago. Perhaps it's the immensity of a disaster even quite innocently involved in. But the tears are there at the mention of Bath—and the sadness. And just as within the Kehoe family, the need has prevailed to strike all evidence of the association from the observation of newer family members. Just as in the Kehoe descendents, the need can be seen in the protective covering of a censored family history. It can be seen in Nellie Kehoe's gravestone in the family plot, a gravestone marked simply, "Ella A. Price." It is almost as though Nellie's immediate family somehow felt less victimized than responsible. Regardless of the reason, the pain has obviously been real and repression has again been the means of dealing with it.

Repression of the crime may also account for avoidance of the Bath Disaster by news and other publishers over the past fifty years. Although it may rank as the greatest mass murder ever committed on American soil, it is usually omitted in any reference to great American crimes.[12] In commenting on the phenomenom in 1966, James Pooler of the Free Press concluded, "There are some

horrors—like nightmares—which psychologists say the mind tucks
away in forgotten places and tries never to recall."

Fifty Years

More than fifty years have gone by now since the disaster struck
Bath. In a way, of couse, one can't go back to the beginnings of it all,
but then again history has lingered at Bath.

Andrew Kehoe, of course, came up from the Clinton/Tecumseh
area. The old school he attended still stands, but its remodeled
inside, ironically sanctified as a rural church. The small homestead
exists much as it did in the days Andrew lived there with his proud
Irish parents. Even the once grand home built for Philip's third wife,
stands where it did across the road. Shorn of its grandeur, the years
have been kinder to the original frame homestead!

In nearby Clinton, evidence of the hard work and prominence of
the Kehoes remains—in the quiet churchyard family plots and in the
single monument marking the grave of the family patriarch. Beside it
is the aging, but well maintained white framed Catholic Church. It is
a picture of dignity, simplicity, and peace—a peace that Andrew
Kehoe somehow never knew.

The few Kehoes remaining in the area are a respected lot; and
community folk, those few aware of a connection, make an effort not
to bring up old humiliations and embarrassments. It's an adjustment
found throughout the chief connections to Andrew Kehoe (close
friends and relatives). The need is to "let sleeping dogs lie." The
need is to protect the innocent.

**

Up at St. Johns, Andrew Kehoe remains as isolated and
undisturbed as the day he was laid at rest. The scraggly maples in
the pauper's section of the cemetary have grown or given way to
large, protecting shade trees. His unidentified grave rests
permanently beside the grave of a child. There is no sign of the
wreath of thorns which was once said to have decorated the spot. It's
a beautiful quiet area, secluded at least temporarily from the world
Kehoe could no longer tolerate. There are no visitors here; and likely
there never will be for whether by design or ignorance, the secret of
Andrew Kehoe's precise gravesite is officially maintained.

Of course, enormous changes have taken place in the surrounding area. St. Johns with great pride in its past has hung onto its
nineteenth century heritage as best it can—but even it is
succumbing a little to the price of modern America. The shopping
centers have sprung up, the drive-ins and the franchises. But the
strong center of the place is bedded in a conservatism and love of
old values that still pervades the county.

Lansing is something else. Since Bath, it has occasionally been Michigan's fastest growing city. Urban sprawl has threatened to overcome the very nature of its early character. The three bastions of its economy (government, Michigan State University, and the automotive industry) have all grown at a pace undreamt of in the 1920's. In the process, Lansing has grown outward and has become increasingly dominant in the lives of the nearby villages, including Bath. (Among the key buildings which sprung up after 1927, is the still splendid former Auto Owners Building—monument to the sprawling insurance empire which prospered under its chief, Bill Searl, the former Bath prosecutor.)

Actually, fewer and fewer of the 1927 Lansing landmarks remain. Gone is the Prudden Auditorium. Gone also is the Home Dairy, delight of Bath's 1920 teachers; and gone are the famous downtown theatres of the time. The home of the Price sisters till stands, however, within sight of the stately Capitol building. The old frame house of another era seems a rather darkened, gloomy place, as if reflecting even yet the tragedy to the close knit Price girls who cloistered there and then moved on.

Sparrow Hospital, which heroically treated most of the injured and dying children of Bath in its crowded rooms and corridors, and in turn, became the beneficiary of a grateful community, survives among new buildings and equipment. The Bath memorial ward which was planned after the disaster apparently became the victim of a recent modernization program. If the memorial plaque which marked it still exists, no one seems to recall where; and record of the facility's proudest and most distressing chapter is all but lost in time.

St. Lawrence Hospital, Lawrence Price's gift to the Lansing people, has been treated well by the community and the Sisters of Mercy who administer it. Fittingly, its expansive new buildings and facilities boast key community mental health units. The physical plant is the most modern in Lansing—giving little hint of a history which included its treatment and protection of Nellie Kehoe, and the children of Bath who were caught in the wrath of Nellie's husband. Lost, apparently, from the public awareness,[13] but not from its name is its origin as a gift from Lawrence Price.

Time has also taken its toll of much of the public record of the disaster which once existed in Lansing. The exhibits of evidence which Prosecutor Searl sent on to the Attorney General's Office are nowhere to be found. Nor are there the investigatory reports filed by the State Fire Marshall. A state police record exists, but minus the report of investigation which would have preceded the official inquest.

Aside from the few remnants and photographs existing at the state archives, about the only other artifact is at the state museum. Even there, not much is left of the presentation given by the only person who seems to have recognized the historical importance of the disaster. Shortly after the disaster, big Albert Detluff[14] donated two battered school clocks to the museum, along with the pocket watch Kehoe was carrying when his body was discovered. The school clocks are missing now, probably mistaken during one of the museum's many moves for the junk they resembled.

All that remains is Andrew Kehoe's gold Hamilton pocket watch. Although the Capital News reported that its hands were set at 9:15 when it was accepted by the museum, only the minute hand remains on the face of the watch now. Against the background of a badly scarred and pock marked procelain face, the unstable hand points to eight, nine, or ten after an unknown hour. The stem is gone and the back cover jammed, locking inside any inscription that might have existed. Andrew Kehoe's watch remains, but just barely, victim of the explosion and, possibly, time itself.

Time has changed some other things, as well. Wood Road, which was the main relief artery to the village from Lansing—is now paved, but has been challenged and probably surpassed by Chandler Road as the chief Lansing connecting link. Both roads still lead northerly into Clark Road which then runs easterly into Bath—just as it did fifty years ago. And just as fifty years ago, the road from Gunnisonville passes by the old Kehoe property, before dipping down to the old railroad right of way and then up again toward Bath.

Unless the Kehoe farmland is pointed out, the passerby experiences no vibrations. Somehow the location comes as a surprise. The dwelling place of such consummate frustration and hatred seems more naturally to have been hidden away on some secluded back road.

But once the former farmyard is pointed out, the haunting feeling begins. Actually, it's as though it never happened—as though it was only imagined—just as one must imagine its existence now. Aside from the faint remains of the old driveway, there is no evidence of the farm house. Empty fields slope upward to the rear and away toward the grove of trees which once shaded children at their picnic play.

The scene is probably about as close to the scene Kehoe was striving for as one could get—but Kehoe has gotten a little help through the years. The farm, destroyed as Kehoe intended, was worth only half the price Kehoe had originally agreed on. It sold for $4,990 when the Kehoe estate was closed in 1934 leaving $4,300 still uncollected by the Price estate. The Price estate was probably lucky to get that, especially in view of stories which circulated for a time that the land was still booby trapped with explosives.

In recent years the land has changed hands more than once. The fields which for a time laid fallow have been put back into production, and bulldozers have razed what was left of the old farmhouse and the superstitions which had begun to envelop it.

231

So there it is, nothing, gone with the wind, and one wonders if that is also true of everything else at Bath. What did become of the village, and of its inhabitants? From the Kehoe place, nothing much looks changed. The Harte farm still stands across the road, much as it did fifty years ago—minus the barn that was victim to one of the recent tornadoes which have hit Bath. Otherwise, many of the other farms within eyesight stand basically unchanged from the way they were fifty years ago.

Moving on into the village (turning left on Main Street), the driver enters the brief residential district—essentially intact, and passes by the old school site on the right. The site is vacant now except for the markers. As the road jogs slightly to the left and dips to pass through the old business district, the similarity with old Bath strikes and strikes hard. The shops are basically unchanged. They still recall a western frontier town. A new post office and store merely emphasize the contrast. The other changes are dramatic, but more minuses than pluses.

Perhaps as important as anything else, the railroad that once crossed the road at the bottom of the hill has been paved over. The depot and elevator are gone and with them the spark that gave Bath life and underwrote its existence. If anything, the business buildings remaining are more dilapidated than they were. Even the old Community Hall which centerd Bath social life had fallen into disuse and disrepair. To the casual observer the old business district looks poor; and it looks country—run down. The scene encourages memory of the rinky dink drive-in bank which was up on the corner a year or so ago; and of the press box on the old football field which looked like something out of the Toonerville Trolley.

The scene prompts the inevitable question, "Did the disaster condemn the community to a slow death?"

It's not a new question. Through the years, Bath has been called "dead," "dying," a "hardluck town." As recently as 1973, a resident told a State Journal reporter, that after the tragedy, ". . .the place just started folding up. We'd like to forget about it, but we just can't. And for that matter, outsiders won't let us. When people think of Bath they think of that disaster and not much else."[15]

Four years later another life chapter was closing in Bath. Jack Rounds, a child survivor of the explosion, was going out of business—selling out the village's only hardware store. As he stood by the cash register, it was hard to picture him as the ten year old child he had been when he was knocked unconscious by the explosion (short to medium height, rounded, with round frame glasses, greying hair, and a keen homey sense of humor). The little hardware store featured linoleum squared floors, carelessly strung fluorescent lights, grooved wooden walls of a bygone era, and suspended wooden shelves. The merchandise was a little bit of

232

everything—mouse traps and rat poison were on prominent display, belying the fact that the old barns of Bath are not rat free. Among the items for sale were outmoded thermos jugs indicating that business at the store hadn't been all that brisk for quite a spell. Turned backward at the door, a sign hung reading—"be back in an hour—Driving School Bus.".

As Jack opened the front door for business though, a small parade of customers poured in. To satisfy the first customer Jack needed "to add four inches onto the piece of glass" he had cut four inches too short the day before.

Next, the Standard Oil dealer needed a set of keys duplicated. A young man needed a small can of silver paint (Mr. Rounds was out). A housewife was after some masking tape (Mr. Rounds was out). A repairman asked for some special washers. When Mr. Rounds replied that he didn't have any, the customer persisted, "Oh, for Christ sake, Jack, look around,"—no animosity, just experience.

> Jack: It's getting so I can't remember things. Last night I forgot to go out to dinner.
> Customer: Say, you do have a problem. I forget things too, but never to eat.
> Customer: (buying a lottery ticket) I hate to take a thousand from you, Jack.
> Jack: Well, it doesn't look like you will this time.
> Another Customer: You are charging too much for this.
> Jack: How can you say that, we haven't got to the price yet—but it's $1.19, $1.24 to you because you are taking so long.
> Lottery customer: Dammit, Jack, you've got the best deal going. You don't hardly work at all yet you even make money from the government.
> Customer: That's right, Jack. You don't hardly work now. What are you going to do when you retire?
> Standard Dealer: Well, I'll see you, Jack. Damn. I'll bet not one of these Keyes is going to work.
> Customer: That price is too rich for me. I'll wait until you have your final sale.[16]

It was all in good fun—yet open and frank—a little of Bath at its best. In a way, it seemed impossible that Jack Rounds could be going out of business. It was sad—but Jack Rounds really tells the true story of this place—Jack Rounds and the other survivors. They are in Bath and around Bath—quite a few of them, even quite a few of their parents.

Just to mention a few, there is Earl Proctor, recently retired as Assistant Chief Underwriter of the State Accident Fund. The Proctor place west and north of the village is a showplace, something of a colonial estate. Proctor takes considerable pride in his home, has done much of the work himself. As a child, both legs were mangled in the explosion. Through the years of orthopedic work, he

233

underwent an unbelievable series of bone settings and resettings—some the result of plain incompetency. Even with all the relief which poured into Bath, the question of payment once came up before prosthetic work would proceed. Proctor determined never to be subjected to the indignity of welfare again. Through sheer determination he forced himself up on those legs and worked initially as a barber in utter defiance of his condition. He learned that one day's barbering could feed his family for a week—and it was the barbering that saw him through the depression.

Proctor's foot never did heal properly. Even now a bone juts unnaturally out. The pain which long ago became a constant companion, never left. Today, Proctor is short, verbal and greying and, with it all, a good sense of humor. Proctor is proud of himself, and of his accomplishments. In a way, he stands as proof that any adversity can be overcome. Proctor feels that he has overcome the disaster, but he is still sensitive in talking about it. For instance, he was very upset when he was cut off in a recent TV interview about Bath. The cut came after he said, "I feel sorry for Kehoe," and before he completed his sentence with, "but not nearly as sorry as for the people of Bath who he injured."

In the village itself is Florence Schoals, a tenth grader in the explosion. After first escaping the main explosion completely, she escaped the second explosion with only minor injury. Today, Florence is elderly or about to become so. She's a grandmother, and she has retired from a life of hard work which included support of an invalid husband. More important to Bath, is the fighting quality of the slightly built woman. She has fought the township board almost singlehandedly in saving the old community hall from condemnation, and she holds title (after a court fight) to the property. What others have seen as an unsafe eyesore, crying for destruction, Mrs. Schoals has seen as a heritage which absolutely must be preserved. For the time being, the township board has been held at bay; and Mrs. Schoals is moving ahead with her own resources to rehabilitate the building.

One thing is certain. Mrs. Schoals is a sentimental battler, cast in the popular role of the underdog. If she succeeds in getting the historical society on her side, there is no telling how much of Bath's business district might be saved.

Out Webster Road, lives Walt Kyes, married now to Alice Webster, a member of the 1927 class whose graduation exercises were called off by the tragedy. Walt, of course, was the younger son of Andrew Kehoe's chief antagonist on the board—the member who, above all others, distrusted Kehoe and fought him—the member who perhaps more than anyone championed the better education of consolidation for Bath children. Walter Kyes is himself retired from his right of way position with the highway department, and his wife is sorely crippled from arthritis. Of course, much of the early beginnings of the consolidated school in Bath are due to the efforts of the Webster and Kyes families. Walt Kyes, now white haired, aging has simply followed in the family tradition. Around Bath he's been just about all everything. Through the years he's anchored the community planning board, acted as chief of the volunteer fire department, and he's been a board member of the Clinton County intermediate school district since about the time the school district was formed. He is a modest, thoughtful, and giving man. The special school outside of St. Johns is named for him.

Down at the school, you'll find two more of the survivors. Raymond Eschtruth and Lee Reasoner. Raymond Eschtruth has been janitor at the elementary school for probably more years than he would care to remember. He is a warm, honest and sensitive man, gentle, almost shy—briefly, but plainly spoken. He's suspicious of writers. He's been misquoted once too often. It's important to himself and for the others to be quoted just right about Bath. He says, "Well, it seemed funny to me that a man who wasn't here and didn't have any part in it could write a book about it—but, well now, we'll wait and see."

Raymond Eschtruth is a helpful man though—the caring, gentle person most elementary schools seek, but rarely find in their custodial staff. Through the years, Eschtruth has remained extremely identified with the school. He has been a constant strength to the sacred Methodist Church and he has been instrumental in developing the memorial at the old Couzens school site. Raymond Eschtruth has overcome the injuries he suffered but, after all these years, still trembles at the sound of an explosion.

Lee Reasoner is at the middle school, supervising the bussing operation. Lee was hospitalized from the explosion with cuts and a broken ankle. It was Lee's father who defeated Kehoe in the latter's last bid for public office. Reasoner today is precise and serious in appearance, wears glasses. From his office he supervises efficiently a bussing operation considerably larger and more sophisticated than the operation which made the original consolidation possible. It's also an operation which has not spawned the bitter battles of the old system. It's an extremely responsible position, and Lee Reasoner takes it seriously.

Of course, some of the survivors, you'll find together. Adabelle Dolton, the pretty little sixth grader who was blown nearly out of the building, is married to Chester McGonigal. He's self employed as an electrical contractor. She is going on thirty years as clerk at the village post office.

As for the marriage, Mr. McGonigal laughs and says it was just a matter of time and biology. Of course, the two know Bath and just about everyone in it. If there is a community pulse here, they have their fingers on it.

Parents of the dead can also be found around Bath. Mable and

Walt Geisenhaver still think mournfully of their first born who was lost in the explosion. Farm folk, they avoided the village proper for years—but they raised seven more children; and their children were all schooled in Bath. They also stored all those unsold books that belonged to Mrs. Geisenhaver's brother, Monty Ellsworth.

Across from the old Kehoe site live two other surviving parents who found each other long after the tragedy. Mr. and Mrs. Roscoe Witchell each lost children in the explosion, but by different marriages. Mrs. Witchell was formerly LaVere Harte's wife, the daughter-in-law of the Harte's, the nosey neighbors who broke off with Kehoe when he killed their dog. The Witchells are getting up there now; and Mr. Witchell has needed to recover from a stroke— but they are a charming couple. The fact that their house overlooks the Kehoe land simply doesn't disturb them. For years, strangers stopped by asking to have the Kehoe property pointed out, but now that's all but over. It's been that way for about ten years now—with the exception of a slight revival of interest when anniversarys and commemorations come up. Each year the Witchells dutifully and lovingly place flowers for the children they lost.

As Mrs. Witchell recalls the death of her little boy, LaVere, she says, "I believe he had been killed instantly." Tears well in her eyes and she controls her breaking voice, "I anguished for weeks," she says, "hoping that was so."

Mrs. Florence Homer lives a little further out from Bath, but not too far from her family's old homestead on Peacock Road. Florence is the daughter of Enos Peacock and she's exemplified the family dedication to education which was started by her father. She wears the same severely bobbed hair style she wore as a Bath school girl. She's worn it all her teaching life. The identification with Bath is inbred—and the rustic quality to her speech hasn't been dented much by her advanced education. Florence Homer was a second generation Peacock to graduate from Bath. Now, a third and fourth generation are represented in the graduates. It's hard to imagine Bath without Peacocks.

There's also Don Huffman—the most mangled of the children to have experienced the explosion and live through it. Huffman is the son of the Bath station agent who stuck at his post longer than anyone could have expected him to. Huffman is retired now. He's on the short stocky side. His hair is sharply receding, but he simply doesn't look his age. One eye doesn't focus. Occasional tears flow because of injury to the tear duct. He wears glasses, but there is no ready sign of impending blindness. A noticeable scar cleaves his right cheek and there is a malformation, possibly, of facial structure with an occasional twitching of the cheek. The damage to what could have been a truly handsome face has worn well. Other scars and trauma are hidden—a lengthy scar extending up the arm from the left thumb; a maze of scars lacerating the back, an amputated heel, jammed feet, and arched toes. Huffman has been exposed to the surgical knife too often to be completely trusting of doctors. He speaks bluntly and in a clear tenor voice. In a way, he is an anamoly. He's fiercely independent, but mad as hell at the state's failure to assume full responsibility for the children injured in a system of compulsory attendance. Most of all, he hits the lack of adequate vocational preparation. He speaks specifically to that when he says, "I would have been better off never to have attended that school."

There are others around, too: The wife of the heroic postmaster, who also lost her father—remarried to a brother of her husband. There's Harold Burnett, husband of the township clerk. As a child Harold lost a brother in the explosion. Now, Harold Burnett is the township's erstwhile historian.

It's hard to take these people as a group—they are individuals. They exist as a proof and a recollection of survival. Of course, survival is a matter of degree and time. Some have required professional help to deal with guilt and grief, and some never have adjusted. For example, the parent who through the years has treated his surviving family as though they didn't count. In general, though, one thing is clear—the survivors have been relieved of pain more agreeably and fully than those who felt identified by some relationship to Andrew Kehoe.

In retrospect, though, most call up a state of shock following the tragedy which lasted only a matter of weeks. It was a state which was followed by a time of painful avoidance—avoiding places and acquaintances which would bring the pain to mind. Then came a time of quiet healing when the tragedy wasn't brought up in discussion, but relationships became natural and normalized again. Finally, for most, an openness of discussion returned and the tragedy became not part of a repression, but part of identification, of full reconciliation. The openness is not complete quite but silence now is confined to the area of old animosities and suspicions. Without question, the disaster became for a long time the key community identifier—imbedded in the community conscience.

As the disaster becomes more legendary, the memories of the survivors become more blurred, obscured both by time and the recollections of others which have been heard or seen in the meantime. As everywhere else, eye witnesses can become confused by later events and by other accounts.

One example of innocent distortion may be the legend which now surrounds the memorial statue "Girl With A Cat." The people of Bath, many of them, are quite convinced that the bronze memorial was actually created by melted down pennies. Truly, the statue was made possible by the pennies collected by the school children of Michigan; and, possibly, those pennies were truly melted down. However, a search of accounts of the time reveals no such literal plan; no such plan was relayed to the Governor; and if such specifics were passed on to the children of the sculptor, they were forgotten. For some reason, however, it is important that the statue actually be made of pennies. Undoubtedly, the verdict of time will side with the people of Bath.

Time may also be a factor in the recollection that one of the churches housed school classrooms after the disaster. School Board records indicate only that a village building belonging to Menzer Church was rented for school purposes.

Time also seems to be on the side of Andrew Kehoe, himself. The belief is now expressed in Bath, and repeatedly, that Andrew Kehoe never really intended to kill and injure the children. It would be nice if that were true. The alternative is so completely intolerable not only for the people of Bath but for the truly fine relatives of Andrew Kehoe. The evidence, unfortunately, doesn't point that way—but time may yet be the court of last resort.

If memory has become obscured, the opinion of the people about the survival of the area is not. First of all, residents make a distinction between the village (business district) and the rest of Bath Township. The old business district is run down. It looks in part like a neglected remnant from another age. There are few dissenters to that. On the other hand, residents are convinced that Andrew Kehoe never was the undoing. The problems were something else—the depression hitting hard on top of the disaster; the decline of the railroad; the automobiles which made village necessity obsolete; the huge shopping complexes nearby; and the lack of imagination and leadership within the village and township (some call it obstinacy) in past years.

Just now, the old business district is old, but it's not dead. (Jack Rounds went out of business, all right, but he found a buyer.) It's simply that its future is in doubt.

As for the rest of the township and the old press predictions that the mass murder had doomed Bath, Mrs. Witchell laughs and says, "Well, now, it didn't turn out that way, did it?" In this, Mrs. Witchell has unanimous support and evidence to back her.

On the 18th of May, 1927 the people of Bath took homicidal losses unparalleled in village and American history. But Bath gave more than she got. Even in the half hour before massive relief forces started to arrive, the courage of response was heroic. In recalling the experience for American communities facing the threat of World War II bombing, the Detroit Free Press stated, "As no American town ever had passed through such a succession of terrifying occurrences as Bath, the courage and self sacrifice with which it responded should be remembered. Indeed, the example which it set that day should serve as an inspiration to all communities when and if Hitler's bombers come."[17]

Bath was surely jolted by the disaster, and some may have feared that its efforts were in a lost cause. The township, however, with Couzen's help, charted a bold new course for the school. Perhaps the most dramatic evidence of that vitality was in the strange new world of interscholastic athletics. In the early thirtys Bath's fledgling basketball team finished number two in the state. It wasn't quite number one, but it also was no achievement of a deceased community.

Approximately one generation after the Bath disaster, the community made it all the way. Playing for the State Class D championship in Michigan State's Jennison Field House, Bath fell into a fifteen point deficit. Then. before a suspense filled audience that included practically the entire Bath community, Bath came back. The sports headlines of the March 20, 1960 State Journal announced, "Bath Wins Class D. State Title." The sports page also featured a large photograph of ecstatic Bath fans screaming and showering the rest of the crowd with confetti. The Journal photograph didn't capture the lumps in the throats, but they were surely there.

If there were still doubts left after all the years, they were probably overcome by the events commemorating the fiftieth anniversary of the Bath School Disaster. Harold Burnett, himself a survivor of the explosion, organized the formal program of commemoration which was held on a hot and bright Saturday afternoon, May 21st, 1977.

For the occasion, a large speaker's stand was erected at one end of the old school grounds. Seated there were the several speakers, dignitaries and honored guests. To the left was the Bath School Band; to the right the community chorus—and back of them a squad of national guardsmen. Emory Huyck's frail widow was on hand; so was Floyd Huggett the former principal; so was the revered Nina Matson, the now elderly woman, who had once returned to the gratified community to teach for a time after her recovery from the explosion.

Large numbers of seats had been placed before the stands to accommodate the crowds, but there weren't nearly enough. Spectators who could, found refuge in the few shady spots on the grounds. The ceremony was brief, really, the addresses short. A son-in-law read Nina Matson's recollection of the day (she feared it might be too emotional for her to read herself). The guardsmen fired volleys after the name of each dead victim was announced; and Superintendent Hixon gave the main address. The band closed the occasion then, as Nina Matson unveiled the brick historical marker. Immediately afterward, the school board hosted with coffee and refreshments over at the middle school.

The occasion was truly significant, not so much for the events of the program, but for the turnout and the quality of happy reunion. Some of the survivors and parents of the survivors had initial qualms

239

about attending such an event, a few simply couldn't bring themselves to attend. Most, it seems, did attend—and at the commemoration and reception which followed experienced a warm and memorable fellowship. (A landmark had been reached.) A few days later, in the spirit of the times, the 1927 Bath High School Seniors joined the 1977 class in receiving diplomas—and in participating in a graduation exercise that had been denied them for fifty years.

In a way, the ceremony on the old school grounds was made possible by the fact which was seen as an affront to the survivors of the disaster. The disaster generation has never been able to accept or understand the mentality which allowed the great Couzens gift to be neglected and then destroyed. Instead of the sacred school the community now has the memorial park on the site. (Forgottenly—what the townspeople preferred in the first place). To the center is the martyred belfry, surrounded by shrubs, graced by the American flag which waves from its modest flagpole. At night a light reverently illuminates both the flag and the belfry.

The new historical marker is placed to the front, just off the road—and tells the story. The inscription concludes the story of the site, the demolition by Andrew Kehoe, and the Couzens rebuilding with this masterful update and seeming reprimand, "In the year of 1975 *by decision of the School Board* approved and contracted the demolition of this school building that had stood as a symbol of higher education for many years in this community."[18]

The site marks the past for Bath, but it has also signaled Bath's future. In truth, Bath had leaned on Couzens while it needed to, even borrowed a bit of his identity—but the movement to fully regain its own identity was irreversible! When it was time, the old building nearly had to go. As townspeople and survivors point out, Bath is no longer the community of 1927. Bath's very nature is changing. No longer is it simply a remote, but self sufficient farming community. The pastoral air is still there, so are many of the farms—and families which backboned the area—but so is a great influx of new people. For the most part, these are people and families, whose jobs are in Lansing —people who want to work one kind of life and relax another.

The evidence of their impact is not too hard to find—and the evidence is growing. Outside the village, the subdivisions have started, some modest, some estate-like. Down the country roads more and more expensive single dwellings are going up. From all the signs, the Bath area will be booming. The planners see it; the contractors see it; and the sharp new bank building on Clark Road is no accident. Down Webster Road prosperous new township offices have gone up; and Federal funding proposals are on the drawing board. A new business district, away from the old one and at the main four corners is just a matter of time. Even the church makeup has changed. The Methodist Church has stayed pretty much the way it was repaired after the disaster—but it has been replaced by the Baptist Church as the dominant church in the village.

These are a lot of changes. Some of the old timers don't like it. A few will end up moving to an area more like they remember Bath. But most will stay. They'll stay and continue to backbone this place.

Of course, the school has also changed. It's a system of schools now—the elementary and middle schools to the rear of the old school site; the modern expansive high school built up on the old Wilkins property.

In some ways the school might be considered even more important to area residents today than it was fifty years ago. As the business and social loyalties of residents have become more diverse, the school has become the only institution which ties the entire population together. On the other hand, Bath's ranking among Michigan school districts (using selected data put out by the Department of Education) is not impressive—basically held back by the poor equalized valuation of the district. That continuing liability has not been accompanied by any distinguishable sacrifice to compensate for it; and the district even suffered a temporary loss of accreditation last year.

Sports, however, are something else. Bath school district residents support an athletic program which regularly produces winning teams in what is becoming a tradition of winning teams. And like everywhere else, loss of accreditation doesn't claim any space in the media, sports do. For Bath, though it's a change. Fifty years ago (when the boys were needed at home uninjured to work the farm), sports were practically taboo.

Nonetheless, the residents also take definite pride in the modern school plant and grounds, built on land made available by Doris Wilkins, a teacher who has taught Bath youngsters from the Kehoe era to the present. The plant is one example of the past joining with the present in Bath to build the future. It's the "Bath High School" again, as it has been for a long time now. The "Couzenites" of the Couzens Agricultural School, are a chapter in the past. Most likely, Jim Couzens would have liked it that way.

The fact is, that the Bath of today looks to the future with a generally new population. Only 15 percent of the student body or thereabouts have or had relatives in the school disaster. Students know about the disaster, of course. Most seem to have an appreciation for the fact that the disaster was a terrible thing which has had a continuing impact on the old timers. They are also aware of some continuing derivatives of the disaster at the school. (Callers to the school are informed that their calls are being monitored. Bomb threats are handled with dispatch—no waiting around for searches, and the children are sped home by school bus. Another derivative

241

the school children are aware of is the still cherished statue "Girl With A Cat.")

What the children and even the school officials may be missing today is the tremendous pride of educational accomplishment which the people of Bath took in their first consolidated school. What they may also miss is the spirit of challenge and unity which was accepted by the community in rebuilding a system born in bloodshed. Old John Phelan of the Agricultural College had thrown down the challenge; and the community had resolved to meet it. "The test of the future," he said, "is that you will make this school a great school."

**

In a way, "Girl With A Cat" looks out of place as she stands on her encased pedestal just inside the school's main entrance. The building is sharp, modern. It's for this time. The statue is timeless, haunting, and it brings back memories. Kehoe, of course, hated cats. There's some justice in that. As the statue is positioned, the girl looks, smiling, across the hall and across time toward the all purpose room, observing perhaps the strange sights and sounds of a 1979 school dance—youngsters dressed in the unisex, dancing to the exploding piercing sounds of disco. Jeans, white jeans, blue jeans, blouses, polo shirts. Red and blue propeller lights, shuddering white lights, rotating and blinking, immersing the dancers in changing patterns of color. The motions are frenzied, pumping, jarring. The children of Bath are at play.

A circling beam of light reaches out from the sound station and barely reaches the "Girl With A Cat." One can almost imagine her smile to be an approving one—approving of the modern Bath girls with "cats." The beat is a very different beat, but the beat goes on. Bath is dead. Long live Bath.

Outside, it's cold and snowing. The winter goes relentlessly on; and more and more the people of Bath look forward to the warm days of May.

NOTES

Chapter II. The Village

1. Letter to Governor Blair of Michigan, February 11, 1861—attempting to thwart a peace conference.
2. Clinton County Republican, August 5, 1920.

Chapter III. End Of The Little White School House

1. Clinton County Republican, May 3, 1921.
2. Lansing State Journal, August 11, 1921.
3. Warden Kyes interview, July 30, 1977.
4. Clinton County Republican, April 28, 1921. Kehoe's name is misspelled "Kebol."
5. Ibid., July 28, 1921.

Chapter IV. Building the Dream

1. M. J. Ellsworth, *The Bath School Disaster*, p. 5.
2. Bath School Board Minutes, 1921.
3. Clinton County Republican, October 12, 1922.

Chapter V. To Make It Work

1. President Coolidge Speech to National Education Association, July 3, 1924.
2. Lansing State Journal, July 15, 1924.

Chapter VI. Challenge

1. George May, *A Most Unique Machine*, Eerdmans Publishing Co., Grand Rapids, 1975.
2. Lansing State Journal, February 12, 1917.
3. Ibid., February 13, 1917.
4. The beneficiaries of Price Estate included the Good Samaritan Hospital of Cincinnati; St. Aloysius Academy of Fayettesville, Ohio; Little Sisters of the Poor in Detroit; Sisters of Mercy Hospital in Jackson; Associated Charities; the poor children of Lansing; and the Lansing Boys Industrial School.
5. Will of Lawrence Price—Ingham County Probate Records.
6. The Patrick Price existence in Bath Township is confirmed by birth records and early accounts of residents who knew Nellie Price as a teenager in Bath.
7. There were probably three reasons for Kehoe's break with the Farm Bureau; (1) His activity with it robbed him of the opportunity for earlier attack on the consolidated school; (2) His political philosophy was increasingly at odds with that of the Bureau; (3) Mel Kyes, a key force for consolidation, was himself gaining power and stature in the Bath Farm Bureau.

Chapter VII. The People's Choice

1. Recollection given in Thelma Cressman Weismiller interview, November 8, 1977.

Chapter VIII. A Dip In Popularity

1. Clinton County Republican, May 26, 1927.
2. *The Bath School Disaster,* p. 36.
3. The inquest record.

Chapter IX. The Underdogs

1. Chapter contents find their source in the school board minutes as well as the inquest transcript.

Chapter XI. Foreclosing

1. Inquest transcript.
2. Ibid.
3. Ibid.
4. Ibid.
5. Ibid.
6. Disaster Scrapbook, Bath High—Kirker Realty Company.
7. Incident from *The Bath School Disaster* and Fordney Cushman Interview.
8. Inquest Transcript.
9. Ibid.
10. Ibid.
11. Bath school board minutes.
12. Clinton County Republican, April 7, 1927.

Chapter XII. Preparations—The Last Month Begins

1. Howard Witt Interview.
2. Inquest transcript.

Chapter XIII. Signals, Blunders, And Rebuff

1. Inquest Transcript.
2. Ibid.
3. Ibid.
4. Ibid.
5. Ibid.
6. Ibid.
7. The date given is estimated based on inquest testimony.
8. *The Bath School Disaster,* p. 33.
9. Op. cit., p. 32.

Chapter XIV. A Matter Of Timing

1. Based on account in inquest transcript.
2. All quotes of this chapter are from the inquest transcript.

Chapter XV. Daybreak—The Nightmare Begins

1. The reconstruction of this chapter has relied heavily on the inquest transcript.

Chapter XVI. Mayday

1. This is the precise description recalled by Ward Kyes at the inquest which, together with numerous interviews, is the source of the reconstruction of this chapter as well.

Chapter XVII. End To An Orgy

1. Lansing State Journal, May 19, 1927. Detroit News, May 19, 1927.
2. Detroit Times, May 20, 1927.
3. Inquest transcript.
4. Ibid.
5. Raymond Eschtruth interview (all quotes of this chapter are taken from the transcript. The reconstruction is from the transcript supplemented by interviews in 1977 and 1978.)
6. Inquest transcript.
7. Ibid.

Chapter XVIII. The Relief Columns

1. State Police Reports.
2. Dr. Shaw Interview.
3. State Police Report.
4. Leona Weldon.
5. Majority view reported in news accounts and recent interviews.
6. Detroit News, May 19, 1927.
7. Christman and Reniger Construction Companies.
8. Owosso Argus, May 19, 1927.
9. Ibid.
10. State Police Reports.
11. Lansing State Journal, May 19, 1927.
12. Owosso Argus, May 19, 1927.
13. *The Bath School Disaster*, p. 41.
14. State Police Reports.
15. Letter by Sparrow Hospital Administrator to Governor Green, May 26, 1927.
16. Detroit News, May 20, 1927. Owosso Argus, May 19, 1927.

Chapter XIX. Shock Waves And Ashes

1. Letter photo copied in numerous newspapers.
2. Lansing State Journal, October 16, 1926.
3. The Governor's appeal issued earlier on Thursday the 19th was followed within hours by Haarers instructional release. The Haarer instructions were printed in full in the May 20 Lansing State Journal as well as other papers. The coverage was considerably less extensive than that given the initial appeal by the Governor.
4. The Detroit News, May 21, 1927.
5. Lansing Capital News, May 20, 1927.
6. Ibid.
7. Ibid.
8. Detroit News, May 21, 1927.
9. NEA Wirephoto, May 21, 1927.
10. Detroit News, May 23, 1927.
11. Lansing Capital News. May 20, 1927.

Chapter XX. The Inquest

1. All testimony recorded here is from the official transcript.

2. For the broader American Community, direct soul searching because of Bath never did materialize. There was no resultant push for mental health programs (see Return to the Village for the significant exception); there was no demand to re-examine the private proceedings, crypitcally recorded, of public bodies. Nor was there any demand to re-examine the required qualifications of school board members, or the public means of financing the schools. True, there was a temporary outcry for greater explosives control and for return of the death penalty, but nothing came—possibly, in Michigan at least, because the legislature was not due to convene again for another year.

Chapter XXI. Attempt At Revival

1. Governor's File, Michigan State Archives.
2. Ibid.
3. Bath School Board Minutes.
4. Governor's File, Michigan State Archives.
5. Lansing State Journal, May 20, 1927.
6. "The Last Bell," 1927.
7. Governor's File, Michigan State Archives.
8. Harry Barnard, *The Independent Man,* Charles Scribner's Sons, New York, 1958, p. 20.
9. Detroit News, October 23, 1936.
10. Speech to Brotherhood of Locomotive Firemen, September, 1925.
11. *The Independent Man,* p. 187.
12. Detroit News, May 21, 1927.
13. Detroit Times, May 21, 1927.
14. Lansing State Journal, May 21, 1927.
15. Lansing Capital News, June 17, 1927.
16. Detroit Times, May 21, 1927.
17. Lansing State Journal, June 24, 1927.
18. Lansing Capital News, June 24, 1927.
19. Open Letter to Congregation, June 23, 1927.
20. Lansing State Journal, May 24, 1927.
21. Ibid., June 21, 1927.
22. August 15, Bath School Board Minutes.
23. Lansing State Journal, July 21, 1927.
24. *The Bath School Disaster,* p. 130.
25. State Police Report and newspaper accounts.
26. Lansing State Journal, October 3, 1927.

Chapter XXII. Challenge To Greatness

1. University of Michigan Accreditation Report.
2. Lansing State Journal.
3. Clinton County Republican, November 17, 1927.
4. Ibid., February 2, 1928.
5. Ibid., November 3, 1927.
6. Associated Press, August 18, 1928.

Chapter XXIII. Kehoe

1. Detroit Free Press, May 20, 1927.
2. Portrait and Biographical Album of Lenawee County, Chapman Brothers, 1888.
3. Michigan Birth Records.
4. Tecumseh Herald, December 4, 1890.
5. Ibid.
6. Ibid., March 22, 1888.
7. Ibid., December 20, 1888.
8. Ibidi., July 4, 1890.
9. Ibid., July 3, 1890.
10. Ibid., December 4, 1890.
11. Battle Creek Enquirer, May 19, 1927.
12. Detroit News, May 20, 1927.
13. Clinton Township Records.
14. Reconstructed from interviews with Hettie Murphy and the half sister of Andrew Kehoe in 1977, as well as newspaper accounts in the Tecumseh Herald, 9/19/1911 and the official recording of death.
15. Hettie Murphy Interview.
16. It might well be suggested that the will represented Philip's attempt to keep the farm in the family by giving Andrew and Lewis the opportunity. The appointment of a second executor might have been made to protect Andrew from any possible question as to his objectivity in disposing of the estate. However, even if done with the best of intentions toward Andrew, his perception of the motive could well have been something else.

Andrew's perception of the disposition of the safe might also have been less than accepting from another standpoint—the apparently already favored half sister would also receive anything that the father had chosen to place in it before he died.

Finally, the father's warning to the beneficiaries could have been standard language of the day without special significance, or it could have been standard language which, nevertheless, was particularly applicable to Philip Kehoe's situation.

17. Of the siblings not mentioned here, Helle, single and thirty died following surgery. Margaret, who had fielded reporter's questions about Andrew, lived to old age as an office clerk. Lydia, died following childbirth, but was survived by a husband and two boys who grew to live creative and productive lives. Irene, also married, worked as a clerk and raised a family. Patrick Lewis the only other male offspring, was a successful farmer.

18. Church Archives.
19. Ibid.
20. Detroit Free Press, May 21, 1927.
21. Battle Creek Enquirer, May 28, 1927.
22. Detroit News, May 20, 1927.
23. Owosso Argus, May 21, 1927.
24. Detroit Free Press, May 16, 1943.
25. As a writer I have laid down suggested diagnoses which a psychiatrist might be hard put to conclude. There simply are too many gaps in information to satisfy professional diagnosis. A psychiatrist would definitely want to know more about Kehoe's very earliest years. The mother's subsequent illness and death might more certainly have caused the trauma depicted here if an earlier preschool trauma had taken place, one which was then reenforced by the mother's illness and death. Such earlier trauma, if it existed, was not available to us except as I have suggested. In addition, too little is known about Andrew's precise relationship with his father. In short, the dynamics laid out in this chapter are by no means the only possible dynamics.

Chapter XXIV. Return To The Village

1. *The Independent Man,* p. 189.
2. Op. cit., p. 185.
3. Elba Morse, the veteran Red Cross official who helped bring organization to the emergency operation at Bath, headed the clinic at Marquette.
4. *The Independent Man,* p. 324.
5. Roosevelt, Public Papers, 1936, p. 531.
6. Alma Record, May 26, 1927.
7. Ibid., June 16, 1927.
8. Michigan State University Series No. 20. *Planning For Continued Improvement* —A study purchased by the Bath School Board, 1967.
9. November/December interview with half sister of Andrew Kehoe, 1977.
10. 1977 interview with nephew of Andrew Kehoe.
11. Through the adopted daughter of Lawrence Price.
12. Exceptions to the magazine blackout appeared in the September 1939 edition of True Detective and the September 1952 edition of Inside Detective. There may have been others.
13. The Price origin of St. Lawrence Hospital is omitted completely from the history of that institution printed in the June 4, 1978 Lansing State Journal.
14. The sensitive blacksmith was also responsible for entering into the official board minutes, the sympathy letters from the school children of Italy.
15. Lansing State Journal, June 24, 1973.
16. On waiting for interview with Jack Rounds.
17. Ralph Goll and Donald Scram, "The Strange Case of the Village Hitler and the Slaughtered Innocents." Detroit Free Press, May 16, 1943.
18. The emphasis is mine.

BIBLIOGRAPHY

Adrian Telegram.
Alma Record.
Ann Arbor Times News.
Barnard, Harry, *Independent Man,* New York, 1958.
Bath High School Student Handbook 1976, 1979.
Bath High School Yearbooks (including Couzen's Agricultural School Yearbooks).
Bath School Board Minutes.
Beckett, J. C., *The Making of Modern Ireland,* New York, 1966.
Carson City Gazette.
Chapman Bros., Portrait and Biographical Album of Lenawee County, Philadelphia, 1888.
Chicago Herald and Examiner.
Clinton County Republican News.
Coffey, W., *Consolidated School: A Study of hte Consolidation of Rural Schools in Michigan,* Lansing, 1919.
Cullen, L. B., *Life in Ireland,* New York, 1968.
Detroit Free Press.
Detroit News.
Detroit Post and Tribune, *Zachariah Chandler—An Outline Sketch of His Life and Public Service,* Detroit, 1880.

Detroit Times.
Ellsworth, M. J., *The Bath School Disaster,* 1927.
Goll, Ralph, "The Great Bath Dynamite Massacre," True Detective, September, 1931.
Harris, Wilmer, *Public Life of Zachariah Chandler,* Lansing, 1917.
Hirsch, Richard, *Crimes That Shook the World,* New York, 1949.
Ionia Sentinel Standard.
Ithaca Herald.
Jackson Citizen Patriot.
Laingsburg Press.
Lansing Capital News.
Lansing State Journal.
London Times.
Los Angeles Times.
Lunde, Donald T., *Murder and Madness,* Stanford, 1975.
May, George, *A Most unique Machine,* Grand Rapids, 1975.
McClung, Paul, "The Last Class," Inside Detective, September, 1952.
Miami Daily News.
Michigan Department of Education, Ranking of Michigan Public High School Districts by Selected Financial Data, Bulletin 1012, 1976-77.
Michigan Patron.
Michigan State News.
Michigan State University, College of Education, *Planning for Continued Improvement,* a study purchased by the Bath School Board, East Lansing, 1967.
New Orleans Times Picayune.
New York Daily Mirror.
New York Times.
Owosso Argus Press.
Roosevelt Public Papers, 1936.
St. Louis Post Dispatch.
San Francisco Examiner.
Tecumseh Herald.
Tecumseh News.
Usher, Frank, *The World's Worst Murderers,* New York, 1965.
Washington Post.
Whitman, Glenn, Transcript of Testimony: In the Matter of the Inquest as to the Cause of Death of Emory E. Huyck, Deceased.

Special Note—The History of Bath Charter Township, by Harold Burnett was not available at the time of writing, but has been invaluable in my editing.

DEAD

Bauerle, Arnold Victor
Bergan, Henry
Bergan, Herman
Burnett, Floyd Edwin
Bromund, Robert
Bromund, Amelia

Chapman, Russell
Claton, Cleo
Cockran, Robert
Cushman, Ralph Albert

Ewing, Earl Edwin

Foote, Katherine Onalee
Fritz, Margory

Geisenhaver, Carlyle Walter
Gibbs, Beatrice

Harte, Blanche Elizabeth, teacher
Harte, Stanley Horace
Harte, LaVere Robert
Harte, Gailand Lyle
Hall, Willa Marie
Hall, George
Hart, Iola Irene
Hart, Vivian Oletta
Hart, Percy Eugene
Hoppener, Francis Otto

Hunter, Cecial Lorn
Huyck, Emory E.,
 superintendent

Johns, Doris Elaine

Kehoe, Andrew P.
Kehoe, Nellie

McFarren, Nelson
McFarren, Clarence Wendell
McDonald, Thelma Irene
Medcoff, J. Emerson

Nickols, Emma Amelia

Richardson, Richard Dibble
Robb, Elsie Mildred

Shirts, Pauline Mae
Smith, Glenn O.

Weatherby, Miss Hazel Iva,
 teacher
Witchell, Elizabeth Jane
Witchell, Lucile June
Woodman, Harold LeMoyne

Zimmerman, George Orval
Zimmerman, Lloyd

INJURED

Babcock, Lloyd
Babcock, Vera
Babcock, Norris
Barnes, Ruth M.
Braska, Anna
Burnett, Gertrude

Chapman, Earl

Delau, Arthur
Delau, Ida
Detluff, Marcia
Dolton, Adabelle

Eschtruth, Iva
Eschtruth, Raymond
Eschtruth, Marian
England, Josephine

Foster, James
Frederick, Aletha
Fulton, Dorothy
Fritz, Mr. F. M.

Geisenhaver, Kenneth
Gubbins, Miss Eva, teacher
Gutekunst, Miss Leona, teacher

Hart, Elva
Hart, Perry
Hobart, Helen E.

Hobert, Helen E.
Hobert, Ralph R.
Hollister, Carlton E.
Huffman, June Rose
Huffman, Donald J.
Hunter, Florence Edith

Komm, Helen
Komm, Florence
King, Lester

Matson, Miss Nina, teacher
McCoy, Pauline Mae
McCoy, Willis
McKenzie, Harold
Mast, Lee Henry
Medcoff, Thelma

Nickols, Ruth
Nickols, Ottelia

Perrone, Mrs. J.
Proctor, Earl Fred
Proctor, Ralph Edmund

Reasoner, Lee
Reed, Lillian M.
Riker, Oral
Richardson, Virginia Blanche
Richardson, Martha Harriette
Rounds, Jack

Sage, Norman
Seeley, Ivan Freemont
Stolls, Lester
Stebleton, Gail Edmund
Stivaviske, Steve
Sweet, Ava Thelma
Sweet, Dean

Wilson, Ardis
Witchell, Kenneth

Zavistoski, Cecilia

GENERAL INDEX